To Rob _____ ly

B' Mahon

Mike Brown

A PROPHETIC PEACE

A
PROPHETIC
ᨿᨿ PEACE

JUDAISM, RELIGION, AND POLITICS

ALICK ISAACS

Indiana University Press
Bloomington and Indianapolis

This book is a publication of

Indiana University Press
601 North Morton Street
Bloomington, Indiana 47404-3797 USA

iupress.indiana.edu

Telephone orders	800-842-6796
Fax orders	812-855-7931
Orders by e-mail	iuporder@indiana.edu

© 2011 by Alick Isaacs

All rights reserved

No part of this book may be reproduced or utilized in any form or by any means, elec-
tronic or mechanical, including photocopying and recording, or by any information
storage and retrieval system, without permission in writing from the publisher. The
Association of American University Presses' Resolution on Permissions constitutes
the only exception to this prohibition.

⊚ The paper used in this publication meets the minimum requirements of the
American National Standard for Information Sciences—Permanence of Paper for
Printed Library Materials, ANSI Z39.48-1992.

Manufactured in the United States of America

Library of Congress Cataloging-in-Publication Data

Isaacs, Alick, [date]–
    A prophetic peace : Judaism, religion, and politics / Alick Isaacs.
      p. cm.
    Includes bibliographical references and index.
    ISBN 978-0-253-35684-0 (cloth : alk. paper) — ISBN 978-0-253-00564-9
(pbk. : alk. paper) 1. Lebanon War, 2006—Personal narratives, Israeli.
2. Soldiers—Israel—Biography. 3. Arab-Israeli conflict—Peace. 4. War—
Religious aspects—Judaism. 5. Israel. Tseva haganah le-Yisra'el. I. Title.
    DS87.65.I83 2011
    956.9204'5242092—dc22
    [B]
                                   2011011594

1 2 3 4 5   16 15 14 13 12 11

For Shuli

Contents

Acknowledgments

As with all books, *A Prophetic Peace* is the product of a group effort. While the responsibility for everything I have written is my own, I am extremely conscious of the many others whose inspiration and teaching have helped me as I have engaged in the processes of studying, thinking, and writing. I have been blessed with wonderful friends and colleagues, who have generously shared their thoughts, knowledge, and ideas with me, as well as with students who have taught me a great deal. A number of people have been kind enough to give hours of their time reading drafts, making corrections, and offering suggestions.

First of all, I would like to mention Jeffrey Perl, the founding editor of *Common Knowledge,* with whom I have shared a thrilling correspondence for a number of years. It is sometimes hard to acknowledge the influence of someone whose ideas and creativity have affected me so deeply that I cannot always distinguish his thinking from my own. Jeffrey was the first person to help me articulate clearly that my true passion is the pursuit of peace and that a combination of post-linguistic-turn philosophy and classical Jewish thought might be my path toward it. He has been a wonderful guide through much of the literature quoted in this book and a sounding board for my evolving ideas. He is a brilliant thinker and a remarkable editor to whom I am honored to express my deep gratitude.

I thank Michael and Geulah Rosenak for years of love and support. Michael spent hours in discussion with me at the dinner table and in coffee shops after reading the entire manuscript and offered his unique words of wisdom and gentle encouragement. Avinoam Rosenak deeply influenced my ability to connect with the teachings of the Maharal and Rav Kook and through them to present authentically the notion of peace's centrality to Jewish thought in the classical Jewish tradition. Tova Hartman has shared hours of discussion with me and has generously given of her time to read various drafts of many of the chapters of this book.

Thanks to Vivienne Burstein for her extensive and attentive editing. Without her, this book would never have been completed. I also thank Richard Wolffe, Benjamin Sommer, Yishai Rosen-Zvi, Adam Afterman, Marc Brettler, Moshe Meir, Yair Lifshitz, Susan Handelman, Avi Sagi, and

Menachem Fisch, all of whom read sections of the book and offered their comments, encouragement, advice, and criticisms. Thanks also to Janet Rabinowitch, Brian Herrmann, and Merryl Sloane and also to the readers appointed by Indiana University Press, whose insights, comments, and corrections have been most helpful. I am very grateful for them all. I would like to make a special mention of Sharon Leshem-Zinger and Stephen Markowitz who, together with Avinoam Rosenak, have worked with me on the Talking Peace project briefly described in chapter 8. This project has provided me with the rare opportunity of trying to put ideas into practice in the hope of helping to make peace in today's Middle East.

I would like to acknowledge the support of the two institutions where I am privileged to work, the Melton Centre for Jewish Education at the Hebrew University and the Shalom Hartman Institute. Both of these have provided a stimulating environment in which to test my ideas with both students and colleagues. The members of the seminars "Political Theology," "Torah from Sinai," and "Violence" at the Hartman Institute will no doubt recognize the impact of our shared study on many of the arguments outlined in this book. My special thanks go to David Hartman and Donniel Hartman, the co-directors of the Hartman Institute, and to Howie Dietcher of the Melton Centre for their spiritual and financial support of this project.

A special mention is due to the soldiers of the Alexandroni brigade who shared the experiences with me in Lebanon that spurred the writing of this book. In particular, I thank Josh Amaru, Shachar Hoshmand, Shaul Vider, and Lee Golan without whom I would quite literally not have survived.

I would like to thank my beloved family. My father, Bernard Isaacs, died long before the writing of this book began, and my mother, Dorothy Isaacs, passed away as I was preparing the final manuscript for publication. Their love of Torah and of peace—as well as my father's tutelage in the art of writing—is a beacon of inspiration to me. I thank my brothers, Lionel, Aubrey, and Michael, for their love, encouragement, and comments on various aspects of the manuscript. I also thank my wonderful children, Hillel, Noam, Talia, Ori, and Hadas, for whom I wrote this book and who provided me daily with the practical challenge of keeping the peace! Finally, I thank my wife and companion, Shuli, for more than anyone should ever write in a public acknowledgment. To her, for that and for so much more, I dedicate this book.

ALICK ISAACS
Jerusalem

INTRODUCTION

Lebanon II

The second Lebanon war, which took place in the summer of 2006, is the event that spurred me to write this book. I participated in that war as a reserve soldier in the Israeli army. At the time, I was thirty-eight years old. The confusion that surrounded the Israeli army's handling of the war, the lack of supplies, the discussions and debates that took place during the course of the conflict—all had a profound effect upon me. I returned from the war with a compulsion to rethink my attitudes toward Judaism, Zionism, war, and peace.

In the thick of combat I realized how complex the challenge of honestly reconciling the potential belligerence of religion with its messages of peace is. It became clear to me that dismantling the connection between violence and religion would take more than a dovishly selective reading of the Bible or the Talmud or a prayer book. But I came away from the war equally convinced that secular political philosophies were unequal to the task of winning widespread support for peace in Israel. During the war, as much as I was challenged by my thoughts about religion, I felt implicated by the ominous side of statehood. I shuddered at the potential dangers of the brand of militarism that secular liberal Zionism had introduced into the Jewish story.

When I returned from the war, I wrote a detailed account of my experiences, which was published in the interdisciplinary journal *Common Knowledge*.[1] While I will not reproduce that account in its entirety here, I feel that some of the events that took place in the latter stages of the war will serve as a meaningful opening to this book. My story begins with the burning of the trees, which took place outside the southern Lebanese village of Ras-Bayada.

The Burning of the Trees

> *When thou shalt besiege a city a long time, in making war*
> *against it to take it, thou shalt not destroy the trees thereof by*
> *wielding an axe against them; for thou mayest eat of them,*

but thou shalt not cut them down; for is the tree of the field [a] man, that it should be besieged of thee?

—Deuteronomy 20:19

Open thy doors, O Lebanon, that the fire may devour thy cedars. Wail, O cypress tree, for the cedar is fallen, Because the glorious ones are spoiled; Wail, O ye oaks of Bashan, For the strong forest is come down.

—Zechariah 11:1–2

In the last few days of the war, my unit reached its final destination—a small cluster of houses facing the town of Ras-Bayada in southern Lebanon. Our mission was to hold the coastal road that ran from there to the Israeli border above Rosh Hanikra. I remember that when I first saw the place, I thought to myself, "What the hell do these people want to make war for? They must be mad. The sun glistens on the sea. The air is fresh and the land is fertile. This little place is a paradise."

The house my unit was assigned to occupy was primitive, poorly equipped, and ugly. But the ground and the setting were quaintly beautiful. With a washing of paint and some well-chosen pieces of furniture and lamps—I thought to myself—the people here could make a fortune renting out their homes as holiday cottages. The house was strategically well positioned over the coastal road and had potentially good views of the hostile village below, as well as of the even more hostile Tyre that languished in the distance. Fruit trees surrounded the house. About fifty meters below, there was a banana orchard; there were sabras (prickly pears) growing on cactus bushes at the entrance to the orchard. There were vines and fig trees dripping with luscious scents and ripe fruit, carobs too. Why make war here?

The house had a second floor. Shimon, my company officer, took us (in shifts) on a guided tour of the whole complex to make sure that each of us knew his way around and knew where each of the other companies and platoons in the division was positioned. We entered the upper level of our house cautiously. We did not shoot our way in as we had on previous occasions during the war, but we were cautious and conscious of the possibility that the house had been booby-trapped. The upper floor was a mess. There were clothes strewn all over the bed, there were pictures scattered around, a VCR and a broken-down TV, an aged hi-fi system. It looked like the bedroom of a teenage son living above his elderly parents. This level of the house was littered with Hezbollah paraphernalia. There were flags and bandannas, pictures of uniformed men brandishing weapons and wearing combat vests like those used by the Israeli army in the 1960s during the Six-Day War. Groups of men and women wrapped themselves proudly around the soldier in the family, posing with their pride and joy smeared all over their faces. We felt revolted by them all. Standing in our helmets and our vests, our guns at the ready, the provocation was too much to resist. The room was ransacked. Some of the booty was carried off for army intelligence; most was destroyed or left where it was. Some of it made its way into backpacks, and at least one item—picked up by a professional comedian in our company—became a prop in a Tel Aviv stand-up comedy act. I shuddered and got the hell out of there. There was running water for a few days, until it ran out. I never used it and I never used the toilet, not there.

Nehemiah, an Ethiopian officer in our company, came to visit his buddy Shimon and to see our house. It was a little more spartan than the other houses in the division, but it had a lovely porch covered with vine leaves where we sat and chatted whenever we had the chance. We were encouraged to stay inside as much as possible for our own protection, but this was a rule never really enforced, not until Ze'ev, the platoon commander whose mother had died on the first day of the war, joined us later in the week.

Our officers Nehemiah and Shimon along with my friend and NCO Ari set about securing the house and establishing a military routine. The missions were defined and remained more or less the same throughout the whole week we stayed there. We were to guard the house from two posts during the day, with one man in the front and one in the back. During the night, two men were positioned in the front and two in the back. Each pair was given night-vision equipment and a field radio. There were two ambush lookout points that Shimon placed at the entrance to the banana orchard. Five soldiers manned each of these at night; one of the positions was also manned throughout the day. Our company's mission was to protect the encampment from the west. Even though we did not move for a week, we were kept fairly busy. Other companies sent out night patrols and positioned men to the south of us, while other platoons covered the east and the north with ambushes and patrols conducted in shifts that sometimes lasted up to seventy-two hours. The roof of the tallest building in the enclave was manned by snipers under Nehemiah's command; they used their telescope sights in the day and magnifying night-vision equipment during the night.

Securing the house was an awkward business. We were clearly vulnerable to a sneak attack from Ras-Bayada and—although the intelligence information we had was both sparse and imprecise—we knew the village was populated by Hezbollah units. We could not allow ourselves to cross the contour of the house and expose ourselves to enemy sniper fire. We needed to find some way of defending ourselves from the southwest. Shimon, Nehemiah, and Ari put us all to work. The first stage of the "operation" was to find as many plates, dishes, bowls, and bottles as we could. We were looking for anything that would make a noise if somebody bumped into it or kicked it unexpectedly while approaching the house in the night. We shattered and scattered all the household china, all the tools in the toolbox, all the plates in the kitchen, all the pots and pans, all the empty bottles and plastic bowls, all the cooking utensils, spatulas, forks and spoons, vases, everything we could get our hands on that would make a noise. We took it all and spread it around. It was like a game and we were like children bursting with pride at our own genius. It was as if we could hardly wait for the enemy to come along and fall into our noise trap, to come along and see how clever we were. Nehemiah laughed and joked: "All those years reading Marvel comics and watching action shows like *MacGyver* have finally paid off."

As pleased as we were with ourselves, there was still one major problem. The trees. As well protected as our house now was, with guards, lookout points, and broken dishes, we still could not see very far. We had altitude; we were brilliantly positioned at the top of a hill that dominated the coastal road. But our view of Ras-Bayada was still blocked by the fruit trees. It was as if they were captive sentinels bravely spying on "us" for "them" from behind enemy lines. The trees felt to me as if they were loyal to the men who had planted, watered, nurtured, and milked them for years and years. They stood silently, surrendering their fruit to our appetites without resistance, all the while obstructing our occupation of the land.

It was a hot day and we were sweating hard, but we got to work cutting down the enemy trees. Someone had found a chainsaw in one of the houses and had already made good use of it in other parts of the enclave. Dan, the oldest man in the platoon (he is a year older than Ari and me), was the chainsaw man. He was soon cutting away at the tree trunks. They fell without retaliating. He cut and we dragged. We dragged the long, bushy, pregnant stumps—heavily laden with leaves and fruit—and stuffed them into the back courtyard of our house. Again, the move was gleefully brilliant. Stuffing the cut-down trees into this courtyard blocked access to our position from yet another vulnerable route to the house. We slaughtered the trees in every direction and stuffed the carcasses into our courtyard. The roaring of the chainsaw ripped through the air, piercing the wood of the trees and the military silence of our position. The noise must have instilled the fear of God into the heart of every bush, plant, and shrub in Ras-Bayada. I imagined the Hezbollah members wondering: "What the hell are those morons up to now?" I am not sure if it was their hatred of our destructiveness or their bewilderment at our madness that I felt and feared more—but the trees had to come down. It made strategic military sense. It was a sacrifice that the god of war was lusting after.

And yet, the stumps that were left behind after Dan had finished were still blocking our view, and the number of trees he had managed to cut down was clearly inadequate to the need. It was the height of summer. The day was broiling hot and dry, with a sea breeze. The weather was perfect for a burnt offering. The trees easily burned, and we sucked in the fumes of their smoke for hours. It was the next morning before the black smelted earth had settled down to quietly mourn the loss of its cremated limbs.

We had good reasons to burn down the trees. We needed to be able to see in every direction all around us. We had to see Ras-Bayada with our binoculars. We had to invade southern Lebanon to protect the northern villages of Israel. We needed to fight a war to bring the hostages taken at the border back home to safety. It all made sense. It all really did make sense. The trees had to go.

Breaking Shabbat

We settled into a routine opposite Ras-Bayada. Night after night, we went out on the same patrols and performed the same guard duties. We switched things around a bit to keep the enemy on his toes, but mentally we were slipping into a routine. For some, fear subsided a little. We started to make ourselves at home. We readjusted the furniture, spread blankets on the stone floor, koshered pots and pans, and rummaged through the cupboards in the kitchen in search of "kosher" cooking ingredients. We found rice and vegetables and the like, which we mixed with the army food that was now arriving in more plentiful supply. Soon enough, our improvised kitchen was churning out hot kosher meals. We fried vegetables and sausages, boiled rice, and served sweet tea (made from leaves we found in the garden) with fruit for dessert.

My fear was slowly turning to depression. The thought that we might be stuck in Ras-Bayada indefinitely was plaguing my mind. We were no longer on the move. We had "accomplished" our mission and were now waiting indeterminately. Uncertainty was in the air and—after the experience of the first Lebanese war—I knew that the Israeli army was capable of staying put in a place like this for years and years and years. The more we settled in, the more despondent we became about getting out. Ari's wife and their kids were leaving for a family holiday in the United States without him. He had hoped the war would be over in time for him to join them, but it was becoming clear that "over" was not happening. Ari, who had never succumbed to fear, was now showing signs of misery and homesickness too. Like a mountaineer looking back at his path of ascent, I looked backward and downward at the progress of our campaign—through Sham'ah and Raj-a-Min, past Zar'it, Kerem Ben Zimra, and Metulla. I looked all the way back. Home. Many of the men complained that they had not been home for nearly a month. We had been away from showers, phones, toilet paper, homemade food, soap, shampoo, toothpaste, and fresh underwear for nearly two weeks, and I had barely removed my boots since Tishah b'Av. I had not changed my uniform or washed a body part. The mere forty-eight hours that we had been told we would spend inside Lebanon were a long-forgotten lie. Every promise of a deadline for going home, however gloomy, had now faded into the fanciful distance behind us. I was becoming more and more aware of my dirty, smelly body in Ras-Bayada—a little like Adam and Eve when first sensing their nakedness. Inertia and complacency are the fruits that the god of war forbids. Ras-Bayada was a garden full of enemy trees.

We broke a hole in the seat of one of the chairs we had found and, positioning it over a well in the garden, turned it into our sit-down toilet. My body had got so used to crouching that I found it a little hard to use. The well offered no privacy (it was in full view of Ras-Bayada and of the rear guard of the house), but most of us were beyond caring. We found some Lebanese shampoo and used it to shower. The spare underpants and socks that I had stuffed into the pouches of my combat vest got their first taste of action. I received a new uniform and was able to change clothes. We were provided with a satellite phone and three minutes of air time each to call home. (I called home badly, saying all the wrong things, expressing all the anxieties I should have concealed—failing to carry my share of the weight.) We were settling in.

Before our first Shabbat in Ras-Bayada, rumors began circulating that one of the companies was going on leave and that Colonel Motti—the battalion commander—was coming to visit. For the first time, we felt anticipation of something other than the end of the war. It was Friday and the men wanted to phone home; they wanted to *go* home. Tempers were rising. Shimon was talking about the letters he was going to write when we got home: letters to the army and the government, letters to the press. I could not help thinking how misplaced this letter-writing-threatening banter was. After the war was over, the press campaign (launched and led by soldiers from our battalion) was equally misplaced and trivial. By the time we had reached Ras-Bayada, the lack of food, water, and supplies that annoyed everyone so much struck me as part of the chaos that one can and should expect from war. I was so sick with fear that I hardly cared about the food. No one had died of either starvation or dehydration. (From the smells coming from our kosher kitchen,

I'd say we were muddling through quite well.) It was the lack of consistent and carefully thought-through orders that upset me, the lack of willingness to follow the orders we were given, the absence of sufficient air and artillery support for our infantry advances, the lack of faith in the purpose of the war itself, the lack of purpose for the war, the senior officers' blatant disregard for human life, along with the soldiers' unacceptable over-concern for their own skins (mine included), the absolutely paralyzing and interminable fear that was bothering me.

As the rumors took shape, it became clear that Dan's company would be the first to go for a twenty-four-hour break. They were scheduled to leave on Friday afternoon in a convoy of armored personnel carriers that would bring them to Zar'it just before Shabbat. After that, they were on their own, free to travel home or stay put at the border as they wished or (for the Shabbat-observant ones) as God commanded. Their orders were to be at the Israeli border by sunset on Saturday night, ready to move out and be back in Ras-Bayada by morning. These short outings were planned to give as many of the men in the division a refresher break as quickly as possible—before we received new orders. There was a window of opportunity here, and Yoel, our division commander, was determined to seize the day.

Carpe diem is all well and good when the *dies* in question is not the Sabbath. Ari and I were outraged by Yoel's decision. We railed against the flippancy with which wartime is treated as a blanket excuse for every (and any) transgression of Shabbat. Even in the midst of a war in southern Lebanon, not everything is a matter of life and death that justifies Sabbath violation. Does a journey from Ras-Bayada back to the border constitute a necessary military action? And if it does, what justification could there be for the journeys inside Israel to and from Zar'it, both of which would inevitably involve desecrating Shabbat? What were the religious soldiers in Dan's company supposed to do when they reached the border? What about the traditionalist men who now faced an almost irresistible temptation? Many of the nonreligious men also felt uncomfortable with this discriminatory plan. What is more, Ari and I were convinced that this order was in blatant violation of military law. We went to speak with Yoel.

We decided to avoid the religious law argument and chose to navigate the conversation in the direction of military law. Yoel's job was to give and follow orders, and if this one was to be rescinded the reasons had better be military. He listened to us politely. He tried to make a quasi-halakhic case by justifying the men's need for a twenty-four-hour leave as if it *were* a matter of life and death. The point is arguable, but it was outside of Yoel's field of competence to argue it. We were not going there with him. Ari pushed for a military rabbi to be consulted on the matter, and he left satisfied that this was what Yoel was going to do. I came along and chimed in with my two cents' worth here and there, but my heart was not in it. My problem could not really have been solved by a military—or any other kind of—rabbi. I was worried about something else; in the thought of a potential Sabbath violation, I had found a new cause for fear.

On the way to speaking with Yoel, I bumped into Yisrael. We chatted. He asked how I was doing. I asked how he was holding up. He told me that Ze'ev was coming soon. We speculated about what lay ahead. Yisrael knew no more than I did. Nobody did. Uncertainty was in the air. I told him I was on my way to speak with Yoel about Shabbat. Yisrael (who is a rabbi and an officer) thought Yoel was right. The men did need a break, and being at war did—in his significantly more learned opinion—justify leniency with the laws of Shabbat. I could not agree, but my reasons were not strictly halakhic. I told him that I thought it imprudent (I was also afraid) to take chances with God's heart. I told him how I felt about the trees. I seem to have stupefied him: "I'm amazed at you!" he told me. "How do you think the walls came crumbling down at Jericho? How did David beat Goliath? How did the Maccabees prevail? How were the Six-Day and Yom Kippur wars won?" (He seemed to see no distinctions here.) "Where is your faith? Of course, we will win. God is on our side. Our enemies are his enemies, no matter what we do. *God* has no alternative. *He* has already made his choice. *He* will help us kill them all. *He* is always with us. *He* hates them as much as we do. What's the matter with you? Where is your faith?"

I did not reply. I was completely taken aback. I could not imagine why *he* was surprised at *me*. Yisrael seemed to correlate faith (the *kippah* under my helmet) with certainty about whom God loves and hates. I partially envied his ability to take comfort in God. I could not do so. *My* faith would not allow it.

I listened to Ari reasoning with Yoel about military law. I chimed in quite helpfully now and again. But my mind was elsewhere. I felt vulnerable before God. I prayed as we spoke. "Oh God, protect us. Protect us. Shield us." I mumbled the words over and over under my breath. I could not help it. I could not help worrying that—like the Shabbat—God's heart and protective shield had been broken.

The Sneak Attack

The following events are the most important to me in this war story. They are also the hardest to recall in sequence. I know all the things that happened, but I am not sure of the order. I have told this story often since coming home, though it took me a while to start talking about it. I have told it with both forgivable inaccuracies and unforgivable untruths—untruths I cannot allow onto the written page. I am aware.

I know that Ze'ev arrived the morning after all this happened, along with "the hands." But the arrival of the hands is hard for me to pinpoint. I remember the moment I first felt them, but I cannot remember when or where that moment was. Hence I am aware that there are mistakes in the account that follows.

I think it was the night after our brigadier commander, Motti, had come and gone that a Hezbollah terrorist infiltrated our enclave. I was just completing my guard duty around the back of our house when he came. The "night watch" of shattered plates and bowls sounded no alarm. The spatulas and forks remained silent. The tree stumps and the charred earth did nothing to help me see anyone coming. I had finished my shift and was just taking off my vest and loosening my helmet strap when I heard the sound of gunfire directed straight at me. For a single moment—it was really no more than an instant—my fear left me. Like a target to the naked eye in the night, I caught a passing glimpse of something other than fear. But no sooner did I try to focus my gaze on it, then whatever it was disappeared. Thick fear returned and blocked it out. There were shots, and a hand grenade went off. I dived to the ground near the perimeter wall of the house and then heard Shimon screaming orders in every direction. He was quick, clear, responsible, and authoritative. I instinctively followed his orders and ran into the house for cover. Count-off numbers were already in the air around me. I screamed mine when my turn came. I was there. Alive. Everyone in the company was awake. Guns were loaded and ready to fire. We lined up inside the house, waiting for the battle to begin. There was more shooting. We heard shots from the sniper guns on Yoel's roof. But, for fear of hitting our own men, we could hardly do anything except wait. We scoured the night with bulging eyes, calling from house to house to make sure no one shot out of turn.

Then there were more shots, some cries of pain, shouting. We heard the whirling sound of a helicopter overhead. Rumors—accurate rumors—spread through the company. Noah (the deputy division commander) had been hit. He was taking a shit under one of the few remaining trees in the enclave when he saw the enemy. Up close. Crouching and naked, he unloaded half a magazine of automatic fire and missed. He took a bullet in his hand and the enemy ran off. I wondered if the terrorist knew that the man he had hit was the division second-in-command. I wonder if he knows now how lucky his strike was. We were amazed at his fearlessness, at his audacity. "How dare he burst into the heart of an entire combat division at war and emerge unscathed?" Even more than shock, there was outrage. "They just walk in and out of here. We don't scare them at all!" Many of the men admitted later that they envied Noah. A shot in the hand wasn't too high a price to pay for a helicopter ride home. They changed their tune when the war was over and we came home unscathed to discover that Noah was still in significant pain and in need of several surgical operations to repair his hand. I remember worrying about his unfinished Ph.D. Would he be able to type? He told me later that the same thought flashed through his mind when he realized where he had been hit. It's funny what you think of when you are shot. We spent every night after that in ambush, covering all the approach routes to the enclave. We never caught our man.

In the morning, Ze'ev arrived. It was good to see him, reassuring. He showed me the holes the grenade had made in the solid steel bars of our gate. He pointed out the shrapnel marks on the perimeter wall of our house. I saw how close I had been. It was that grenade on the other side of the wall that I held uppermost in my mind when I was able to give thanks for my safe return home. I think it was some time during the course of that morning—after a sleepless night and a very near miss—that I began feeling the hands. Or it could have been the day before. I am really not sure.

The Hands

Whenever it was (the morning after or the morning before the sneak attack), I started to feel the physical sensation of two hands resting on my shoulders. The fingers of each hand pointed inward toward my neck. The palms rested on the straps of my combat vest on either side. The fingers were spread evenly across the front and back of my shoulders. I could feel each finger distinctly and separately resting—thoughtfully—on my shoulders. The hands were weightless. But as long as they were there, I felt their weightless pressure on my shoulders. I could not see them or touch them. I could only be touched by them and imagine them. They seemed to feel blue—a sort of watery, jelly-like, white-colored blue. I remember thinking, from the moment I first felt them until they left, about the burning bush. Their weightless weight pushed down imperceptibly on my shoulders and made me think of harmless flames igniting a desert shrub. The sensation surprised me. It felt impossible. But it stayed with me for three full days.

The easy thing to do—perhaps the safe thing to do, certainly the rational thing to do—would be to say that the sensation I felt didn't mean a thing. If it happened at all, then surely the event took place within the realm of intelligibility. For weeks, I had been carrying around weight on my shoulders that

I was not accustomed to. I had experienced something of a trauma the night before. Both of these could explain the hands away. On the first day, I took off my vest several times and swept my own hands over my shoulders to brush off the feeling, like dandruff flakes. The second day that I experienced the feeling, Ari and I took turns in a waterless shower stall throwing buckets of cold water, drawn from a well, over each other's head while we shampooed and soaped ourselves down. I scrubbed my shoulders with soap. I brushed away the sensation of the hands time and time again during the three days they were there. But it was not in my power to make them go away then, and it is still not in my power to do so. I did not really want them to go away then, and I do not want to explain them away now. They left when they left.

I could say that the sensation was a figment of my imagination. But then, what would that figment be? How would it be any different from the sensation itself? The sensation felt impossible. What could be gained by calling its impossibility a figment? I felt the impossibility of the hands resting on my shoulders over and over again. Over and over again, I thought of God and the bush. I had no revelation, only an association that stayed with me as tenaciously as the hands themselves. I could protect myself now by not writing any more. But I choose not to. I choose to protect (my memory of) the hands instead.

While these hands rested on my shoulders, the war carried on and the routine of life in Ras-Bayada carried on. We ate. We slept, we guarded, we patrolled. Nothing changed. Nothing, that is, except that I felt responsible to God in a way I had not known before. But I knew nothing about that responsibility. There was no content. The hands sat there for three days saying nothing. Nothing.

I imagined that I should feel safer while they were there. But I did not. I could not. I imagined that I should feel somehow more pious, more devout. But I did not. Typically, the sensation of hands resting on my shoulders is a reassuring one. When my father rested his floppy hands on my shoulders— especially in public—I felt like the safest child in the world. When my wife rests hers on me, I feel loved. But these hands just sat there. My fears, worries, and uncertainties were untouched. The hands had no message for me. They offered no comfort and promised no safe return home. *Though I walk through the valley of the shadow of death, I will fear no evil for thou art with me.* I muttered the words to myself in Hebrew, but they did not fit. I tried them in English, but they still would not fit.

I walk through the valley of the shadow of death. I fear evil, and thou art with me. Amen.

A PROPHETIC PEACE

CHAPTER 1

Politics, Anti-Politics, and Religion

Self-justification *is the heavy burden because there is no end
to carrying it; there will always be some new situation where
we need to establish our position, dig the trench for the ego to
defend.* . . . Self-accusation, honesty about our failings, is a
light burden *because whatever we have to face in ourselves,
however painful is the recognition, however hard it is to feel
at times that we have to start all over again, we know that the
burden is already known and accepted by God's mercy. We do
not have to create, sustain and save ourselves; God has done,
is doing and will do all. We have only to be still, as Moses says
to the people of Israel on the shore of the Red Sea.*

—ROWAN WILLIAMS, *Silence and Honey Cakes*

The Temptations of Political Discourse

The walk back over the Lebanese border was no easy hike. We retraced
our steps through the ruined villages and finally approached the border along
a very steep uphill path. The war was over. Our journey home was supposed
to be safe. But, of course, we knew that nothing was over, and the atmosphere
was still tense. The feelings that accompanied me as we crossed the border
on the way into Lebanon are well expressed by Hegel's assertion that war
"seems to be more mechanical and not so much the deed of a *particular*
person as that of a *member* of a whole."[1] When the war was over I felt again
how arbitrary the participation of an individual in a war is. We all pulled out
as mechanically as we had pushed in. With nothing resolved and nothing
accomplished, the decision to bring us home was welcome, but not satisfying. We carried no trophies of a great victory and no new hopes of peace. All
the same, when we reached the Israeli side of the border we began to rejoice.
Our fear was lifted. Our minds were free to make plans.

The thought of political protest entered my head almost as soon as the bullets had been safely removed from my M-16. I felt entitled to express my grievances. My unit had been cut off without food or water for days. Our orders had been confusing and contradictory. It was clear that the war had not been handled well, and I will not deny concluding that there was a political opportunity here to be seized. Many of the men who crossed the border with me in the first days after the war were filled with the prospect of appearing on the news, rallying a popular movement, and trying to bring down the government!

As we headed home and the wheels in my head started to turn, I wondered: what difference would it make if the government caved or not? A change of government is just a change of government. Nothing more. In Israel, where the same politicians are recycled election after election, it is often a great deal less. Why would another government be different or better? Is there nothing deeper to pursue? I avoided the eager conversations that ensued among the protesting war veterans. I felt that their protest—successful or not—had no real purpose or desirable outcome. I shrank away from those who stood outside the prime minister's office for months on end, signing petitions and giving TV interviews. I distrusted their political opportunism. I felt that demanding the prime minister's resignation was too indelicate a response to the complexity and shamefulness of what we had experienced.

It took more than a year for the Winograd Inquiry Commission to publish its findings about the mishandling of the war. The findings were indelicate too. The interim report, published in April 2007, had censured the prime minister, the minister of defense, and the chief of staff. Amir Peretz (minister of defense) and Dan Halutz (military chief of staff) had both resigned by the time the findings of the final report were made public. And so when the publication date of the report drew near, the atmosphere among the Miluimnikim (military reserves) surged with anticipation. Rumors about the political upheaval the report would cause started to circulate. "The prime minister must *take responsibility* for his actions!" the Miluimnikim declared. *Responsibility,* so it would seem, has more than one meaning. To the prime minister, it meant staying in his job for as long as possible.

The Winograd report was a great disappointment to many. The members of the commission were accused of serving the interests of the government that appointed them. Most of the critics had hoped for an explicit call for the prime minister to resign. Since the members of the commission avoided this issue, their report—though severely critical of the military and political leadership—was perceived as dull and toothless. I was also disappointed—but for different reasons. I had been waiting expectantly for the report to precipitate some deep and collective national soul-searching. I hoped—somewhat naïvely—that it would provide an opportunity for the citizens of the Jewish state to take stock of themselves and debate the ultimate purpose and historical significance of Israel's military conflicts. This was not the report's effect.

After the publication of the Winograd report, I was finally moved to write a letter to the *Haaretz* newspaper. I identified myself as a reservist who had served in the war and who had chosen not to join the campaign to overthrow the government. I shared my feeling that Israeli society had been forced to confront itself in southern Lebanon. In my view, the war backfired because the people who fought it discovered they were not committed to winning it for the government that declared it. There can be no doubt that Israeli soldiers showed remarkable bravery under fire. Men fought to protect their injured comrades and sacrificed their lives to save the lives of the soldiers around them. But in my experience, few were willing to risk their lives for the sake of tactical, strategic, or political gains. The members of the Winograd commission briefly acknowledged the changes that had taken place in Israeli society since the country last fought a full-scale war, but did not make detailed observations about these changes and their implications in their final report. I believed that a careful analysis of how men behaved in Lebanon in 2006 would show that Israeli civilians as reservists (on whom the army must depend) had demonstrated that they were no longer ready to fight with the kind of unflinching reckless bravery that is needed to win full-scale wars. Israel had changed and its society had changed. In the minds of Israel's citizens, military combat was no longer synonymous with ensuring Israel's survival. It seemed clear to me that, whatever the idea of sovereign Jewish life in the Holy Land meant today, for many (including myself) it did not automatically demand the personal sacrifices that combat soldiers are called upon to make on battlefields.[2] Given that the political and strategic aims were not perceived by many of the men who went to war in 2006 as ideals worth dying for, surely the time had come to give much more attention to evaluating war's alternatives even in times of crisis. For nothing other than these most pragmatic of reasons, I expressed my view that the Winograd commission would have done better to question how we ended up at war in the first place instead of devoting all its time and energy to examining why we didn't win.

Taking Responsibility

Reality possesses two faces. On the one hand she presents us with a bright, happy smiling face; she greets us with a cheerful countenance and reveals to us something of her essence.

. . . She shows us a bit of her lawful structure and the order of her actions. . . . On the other hand, however, reality is possessed of an extreme modesty; at times she conceals herself in her innermost chamber and disappears from the view of the scholar and investigator. Everything bespeaks secrets and enigmas, everything—wonders and miracles. And reality is characterized by a strange feature. For, at the very moment when she treats us generously and reveals to us a bit of her form, she covers much more. The problem increases as the cognition progresses.

—Joseph B. Soloveitchik, *Halakhic Man*

The pragmatic point of view I expressed in my letter to the press was not really a full expression of how I felt about the implications of the war. After the war I felt dissatisfied with the almost exclusively political and strategic public reckoning that ensued. In truth, I found both pragmatism and politics unequal to the task of absorbing the implications of this war and—for that matter—of the perpetual state of war that has been part of life in the Jewish state since its inception. I came home from Lebanon feeling how much more than politics is disputed in the Middle East and how ill suited the problem-solving mechanisms of political reaction are to the complexities of the fears, the doubts, the moral compromises, the friendships, the bickering, the physical hardships, the pain, the prayers, the paradoxes, and the absurdities of conflict. I felt almost ashamed to draw political conclusions from the war. After all, I had sustained no heroic injuries, sacrificed no brothers in arms. I suppose I felt too grateful to complain, too unsure of why I had been so lucky to emerge unhurt, too imposed upon by my good fortune to demystify it. I found the idea of political change irrelevant and distracting.

At the core of all this political inhibition lay the sense that some problems have implications that transcend their solutions. Some problems are belittled by the attempt to solve them. Certain circumstances cannot endure the simplification that follows attempts to distill their meaning into policy. The deeper significance of the political reality in the Middle East, so it seemed to me, would be lost were I to think of the Arab-Israeli conflict as a problem that could be forgotten once a way to make it go away had been found. It struck me that the alluring (and perhaps illusory) model of peace among Western democracies after the Second World War[3] should not serve as a precedent for the imagined solution of a conflict that touches on such ultimate things as the return of Abraham's sons to the promised land, the construction and destruction of the Temple Mount/Haram-esh-Sharif, and the final boundaries of the Dar-el-Salaam. The Middle East conflict is about more than territory, economics, limited resources, nationalism, sovereignty, and power. The prophecies of Isaiah, Jesus, and Muhammad are at stake here. These ultimate visions that lurk behind the scenes of the conflict are blocked from emerging onto the stage of political reality by each other and by any number of intractable difficulties and obstacles that lie in the way of their realization. It is perhaps a dangerous thing to force an illusion of clarity on a situation filled with such enigmas, but this is what politicians and diplomats must do to reach agreements. How else can one respond? What else can be done to alleviate the terrible suffering of so many people locked in an incomprehensible clash of ancient enmities? Are there responsible reactions to political conflicts other than the attempts to use diplomatic, economic, and military means to resolve them? Can a responsible case be made for allaying the temptation to solve things?

In *Silence and Honey Cakes,* Rowan Williams collects the wisdom and insight of the church fathers of the desert on the impulse to flee. He cites Abba Macarius: "Abba Isaiah asked Abba Macarius to give him a word. The old man said, 'Flee from human company.' Abba Isaiah said, 'But what does it mean to flee from human company?' The old man said, 'It means sitting in your cell and weeping for your sins.'"[4] On this slightly elusive and counter-intuitive passage, Williams comments, "Flight as this saying of Macarius suggests, is about denying yourself the luxury of solving your problems by running away literally or physically from them (sitting in your cell) and about taking responsibility for your sins (weeping)."[5] It is perhaps curious that Williams proposes weeping for sins and fleeing from society as a model for taking responsibility. This is certainly not a typical modern response to adversity. Even in religious circles where faith in God is a given and reliance on his mercy is axiomatic, God's role in our struggles with adversity is most commonly tied to the popular notion that God helps those who help themselves. We tend to censure the phlegmatic indifference that religious submissiveness can engender. People who refuse medical care for their children because they prefer to pray for them are more likely to face charges of child abuse than they are to earn the respect of society (even religious society). Nothing seems more responsible than facing up to a problem and trying to solve it. It is hardly a luxury.

Macarius's point (at least according to Williams's interpretation of it) should not be confused for phlegmatism. The idea here is different and much more subtle. On one level, through his reading of Macarius, Williams is suggesting that praying and repenting before acting can have clear practical advantages. After giving an account to God, we approach the world with a religious sense of sobriety and proportion. We recognize that God created a world full of adversity and that it is beyond our power to change that. We realize that even after a particular problem has been solved another one will always follow. This realization prevents our acting rashly and irresponsibly. The slow consideration of a problem—divorced from the attempt to diagnose and treat it—forces us to take the complexity of the world seriously. While it is possible to shy away from this reality and jump straight to the problem-solving stage, this would be an evasion of responsibility. It is this evasion that Macarius sees as an unaffordable luxury.

On a second level, Williams's reading of Macarius runs deeper, culminating in the suggestion that fleeing is the way to find religious meaning in adversity. His version of what it means to face an obstacle religiously involves resisting the temptation to ignore the enduring theological significance of a problem. "Sitting in your cell" and "weeping" are reactions that acknowledge the complexity of the human condition in a world created by God, whose design for it defies our understanding. Adversity and difficulty are too fundamental to life—too central to the experiences of too many people on earth—to be brushed aside as if they were not supposed to be there. Recognizing the divine origins of the world through its complexity converts our attempts to fix things in the world into humble acts of faith rather than cocky displays of human capability. Problem solving leads people to believe in themselves; fleeing turns their attention toward God.

For Macarius, the broken design of creation is a standing invitation to contemplate the mysterious perfection of God. One must flee the temptation of thinking that all adversity is only a challenge to human ingenuity in order to solve a problem *in his service*. The conviction that the world is irreparably flawed is there to remind us that there will always be something urgent to pray for even after some of our present goals have been accomplished. Similarly, Rabbi Tarfon teaches, "The work is not ours to complete, neither are we free to shrink away from it."[6] We are not absolved of our duty to act. But at the same time, we are blocked from thinking that our actions might lead to completion and absolute resolution. There will always be more work to do. When Rabbi Tarfon says that the work is not ours to complete, it is because the role of humanity is to work in an incomplete and irreparably broken world forever. The ultimate purpose of this endless work transcends its more direct results. However, lest we think that endless work is pointless, Rabbi Tarfon insists that we are not free to shrink away from it. The hopeless task of partial repair is our perpetual obligation because it is the partiality of our successes in a broken and incomplete world that we must observe in order for our work to effectively draw our attention to God. The distinction between fleeing and problem solving, between technology and religion, between those who strive for completion and those who draw meaning from the mystery of brokenness is perhaps epitomized by the difference between those who speak of *tikkun olam* (fixing the world) and those who speak of *tikkun olam bemalchut shaddai* (fixing the world in the dominion of God). This too is the distinction between Soloveitchik's two typologies in the opening chapter of his essay *Halakhic Man: homo religiosus* and *cognitive man*.

Cognitive man experiences the world as a puzzle waiting to be solved. He "does not tolerate any obscurity, any oblique allusions and un-deciphered secrets in existence. He desires to establish fixed principles, to create laws and judgments, to negate the unforeseen and the incomprehensible, to understand the wondrous and the sudden in existence."[7] Cognitive man is driven by his desire to demystify the world. "Cognition, for him, consists in discovering the secret, solving the riddle, hidden, buried deep in reality. . . . In a word, the act of cognitive man is one of revelation and disclosure."[8] Cognitive man is a scientist.

Homo religiosus lives in search of religious experience. He is no less inquisitive than his cognitive counterpart, but his curiosity about the world is driven by a different energy. He digs deep in his search to understand the world with the conviction that ultimately no explanation of its wonder can satisfy him. He is driven by the desire to push human understanding to its limit because of his conviction that there always is a limit. It is at the unavoidable limit of human comprehension that he seeks religious experience. He is skeptical about theories and projects that explain and regulate everything. He questions further in order to expose contingencies and uncover in every illusion of absolute explanation the details that defy comprehension and fuel his enduring sense of wonder. The very semblance of a system is also a mystery to him. How does the world appear comprehensible when ultimately it is not? How come there appear to be laws and general principles when ultimately there are none? In Soloveitchik's words:

> The concept of lawfulness is in itself the deepest of mysteries. Cognition according to the worldview of the man of God consists in the discovery of the wondrous and miraculous quality of the very laws of nature themselves. The mystery of the world is to be encountered precisely in the understanding of the functional relationship in effect between the phenomena of this world. Every clarification

of a phenomenon brings in its wake new enigmas. *Homo religiosus* sees the entire ordered world, the entire creation, which is delimited and bound by the law as a cryptic text whose content cannot be deciphered, as a conundrum that the most resourceful of men cannot solve.[9]

One might mistake *homo religiosus* for a man who rejects progress, flies in the face of science, ignores proofs, and denies evidence. He might seem uninterested in human achievement and comprehension, stubborn and set in his ways, determined to contradict the premises of science come what may. But this is not the character that Soloveitchik describes any more than Macarius's model of fleeing is an excuse for inaction.[10] The *homo religiosus* acts feverishly but modestly. He has no wish to deny human achievement. He is simply unpretentious about its ultimate value. He is a man of God. His belief is not the assumed answer to his unasked questions. It is the secret motivation for his relentless interrogation of the world and its phenomena. Like cognitive man, he is a scientist who asks questions and seeks answers. But he is perennially unsatisfied with his capacity to comprehend. He is forever in search of God. His wonder is not the naïve outcome of an unchallenged faith. It is the product of a passionate humility and an insatiable desire to explore further. The rigor of his questioning protects him from confusing plausible theories with ultimate solutions to the enduring questions that human life—lived in the shade of mortality—stirs in the human soul.

My experiences as a soldier in Lebanon in the summer of 2006 led me to consider the possibility that taking responsibility for the conflict between Jews, Christians, and Muslims in the Holy Land means thinking like Macarius, Rabbi Tarfon, and *homo religiosus*. In this context, it means going beyond the political language of high resolution and clarity in order to conceptualize the conflict and its meaning in the religious language of mystery and conundrum. Taking responsibility means resisting the temptation to hang our highest hopes on the peaks of potential human achievement.

If peace is our highest hope—and I believe it should be—then perhaps its meaning must be reconsidered in anti-political and theological terms in order for us to address more fully its deeper implications without falling into the trap of confusing our ambitions with our prayers.

Theology and Anti-Politics

For behold, the Lord, the Lord of hosts doth take away from Judah stay and staff . . . the mighty man and the man of war, the judge and the prophet and the diviner and the elder,

*the captain of fifty and the man of rank and the counselor
and the cunning charmer and the skillful enchanter. And
I will give children to be their princes and babes shall rule
over them. And the people shall oppress one another every
man his fellow and every man his neighbor. The child shall
behave insolently against the aged, and the base against the
honorable. . . . As for my people a babe is their master and
women rule over them.*

—Isaiah 3

George Konrad coined the phrase "anti-politics"[11] in a book that some
would argue helped to bring down the Soviet regime in Central Europe.
Konrad urged his readers to think of anti-politics as a realistic way of dealing
with political oppression. The book *Anti-Politics* argued *for* standing down
and *against* engaging in confrontation. Written in the context of pre-Glasnost
Soviet Hungary, Konrad believed that peaceful withdrawal from the battle-
ground would serve Hungarians better than triumph: "In the Soviet-American
match there are many who cheer for the American side, but I don't know anyone here in Budapest who would be willing to see our city become a battle-
ground, even if they knew that the Americans would be here afterward."[12]

In Konrad's view, an obsession with political ideology is the sure way to
destruction. He writes, "I consider a permanently open democracy to be the
greatest good, and the ideological war that constantly casts the shadow of
atomic war on the wall to be the greatest evil." Since the Soviet Union could
never be either wished or battled away, Konrad's solution is "de-statification,"
a reduction of power from above. He suggests that political life can be limited and compartmentalized. Government can run things, without perme-
ating them. Instead of politics, Konrad proposes "networks of friends" in
factories, neighborhoods, and universities: people who trust and cooperate
with one another, trading ideas and constantly extending their areas of liberty. "Let the Government stay on top," he writes. "We will live our own lives
underneath it."

The distancing, or the sublimation, of the political away from people's
lives ascribes a matter-of-fact or ordinary role to the structures of government. The task at hand is to find a way of allowing the political process to
continue without hanging high ideological hopes on it. Anti-politics, according to Konrad, has the practical advantage of releasing citizens from the
impossible burden of committing themselves ideologically to the good or
evil embodied in one political regime or another. Political participation is a

matter-of-fact affair. Ultimately, anti-political thought seeks to protect society from the volatile fusion of a grand idea with political power.

The problem of violence that emerges when politics and ideology are combined is not really addressed by Konrad. *Anti-Politics* prescribes a healthy attitude toward political oppression, but this is only useful when one oppressive side is wielding all the political power. It suggests a form of peaceful resistance but does not point to a theory of peaceful government—and perhaps wisely so.

Charles Taylor developed the anti-political notion of an organized society when he attempted the depoliticization of the Catholic Church in the spirit of Vatican II and of the American bishops. In an attempt to articulate a resolution of modernism and Catholicism, Taylor's essay "A Catholic Modernity?" proposes the deconstruction of Catholicism's desire to fully incarnate itself in the political form of Christendom.[13] Taylor learns from modern experience that Catholicism must withdraw from its aspirations to unite the religious with the social and applies this same critique to the exaggerated political aspirations of modern secular humanism. Taylor warns against marrying faith—any faith—with a mode of society because "human society in history inevitably involves coercion." While something of this has been recognized from the beginning of Christianity in the distinction between church and state, Christendom as a project has stifled the potential of this separation with often calamitous consequences. In place of Christendom, on the one hand, and a notion of peace founded on an equally dangerous "post-revolutionary exclusive humanism" (that will supposedly allow for the peaceful coexistence in freedom of people who have relinquished transcendental visions), on the other, Taylor proposes a public sphere where no single philosophy rules. This sphere he imagines as a "locus of competing ultimate visions" that is not controlled, dominated, or facilitated by one single strong idea.

While ideals can inspire noble action, they also drag the actor into the realm of politics. In the political sphere, even the loftiest of modern values still has a Janus face. Thus, Taylor argues, "Philanthropy—the love of the human—can gradually come to be invested with contempt, hatred, aggression. The action is broken off, or worse, continues but is invested now with these new feelings, becoming progressively more coercive or inhumane."[14]

Good intentions and high values that are politicized have tragic outcomes, and the history of the twentieth century abounds in painful examples: "The history of despotic socialism (i.e., twentieth-century communism) is replete with this tragic turn . . . and then repeated again and again with a fatal regularity, through one-party regimes on a macro-level, to a host of 'helping' institutions on a micro-level from orphanages to boarding schools for aboriginals." The combination of high ideals and the politics of real people (along with the distribution of resources and power that political implementation demands) creates a painful irony that has been captured by Dostoevsky, Dickens, and many others. In Taylor's words, "The tragic irony is that the higher the sense of potential, the more grievously do real people fall short and the more severe the turnaround that is inspired by the disappointment." Israel's modern history of wars fought in the so-called pursuit of peace strikes me as one such tragic irony. Taylor supplies the following colorful anecdote to further illustrate the point:

> A Buddhist friend of mine from Thailand briefly visited the German Greens. He confessed to utter bewilderment. He thought he understood the goals of the party: peace between human beings and a stance of respect and friendship by humans towards nature. What astonished him was all the anger, the tone of denunciation and hatred towards the established parties. These people didn't seem to see [that] the first step toward their goal would have to involve stilling the anger in themselves. He couldn't understand what they were up to.[15]

The conclusion drawn here is a form of anti-politics. Taylor refers to it as a "minimum hope in mankind" and proposes finding the correct balance between the extremes of philanthropic action with this minimal hope. He poses the poignant question: "is there a way out?" Can high ideals be put into practice without running up against the failings of humanity? Ultimately, the public sphere must be run by no one ideology (not even an ideology of peace). All ideologies fail unless they are incorporated into a system or structure that has no other interest than the coexistence of them all.

To me, the practicability of this is hard to imagine. Nothing other than a council of angels in heaven might hope to attain such innocence of purpose. (Given the track record of the angels according to Christian theology, indeed not even they seem to know how to pull this off.) All the same, Taylor identifies his ideal system with his notion of Catholicism and believes that Catholics can achieve such wholeness when they internalize the criticisms leveled against them by their opponents. Offering a vote of thanks to Voltaire, Taylor acknowledges that Catholics might get a little closer to the fulfillment of their own ideals—"with a little help from [their] enemies." Such Catholicism demands that the notion of Catholic universalism be supplanted with a principle of "universality through wholeness constituted by complementarity rather than an identity of parts. Wholeness is a unity of parts rather than a suppression of them." This brings Taylor to the crucial conclusion that political societies might be steered away from violence, calamity, and the general abuse of power by a consciousness of transcendence. Religion has failed in the past by losing its genuine orientation toward that which lies beyond and cannot be mastered by the will or by the single interpretation of any human being. Thus, Taylor confesses, historical religion has been no less responsible for violence than politics has been. But a true reorientation toward the mystery of the transcendent, he proposes, might offer a way out: "What it might mean, however, is that the only way to escape fully the draw toward violence lies somewhere in the turn to transcendence—that is, through the full-hearted love of some good beyond life."[16]

Christian spirituality points toward an escape route from the failings of human politics. Turning to transcendence means orienting one's life toward the love of God. It is this love of God that, according to Taylor, reverberates back into the world as *agape,* i.e., in the form of a transcending love of humanity. Such a love, Taylor urges us to believe, is possible "but only to the extent that we open ourselves to God." In Taylor's view it seems that the violence that attends on the use of political power can be neutralized when the sphere of politics is entirely open to all ultimate visions and when "a love of life and what lies beyond life are bound together." Give up either humanist politics or religion, and violence, even a cult of suffering and death, results in religion as well as in secular society.[17]

A long history of Jewish suffering at Christian hands has taught me to be wary even of Taylor's equation of transcendence with pure Christian love. That said, I do wish to adopt the notion that mindfulness of the transcendent might offer a path out of the failings of politics. I would like to suggest, however, that a Jewish (or perhaps it would be more accurate to say biblical or prophetic) formulation of Taylor's hypothesis would reverse the roles of theology and politics. Rather than turning to theology (and love) to solve or resolve the flaws of politics, as Taylor proposes, a prophetic political theology establishes its transcendent awareness by tirelessly drawing attention to the inescapable flaws of politics. In other words, theology deconstructs politics in order to prevent it from having ultimate ambitions. Theology exposes the flaws in politics so that we remain sober about our political aspirations. Political sobriety is not there to calm our passions. Its purpose is to redirect them toward God. Biblical prophecy blames politics for thwarting the project of revelation.[18] The temptation of politics and power to give (inevitably flawed) political expression to great ideals diverts attention from the religious sensibility that those ideals might otherwise signal and cultivate. The attempt to concretize ultimate political ideals (messianism) leads to inappropriate dissatisfaction with ideals as they are. This in turn leads to impatience with them and finally to acts of violence performed in their name. The prophetic critique of politics reinstates our dreams, visions, and ideals by giving them an extra-political role to play in our religious lives.

Like love and humanitarian philanthropy, peace is yet another of the great ideals that politics does not serve well or safely. When pursued with the machines of political power, peace can be a dangerous objective. The political visionary can coax his unsuspecting subjects into making the boldest of sacrifices for this highest, noblest, and supposedly least pernicious of political causes. But in a biblical political theology, the "prince of peace" will join nobody's party nor serve anybody's political interests. Peace is not the trophy of a human triumph. It stands at odds with the deep political interest in war and conflict that Hegel understood and perhaps even celebrated when he wrote:

> Perpetual peace is often demanded as an ideal to which mankind should approximate. Thus, Kant proposed a league of sovereigns to settle disputes between states, and the Holy Alliance was meant to be an institution more or less of this kind. But, the state is an individual, and negation is an essential component of individuality. Thus, even if a number of states join together as a family, this league, in its individuality, must generate opposition and create an enemy. . . . wars will nevertheless occur whenever they lie in the nature of the case [*sache*]; the seeds germinate once more, and talk falls silent in the face of the solemn recurrences of history.[19]

Peace, "as an ideal toward which mankind should approximate," has no obvious place in the political process, which is individual and belligerent by its very nature. The biblical notion of a political theology of peace offers no real political alternative. On the contrary, the biblical visions of peace seem to suggest that an ideal peace for Israel can never be the direct outcome of political action.[20] Thus, biblical visions of peace temper political aspirations, quench social ambitions, and draw attention (away from politics) to the sublime mystery of God. The redirection of religious passion toward the transcendental empties the sphere of political activity of its ideological volatility. With politics disarmed of its ultimate purposes, the difference between prayers and ambitions seems clearer. Religion is better off for this distinctiveness of purpose and so is politics. What I am suggesting—perhaps counterintuitively—is that our collective political interests are well served by the intensification of religious passion for God. When religious passion is focused on God, peaceful living (political peace) might be the coincidental by-product of messianism (prophetic peace).

The Missing Peace

*Peace is our most important challenge and task, from every
point of view and for all religions. But we leave it to others.
We have delegated our conscience to a few diplomats and
generals, and this is a very, very grave sin.*

—ABRAHAM JOSHUA HESCHEL, "No Time for Neutrality"[21]

While I am most certainly not opposed to the ongoing attempts to nego-
tiate a peace settlement for Israel and its enemies, I am also very aware of the
failure of almost every attempt to do so thus far. I believe that insufficient
attention to the religious significance of the conflict has played a considerable
part in the inability of political leaders to make lasting progress. I think, for
example, that Dennis Ross was wrong to claim that the talks at Camp David
between Ehud Barak and Yasser Arafat in July 2000 fell through because the
Israelis and the Palestinians were unable to transform themselves "in sync."[22]
According to Ross, in order for an agreement to be made, "transformations
were required, but each side fell short of what was required."[23] Arafat was
incapable of making the transition from revolutionary to statesman, while
the Israelis were incapable of mirroring the rhetoric they used at summit
meetings in their day-to-day handling of Palestinians.[24]

The fundamental assumption that Ross shares with the other members
of the U.S. administration (whose involvement in the Oslo peace process he
describes) is that people on all sides will—and should—always prefer peace
to war when given the choice. Hence, he acted on the premise that even an
agreement built on concessions elicited from leaders under extreme diplomatic pressure will do. As long as the leaders come home from a summit with
an agreement in hand, the people on both sides will come around!

The problem is that they did not. The negotiation strategy that Ross
describes overlooks the ultimate, religious dimensions of the conflict and its
resolution. This, I believe, is a significant oversight. Religious values, as well
as people who are prepared to endure tremendous difficulties in order to preserve them, were involved in resisting the Oslo process on both sides. It was
the recurrent cycles of violence and popular opposition to the agreements
on both sides that were responsible for what Ross calls a lack of synchroni-
zation. The opposition to the proposed diplomatic solutions expressed profound objections to the entire philosophy of peace that Oslo proposed. Oslo
uncovered the deepest concerns and convictions of actual people involved
in the Middle East conflict—concerns that the political leaders were clearly

not authorized to compromise. Arafat, I would suggest, understood this. This is at least part of the reason that—despite the powerful diplomatic pressure generated at Camp David—he bolted from signing an agreement with Barak. Similarly, Barak—whose willingness to make territorial concessions was unprecedented—encountered such overwhelming religious opposition at home that his coalition government collapsed.[25]

This clash of religion and Middle East peace raises the question that is at the heart of my purpose in writing. The work is not mine to complete and I am not in a position to tackle this question in either Christian or Islamic theology; but neither am I free to shrink away from it. Therefore as a Jew, I have set myself the task of rethinking the relationship between religion and politics in my faith. While the history of religious Zionism is one of actively blurring the boundaries between political ambitions and prayers, I am suggesting that religion's ultimate concerns are better served by the depoliticization of its purposes. What I propose is a path to peacefulness achieved through the intensification of religion rather than its secularization.

In this vein, I submit that the secular politicization of the Middle East conflict should be noticed as a wasted opportunity for *homo religiosus,* who should be thinking about the meaning of "peace." Since the founding of the state of Israel, public political discourse in the Middle East has been dominated by one narrow, secular understanding of peace. The result is that "peace" is a dirty word among many religious people and—conversely— religion is generally perceived as an obstacle to peace. But *shalom* and *salaam*—in the vast and deep historical cultures of Judaism and Islam—are crucial concepts that stand for much more than a ceasefire achieved through the exchange of land. I believe that the prospects for peace in the Middle East would be improved if religious discussions about peace—as opposed to political attempts at conflict resolution—were amplified. A more vigorously religious discussion of peace could replenish the political debate with new ideas drawn from the religions and cultures of the peoples engaged in the conflict. But beyond the political gains that might stem from the articulation of new religious visions of peace, peace is a concept powerful enough and important enough in Judaism, Christianity, and Islam to bear the weight of absorbing the significance of the conflict in religious terms. By this, I mean to suggest something much deeper than the idea that messages of peace can be extracted from each religious tradition. I would like to suggest that, in the same way as the resettlement of the land of Israel by secular Jews during the first decades of the twentieth century generated a powerful religious ideology that defined Judaism as the religion of the land, a theologically intensified, depoliticized attitude toward the conflict might inspire a religious disposition or consciousness that understands Judaism, Christianity, and Islam as religions dedicated to peace. If the fuller and richer meaning of peace could be utilized to motivate the hearts and souls of the faithful in the Middle East, the well-being (*shalom*) of both religious and political life would be served.

Religious ideas and religious people have a role to play in peacemaking, but this requires a serious commitment to cultivating the peaceful potential of the respective religious traditions involved in the conflict. The scholarly discussions that I will develop in this book are an attempt to go beyond harping on references to peace in Jewish texts. My purpose is to articulate a holistic and passionately peaceful religious philosophy of Judaism. The following chapters are dedicated to theological readings of biblical, rabbinic, and prayer texts in an attempt to make good on both biblical and rabbinic statements that present the entire Torah as a path to peace. In the final analysis, I will present a notion of Jewish monotheistic theology that is geared toward the acquisition of humility, the radical acceptance of diversity, and, ultimately, peace.

I will make extensive use of hermeneutics and deconstruction in an attempt to probe the use of language in Jewish texts and to show that the classical genres of Jewish literature (rather than the specific content of either prophetic or rabbinic statements) are founded upon notions of revelation, theology, and law that are expressly peaceful. Since many Jewish texts speak approvingly of war, the strategy for accomplishing this is necessarily complex. I will suggest that biblical and rabbinic texts utilize paradoxes, metaphors, oxymoron, dissent, contradiction, and enigma in order to prevent the concretization of God. Thus, biblical and rabbinic texts ground Jewish religious tradition in a paradoxical foundation in which revelation and concealment are combined. It is this translucent combination of concealment and revelation that stands guard against those who wish to declare holy war in God's name.

Applying the principle of the translucense of revelation (which echoes theories about the translucense of language proposed by Ludwig Wittgenstein, Jacques Derrida, Gianni Vattimo, and John Caputo) to the interpretation of Jewish texts allows the Jewish tradition to emerge as one that simultaneously makes claims to prophetic/rabbinic knowledge of God while remaining insistent upon the partiality and imperfection of that knowledge. This book suggests that a perpetual experience of this partiality and the mysterious yearning for God that it engenders is an essential complement to the more conventional notion that Jewish practice is founded upon obedience to the explicit principles of Jewish law (halakha). I will propose that the combination of theological mystery and explicit law makes Judaism perennially resistant to fundamentalist religious impulses. In sum, this book calls attention to the irenic (i.e., conducive to peace) value of the linguistic mechanisms in Jewish texts that allow revelation and law to function in human hands without giving prophets and rabbis the power to impose a single view of God's will as self-evident.

Repair

Jews have responded to violence against them in a variety of ways—for example, by persuading, buying off, and otherwise appeasing or mollifying their oppressors; by preaching and practicing nonviolence and other forms of passive resistance; by flight and emigration; by prayer, inaction, and passivity; and by seeking salvation either by repairing the society in which the violence against them occurs, relying on divine or messianic intervention, or achieving political independence by means of establishing a sovereign state. Finally, the actual achievement of Jewish sovereignty, and the need to govern and defend the state of Israel radically broadened the scope and incidence of violence by Jews, both against fellow Jews and against others.

—PETER Y. MEDDING, *Jews and Violence: Images, Ideologies, Realities*

My service in the Lebanon war in 2006 was the end of my military career in the reserves. It was the culmination of a civilian process of acclimatization to life in Israel that began twenty years previously. On completing my regular military service in 1987, I discovered that I had been very hurt by my experiences in the army and that it was the Israelis with whom I served who had hurt me the most. Like everyone else in basic training, I had been the object of insults and jeering. I experienced physical exhaustion and extreme duress trying to meet absurd deadlines (thirty seconds, two minutes) for performing tasks that I could not have completed in an hour. Contrary to popular mythology, the tension that this method of training created had a severely detrimental effect on the social bonding of my unit. We helped each other, but often resentfully and with openly expressed bitterness. Insults of the most personal nature flew around the tent. Hardly a day went by without my being told that I was "a nothing," "a bastard," or the son of all manner of nature's females—human and animal.

Though only a small fraction of Israelis actually serve in the kind of unit I served in and actually experience the training I went through, when I completed my military service I felt sure that I had found the key to the heart of Israeli culture. Relatively speaking, I was still a newcomer to the country, but I believed that I had been given a glimpse into the soul of Israel's inner sanctuary and that I had found it filled with maggots. I saw the behaviors of my officers and comrades duplicated in the everyday conduct of police officers, shopkeepers, bus drivers, bank tellers, government officials, politicians, and journalists; everywhere I went, the rude, bitter, coarse familiarity with which Israelis often interact struck me as the product of a shared burden, a shared sense of national duress and collective resentment. Israeli society seemed to me like one big military base, full of exhausted, bitter, angry, selfish people, wrestling each other for a minute's extra sleep. I could not put the army behind me. I felt guilty and misunderstood. I felt that I had become too Israeli to turn back and that I could not (or would not) become Israeli enough—militaristic enough—to fit in. I became impatient and resentful, bitter, arrogant, and lonely.

I had entered the army as part of the *hesder* program, which combines military service with religious studies in a yeshiva, allowing religious boys to serve together in the same military unit. When I returned to study in yeshiva along with the same boys that had been in my unit, I continued to observe their militarism. They told interminable army stories at meals, laughing loudly at the same jokes over and over again. They used military jargon in conversation and military metaphors for everything—even in their Talmudic studies. They relished the opportunities they had to carry guns on guard duty at the yeshiva and regularly demonstrated their skills dismantling them and putting them back together. Even in civilian life, they wore regimented clothing consisting of flannel shirts and sandals with blue or gray trousers, a pen in their buttonhole, and a small notebook in their chest pocket. I was neither mature nor wise enough to forgive them for reliving the most thrilling and meaningful experience of their lives in the years that followed their release. Instead, I concluded on scanty evidence that the army—above all else—was responsible for forging the social, religious, and political behavior of Israel's religious society. I was wrong—but not entirely. I saw something, but not everything. I saw something, but not all of what I saw was there.

As Peter Medding suggests in the epigraph to this section, one of the ways in which Jews respond to violence is by trying to repair the society in which the violence against them occurs. As long as my characterization of Israel's religious society was founded on my observation of its militarism, I connected this with the militant politics that I believed were responsible for perpetuating the violence in the territories. Moreover, I found myself torn between the secular view that religion was an obstacle to peace and my own deep religious convictions. I sought a balance between halakhic integrity and dovish liberalism and found myself gravitating toward Israel's small and politically isolated religious left. The personal impact of such events as the election of Yitzhak Rabin, the early successes of the Oslo process, the horrific waves of terrorism that came in its wake, the assassination of Rabin (by a religious Zionist), the tenures of Benjamin Netanyahu and Barak, the disillusionment with the philosophy of Oslo that followed the failure at Camp David, the disengagement from Gaza, and the second Lebanon war on someone who was perched so precariously between English and Hebrew, left and right, religious and secular, was immense. However, rather than continuing my account of how these events shaped my thinking in an autobiographical narrative, my purposes now would be better served by switching to a discussion of Jewish literature, philosophy, methodology, theology, hermeneutics, epistemology, prophecy, halakha, and prayer. My story—to the extent that what follows may be called a story—is about an ongoing quest for the reconciliation of my passionate religious and Zionist convictions with my desire for peace and for the demilitarization of Israeli culture. This is all the more complex when one recognizes that neither the state of Israel nor the Jewish religion can be cleaned up, homogenized, and sanitized to suit the standards of a Western culture that presumes to imply its own moral and ethical superiority. Not only is this presumption highly problematic, it is also entirely irrelevant to the challenge of reaching agreement with Palestinians, for whom Western liberalism has virtually no appeal. In short, humane occupations, "just" wars, fair compromises, and good fences do not work. They do not bring peace. It is from this realization that I began my journey away from both the religious consciousness and the political sensibilities of the aforementioned religious left in search of a more complete and holistic role for peace both in Jewish thought and in Israeli political life.

CHAPTER 2

Irenic Scholarship

Rabbi said: All manner of lying is prohibited, except it be to make peace between one and his neighbor.

— Babylonian Talmud, Derech Eretz Zuta
(The Chapter of Peace)

Putting Peace before Ethics

The state of Israel has changed the tone of Jewish history. By way of necessity, it has and must continue changing the way the story of Jewish history is told. Indeed, the impact of the state on the entirety of Jewish intellectual life has been, and should continue being, definitive.

Armed with the ethics and truths of the Jewish state, the Jewish tradition has—all of a sudden—grown sharp teeth. Israel, right or wrong, just or criminal, heroic or demonic, wields a great deal of power. Israel is a powerful society that does not live in peace. Jewish warriors have returned to the battlefields to (re)claim what is "rightfully" theirs, to make good an ancient promise. The enmities of old have been stirred from the safety of an ever-receding past. Amalek, Ammon, and Moab have been summoned to account for the apocalyptic conflict with the (God-fearing) Ishmaelites. This rearmament is a question not only for Jews but also for how Judaism must be understood today. Handling the Jewish return to sovereign power is perhaps the definitive question for Jewish scholarship in our time. As David Hartman puts it:

> Because of national renewal and empowerment, Jews are no longer living metaphors for the "other," the "stranger," the eternal victim. They now wield power in a sovereign state, and so they cannot conceal their moral failures by blaming others. The rebirth of Israel provides the Jewish people with a public arena where they themselves must take charge, drawing on the strength of their tradition to give

a direction to political life and a content to popular aspiration. Now Jewish values must come to grips with Jewish power.[1]

The questions Israel raises for Hartman concern political ethics and justice. Historical weakness has concealed from view the political implications of Jewish law. Zionism has created a new arena that puts Judaism to the test. Sovereignty summons Jews and Judaism to the flag of national and political responsibility. Thus, according to Hartman, the establishment of a heavily armed Jewish state in Israel requires Jews to rethink, reselect, reinterpret, and reconstruct their politico-religious legacy. As the national religion of Israel, Judaism must meet the standards of political and moral accountability that are required of those who wield power.

Hartman's call that "Jewish values must come to grips with Jewish power" is one that I believe should be answered. The question is how and with what kind of response. Throughout his career Hartman has been calling upon scholars to force the Jewish tradition to face the ethical, moral, and political responsibilities that come with sovereignty. He suggests that such a confrontation will help to build the Jewish capacity to use power well. Indeed, this is the voice that I believe reverberates most strongly among those who remain committed to the Zionist idea and concerned for its well-being. But I would argue that the expectation that Judaism can guide the state of Israel to use power well is problematic. Surely, the power of sovereignty to intoxicate religion is greater than religion's capacity to affect political restraint. Where Hartman responds to the challenge of Zionism by turning to Jewish sources for a more robust political ethics, I suggest the possibility that a weak or irenic intellectual ethos might be more helpful. It seems to me that the appropriate response to empowerment involves a softening of Israel's ambitions and convictions and utilizes the religious tradition to undermine the state's moral certitude. Can this be done with integrity within a context that continues to affirm both the validity of state power and the Jewishness of the state? I believe it can but on the condition that we agree to put peace before ethics or even truth. In this chapter, I will consider the implications of this condition as it plays out in the arena of scholarship. What kind of scholarship can put peace before truth?

The brand of scholarship I have in mind might be termed "irenic scholarship." Irenic scholarship in contemporary Jewish context would set out to soften Judaism's basic attitude toward power and would provide significant opportunities for directing Jewish thinking toward peacefulness. It would seek to pacify rather than to either legitimize or delegitimize the notion of Jewish statehood. In the remaining chapters of this book, I will present my proposal for an irenic approach to Jewish political theology, but before I do so, I will examine what the principles and methods of irenic scholarship are and provide two significant examples from which I have drawn inspiration.

A Manifesto for Irenic Scholarship

In May 2005, I had the privilege of participating in a small consultation, which met at Skidmore College in New York for two days of discussion hosted by the college president. The meeting, which was sponsored by Skidmore, the Woodrow Wilson National Fellowship Foundation, and the Fohs Foundation, was organized under the auspices of the interdisciplinary journal *Common Knowledge*.[2] The people who attended the consultation were an illustrious group of scholars associated with *Common Knowledge,* including Caroline Walker Bynum, Clifford Geertz, Sari Nusseibeh, Robert Weisbuch, Israel Yuval, Philip Glotzbach, and Jeffrey M. Perl.[3] The purpose of the discussions was to consider ways in which scholarship in general might be directed toward the advancement of peace. After the consultation, Jeffrey Perl and I wrote a short statement that was signed by the group and published in *Common Knowledge:*

> The humanists and human scientists associated with this journal hold that the deflation of dispute and the facilitation of peace should be primary considerations of scholarship. And this approach, we believe, entails direct personal interaction. . . . We therefore recommend that *Common Knowledge* arrange meetings . . . [that] evaluate the contribution that existing scholarly methods can make to the achievement and maintenance of peace. The methodologies that have characterized the material published in *Common Knowledge* are those that, at least initially, we would encourage. These are methods that foster self-awareness and self-criticism; purposely demythologize the scholar's own collection of beliefs; evade engagement in polemic; enable views of the past resistant to easy moral judgments; employ the techniques of microhistory to discourage tendentious abridgements and synopses of intricate situations; reconsider irreconcilable truth-claims in the context of misunderstandings, mistranslations, and other contingencies that generate and perpetuate animosity; expose irenic tendencies and ambivalences in circumstances where pure hostility is expected; and deprive present-day conflicts of genealogy by identifying retrojections of current antagonisms into the past.
>
> Participants would be asked to consider the enabling or discouraging of peace as a criterion for evaluating scholarly methods.

Would this paper we have just heard, they could ask, contribute to the achievement of mutual understanding and respect on the part of the adversaries with whose disputes it deals? . . . It is our hope that scholars may come to identify with their methodological commitments as much as or, eventually, more than with their national allegiances and partisan aims.[4]

The scholars who signed their names to this document made theoretical room for peace (in place of an indiscriminate commitment to truth alone) in scholarly hermeneutics. Since this is a category that defines purpose, I would say that the voice emanating from this text is "programmatic" in its tone. Add to this the proposal that meetings should be arranged to allow scholars to discuss how their work may be evaluated in terms of its contribution to the achievement of peace and what emerges is a project proposal that could quite comfortably bear categorization as an initiative in intellectual entrepreneurship.

The methodological section of the Skidmore document is one densely packed, long sentence, but it does include precise terminology for what might constitute a peaceful or irenic approach to (particularly historical) scholarship. Causes of enmity and conflict are associated with conflicting metaphysical (and hence irreconcilable) truth claims and sharp binary distinctions that allow scholars to set their sights on "telling the truth, the whole truth, and nothing but the truth." As noble as this ethos sounds in a court of law, this group boldly proposed that the ideal of independent truth is a fallacious ruse that conceals more than it reveals. Insufficiently complex notions of truth are the bubble that scholarship needs to deflate. The document starts with the assumption that there is no truth sufficiently free of contingency that it can be relied upon to overcome intercultural incommensurability—an assumption that Clifford Geertz spent an illustrious career in anthropology substantiating[5]—particularly in situations of conflict. In the absence of such a universal truth, the pretense is volatile if not bellicose. The different methodological recommendations listed here share a common rejection of truth claims that generate certainties and fuel enmities.

Despite the best efforts of the organizers, the Skidmore meeting was not successful in launching an intellectual project of the sort that the document recommends. While I believe that such a project might still help to foster and spread an irenic ethos in scholarship, the journal has continued through numerous symposia and scholarly articles to advance its agenda within the confines of its pages and readership.

Even without the active interventions of an organized group, I think it is clear that scholarly trends can be seen to have an impact even when the kinds of paradigmatic shifts that enable them to take place occur with a lower degree of self-conscious purpose. Two related examples in the field of Jewish studies, I hope, will help to illustrate the point.

Comparison and Reconciliation

> *It is the premise of this book that how the two sides (Israeli and Palestinian) understand—and misunderstand—their own and [the] other's history has a profound influence on their ability—and inability—to make peace.*
>
> —PAUL SCHAM, WALID SALEM, AND BENJAMIN POGRUND,
> *Shared Histories: A Palestinian-Israeli Dialogue*

Since the 1980s, a significant shift has occurred among Jewish historians with the widespread adoption of comparative methods that are used most notably in historical analyses of the interactions between Jews and Christians. Medievalists and historians of late antiquity such as Israel Yuval, Robert Bonfil, Ivan Marcus, Jeremy Cohen, Daniel Boyarin, and others have begun emphasizing in detailed comparative studies the many similarities that can be found between the beliefs and religious practices of Jews and Christians in the past.[6] Their work seeks to account for these similarities by attempting to grasp the nature of Jewish acculturation in premodern Christian societies.

Comparison—according to Durkheim—is the essence of social science and it is therefore no surprise that this method is so widely used in the study of social history.[7] As a scholarly method, comparison is conventionally used by historians to uncover similarities and differences that allow for a sharper understanding of what is unique about a particular historical group. However, I am more interested in emphasizing here the centrifugal effect that, I believe, lends the comparative method its educational significance. Comparisons not only sharpen distinctions, but also construct associations. Comparisons cluster disparate subjects closer together, allowing unanticipated relationships between them to emerge. When the subjects of a comparison are in conflict, comparative methods have the effect of bridging gaps and building relations. It is this quality of the comparative method that makes it irenic.

The comparison of Judaism and Christianity has a long, problematic, and often painful history. Comparison is what Christians have insisted upon for over a millennium and it is what Jews have tenaciously tried to avoid. For Christians, the comparison with Judaism establishes their claim to God's preferential love.[8] Traditionally for Jews therefore, comparison has been almost unthinkable. With its centrifugal direction, comparison was a distraction from what Jews perceived as the central—centripetal—thrust of the Jewish story. Jews have celebrated the tenacity with which they have held onto their faith. The Talmud even proclaims that the distinctive survival of the Jewish people among the nations replaces the ancient Temple in Jerusalem as proof of God's presence in the world.[9] In the telling of Jewish history, contrast and disparity—not comparison and similarity—were the tools used to champion the heroic underdog. If Jews and Christians were at all alike in the past, then the similarities between them were thought to count for nothing more significant than the points conceded by a winning team in a game; they are slip-ups that leave no enduring impression on the final outcome.[10]

Even Fritz (Itzchak) Baer, a pioneer of interreligious comparison in Jewish history, consistently displayed his preference for the historical accounts found in Jewish sources. Baer was especially cautious with medieval Christian sources, suspecting them of tendentiousness and anti-Semitic bias. This was the case, for example, in his famous comparative evaluations of the Jewish and Latin sources of the great thirteenth-century debates in Paris and Barcelona.[11]

Putting one's trust in the prima facie reliability of Jewish sources was so powerful a statement of loyalty to one side of a conflict in Jewish scholarship that Israel Yuval, writing in 1993 amid a plethora of comparative studies in all fields of Jewish history, faced bitter ideological opposition for his earnest treatment of Christian source material. In a fierce rejection of Yuval's thesis concerning the possible Jewish origins of the blood libel, Ezra Fleischer accused Yuval of attaching historical significance to nonhistorical source material (whatever that might be) and of attributing disproportionate import to frivolous superstitions.[12]

The methodological development in Jewish studies pioneered by Yuval, Bonfil, Marcus, Cohen, Boyarin, and many others marks a significant and much-needed shift in Jewish attitudes toward Christianity—a shift that might be framed most effectively as reflecting the primary orientation of most Jewish scholars and indeed the Zionist state toward peaceful relations with the (predominantly Christian) West. The early years of the Jewish state were not a time for Israeli historians to engage in comparison and certainly not a time for settling differences. It was a time of triumphant recovery from the weaknesses of the Jewish past. But the political and now scholarly paradigms have shifted. Even if the accounts of many scholars focus upon polemics and conflicts in the past relations of Jews and Christians, the paradigm they have created is one of a shared history, a shared culture, a shared set of religious concerns. Scholars now require a working knowledge of both Judaism and Christianity in order to understand the history of either one. But, more important, anyone who reads their work now sees Jews and Christians as belonging to the same milieu.

When one considers how little time has elapsed since the Holocaust, the new attitude that this approach to the more distant past has engendered is quite remarkable. An honest representation of Yuval, Bonfil, Marcus, and others must concede that the intentional purpose of their tendency toward interreligious comparison is, first and foremost, historical and not political. However, as their student, I feel compelled to testify that their teaching impressed far more upon me than the scholarly advantages of the comparative method. I noticed in them (and among the other students of my generation) a distinct enthusiasm for Christianity. I learned from them a sense of closeness to Christian history engendered by the discovery of relatedness and similarity.[13] My personal experience of this underlines the terse observation that scholarship has an impact on those who study it or, quite simply, that higher education educates. What remains, of course, is for a similar shift in paradigm: the willingness of Jews at last to live in peace with the West must be supplemented with an equally compelling willingness to discover relatedness and similarity with the Islamic world.

Depriving Present-Day Conflicts of Genealogy

Even between the persecutor and the persecuted mutual relations exist. Historians must therefore learn to take both sides into account when they write their narratives of Jewish life in Christian Europe.

—ISRAEL YUVAL, "Vengeance and Damnation,
Blood and Defamation"

My second example is perhaps a more radical offshoot of the comparative method. Comparison has introduced a broader notion of Jewish historical culpability into the scholarly discourse, which has ultimately led many scholars to tackle the uglier side of the Jewish story in ways that were not previously conceivable.[14] The shift in attitude that I am describing is connected, at least in part, to the maturation of an ironic and complex consciousness of Jewish sovereignty. The result has been a steadily growing number of studies that draw attention to the phenomenon of Jewish violence against others (Jews and Gentiles) in the past. *Reckless Rites* by Elliott Horowitz[15] is an especially helpful example of this because the author openly acknowledges his sense that his work is contemporary and relevant.

In *Reckless Rites* Horowitz challenges some of the implicit assumptions that Jewish scholars have about Jews.[16] With the frequent echo of Ernest Renan's "perhaps" reverberating throughout the book,[17] it is hard to think of Horowitz as a positivist historian just trying to set the record straight and figure out what really happened in the past. It is true that he corrects distortions set in place by both anti- and philo-Semites, resurrects sources, and—with remarkable erudition—offers evidence for phenomena that have generally been ignored. But his study of Jewish violence is quite openly dedicated to much more than a methodologically untenable—Rankean—attempt to simply say what happened.

In my view, *Reckless Rites* is a perfect example of scholarship that rediscovers the past in the light of contemporary experience. This agenda is perhaps most explicit in the introduction to the book (to which I will return), but a review of the rest will help to illustrate the point in all its richness. The book focuses upon the festival of Purim and its accompanying "rites of violence." The first section outlines the complexity of the book of Esther's reception among non-Jews beside a historical account of how the biblical tribe of Amalek was conceptualized by Jews as an appellation for all forms of evil in Jewish history. This appellation was ultimately the foundation of a culture of violence that reverberates through the final chapters of the book of Esther, whose eagerly aggressive finale has often been ignored or suppressed by many Jewish readers. However, as Horowitz shows in some detail, this violence did not escape the attention of Victorians who read it with "bewilderment and with scorn for its sanctioning of ... barbarous deeds against non-Jews."[18]

In the second chapter, Horowitz moves to a review of Mordecai's refusal to bow down to Haman. Given the perilous outcome of this refusal, Mordecai's conduct requires some explanation. Were the ancient tribal conflicts between Benjamin and Amalek at play here, or was Mordecai—as the rabbinic literature suggests—bound to stand straight rather than bow down before the idolatrous amulet that Haman kept hanging around his neck? These two possibilities represent two archetypal responses of Jews to Gentiles. If, as the rabbinic texts suggest, Mordecai was a willing martyr who refused to stoop before an idol, his conduct does nothing to undermine the pervasiveness of the weak (or wimpy) Jewish stereotype that *Reckless Rites* is calling into question. However, if his refusal is tied to an unsettled tribal rivalry (Israel/Amalek, Saul/Agag, Mordecai/Haman) then Mordecai's "reckless" refusal is a wild declaration of territorial war. A subsequent chapter is dedicated to

the implications of the latter option in which the historical characterization of Haman as the eternal symbol of anti-Semitic persecution is the issue.
Horowitz shows how the genealogy of Esau, Amalek, and Haman has been
tied with the Roman Empire, the church, Hitler, and broadly speaking all
those who "in every generation rise against us to destroy us." With the alle-
gorization of Amalek to include all forms of evil, Jews are armed with the
God-given right to destroy their enemies in every generation—perpetually
obliged by biblical injunction to use violence against them in order to wipe
them out.

This allegory has occasionally been applied to such harmless struggles as
the internal war with the evil inclination. But Horowitz is clearly concerned
with the ways in which it has been used to justify more pernicious forms of
conflict. He closes the section with Rabbi Shlomo Riskin's commentary on
a sermon delivered at the Yeshiva University in New York on Israel's eighth
Independence Day by Rabbi Joseph Soloveitchik. Horowitz reminds us,
"Soloveitchik advanced the notion that an Amalekite was anyone, of any
background, who harbored unconditional hatred of the Jewish people." In
Soloveitchik's words, "In the thirties and forties this position was occupied
by Nazis led by Hitler. . . . today [1956] it is occupied by the hordes of Nasser
and the Mufti."[19] Horowitz continues, "And Shlomo (a.k.a. Steven) Riskin,
whose rabbinical career has taken him from New York's West Side to Efrat on
the West Bank, has recently written, on the alleged authority of his 'revered
rebbe' Soloveitchik, 'that the spiritual heirs of Amalek include the Nazis, the
Soviet communists and those Arabs who will not rest until we disappear
from the land.'"[20]

The second section of the book is a detailed historical study of Jewish
violence that ranges in its examples from violence against Christians in medieval Europe to the Jewish legends of the boxing ring in twentieth-century
America. In most cases, this violence is connected with the festival of Purim
or with the notion that the enemies of the Jewish people are figuratively
connected with Amalek. The section "Second Purims" comes to an ironic
halt with the story of Baruch Goldstein, which brings us back to the same
contemporary social critique insinuated by Horowitz's portrayal of Rabbi
Riskin. After "bemoaning" the forgotten custom of declaring a second (or
local) Purim after Jews are saved from persecution, Horowitz wryly recalls,
"After the massacre of the Tomb of the Patriarchs, at least one local rabbi
raised the possibility of establishing a local Purim for the Jews of Hebron and
Kiryat Arbah, who had been saved, many insisted, from a savage attack by
their Arab neighbors on Purim 1994, through the 'martyrdom of the sainted
Doctor Baruch Goldstein.'"[21]

The entire book is written with the ironic consciousness of these lines that bring it to a close. They propel the reader back to the introduction in which Horowitz first mentions the Hebron massacre together with a series of chilling accounts of settler violence against Arab civilians. He weaves these stories together, providing historical glosses that place the rhetoric used by the settlers into a broader historical context. Horowitz seems to feel that including these accounts in his introduction to a historical analysis of Purim ritual is somehow a personal confession or a "coming out." He writes, "Both the Book of Esther and Purim are subjects that have impelled both apologists and anti-Semites to show their true colors, as they have impelled me to show mine in this introduction."[22] But Horowitz's true colors are not those of one political party or another nor are they those of a pacifist, a leftist, or a self-hating Jew. This book's subtle message is not reducible to one or the other side of a political debate. Without ever belaboring the point, Horowitz shows quite plainly that contemporary Jewish violence didn't come from nowhere. However politicized and entangled the conflict with the Palestinians and other Arab nations might be—however deeply one might believe that the state of Israel and its civilian population use force only in self-defense—this perception is neither proven nor vindicated by the popular knee-jerk response to Jewish history that loyally insists, *we must have been provoked because Jews have never behaved like that.* Horowitz's voice rings clear, "Yes, they have!"

The week after I completed reading *Reckless Rites,* I bumped into the author and congratulated him on his book. I told him that I thought he was "very brave." "I appreciate your being able to see that" was his response. By "bravery," I meant to commend his willingness to put something of value at risk for a cause. Horowitz obviously feels that his book is a potential minefield, which is perhaps why he appreciated my praise. What I intended was also to applaud his brave choice of cause—a cause that I understand as making a place for sober and responsible self-reproach in contemporary Jewish—dare I say Zionist?—scholarship.

Reckless Rites is peaceful in that it purposefully inhibits the contemporary abuse of a presupposed impeccable track record by noticing past misbehaviors. While historical weakness has concealed certain—very human—questions of Jewish conduct from view, the establishment of a heavily armed Jewish polity in Israel—in my view—requires Jews to begin the work of conciliation and peacemaking from a position of accountability. Indeed, I can think of no higher purpose for Zionism and no worthier project for contemporary Jewish scholarship than the peaceful conciliation of Jews with the other nations and religions of the world.

Zionist thought and Zionist history present the Jewish people today with the question: how is Judaism to be understood in an era of political sovereignty? My suggestion is that there is a legitimate place—methodologically—for the attempt to answer this question irenically. How must Judaism be understood in our time if it is to become a force for peace in the Middle East? This is the role of irenic scholarship. The work of scholars like Yuval and Horowitz demonstrates how irenic scholarship might change the face of Israel's historical identity. What I propose is an irenic approach to Jewish political theology. This begins with a process that I call *theological disarmament.*

CHAPTER 3

Theological Disarmament

Bar Kappara said: Great is Peace, as among the angels there is no animosity, no jealousy, no hatred, no commanding, no quarrelling, because the Holy One, blessed be He, has made peace among them, as it is written [Job 15:2]: "Dominion and dread are with him: He maketh peace in His high places." "Dominion" is the angel Michael and "Dread" is Gabriel, one of whom is of fire and the other one of water, and still they do not oppose each other, for the Holy One, blessed be He, has made peace between them....

The name of the Holy One, blessed be He, is also "Peace" [Shalom], as it is written [Judges 6:24]: "And called it Adonay-Shalom." R. Jose the Galilean said: The name of the Messiah is also "Peace" [Shalom], as it is written [Isaiah 9:5]: "The prince of peace." Said R. Jehoshua: Israel is also called "peace," as it is written [Zechariah 8:12]: "For the seed shall be undisturbed, the vine shall give its fruit," which is to be interpreted thus: "The vine will give its fruit to the seed of peace" [Israel].... R. Jehoshua of Sachnin said in the name of R. Levi: Great is peace, in that all the benedictions and prayers conclude with "peace." The reading of Shema we conclude with "peace," "and spread the tent of thy peace"; the blessing of the priests concludes with peace, "and give thee peace"; and the eighteen benedictions conclude: "Blessed be thou, master of peace."

— Babylonian Talmud, Derech Eretz Zuta
(The Chapter of Peace)

Approaching Prophetic Peace

The history of religion is soaked in the blood of holy warriors and heroes, pilgrims, crusaders, kings, boys, yeomen, and knights—all sacrificed on battlefields. Their roads to war were flagged with glorious self-justifications and truths, sacred values worth dying—and killing—for. Lives have been spent on unquestioned premises, unchecked totalities, and unexamined convictions.

Historically, it has been a long time since Jews have had to fear their own conceptions of justice and truth. They have generally been disarmed by exile and dispersion. Jews were perennial victims of injustices and libels perpetrated at the hands and mouths of others. They carried no flags onto the field, had no lethal uses for their grand self-justifications and immutable truths. Instead they retreated into a world of powerlessness, taking comfort in toothless theodicies. Some dreamed and prayed for God to take his revenge on the *Goyim*. They dreamed of this promise and murmured his name, Adonay-Elohim, All-Powerful Master of the Universe, yearning (perhaps) pathetically, (perhaps) benignly, (perhaps) maliciously for the crumbled walls of Jericho, the pierced forehead of Goliath, the fateful demises of Sodom and Dagon, Sisera and Agag.

Though historians, political scientists, and journalists are unlikely to conclude that the second Lebanese war was necessarily about religion, my participation in it most certainly was. It was my Jewish religion that took me there and it was my religion that accompanied me throughout, tucked away in the pouches of my combat vest. My path to Lebanon began with a decision that was forged in an act of violence. I gasped "Israel" at the age of fourteen, lying in a pool of my own blood on a sidewalk in Birmingham, England. A gang of teenage neo-Nazi thugs—skinheads—had spotted my *kippah* as I was walking home from a Talmud class and pulled me into the dark corner of a council housing estate. They pushed me to the ground and kicked my face. I lay with my head wrapped in my arms—smarting from the shame at least as much as from the pain—and prayed, "Israel, Israel." There on the ground I made three promises. I vowed to settle in the land of Israel and to enlist and serve in an Israeli military combat unit. Even after I'd fulfilled the third promise and earned a black belt in tae kwon do, my four remaining teenage years in Birmingham were years of fear. I was afraid to walk through the streets and comforted myself with the dream of a life in Israel, where I would feel permanently safe. I dreamed of the kind of peace that follows a triumph—the peace of the daring. That dream of peace led me to war in Lebanon and in Lebanon I parted with it. In Lebanon I discovered a new peace—the peace of the timid.

Peace in the Middle East will be possible when the idea of it is a timid one. For this to be possible we must learn to think about our convictions in softer terms. If religious disagreement has a role to play in exacerbating the conflict, peace will only be possible when our notions of religious obedience are softened. This softening is what I refer to as theological disarmament. Theological disarmament should not be confused with secularization; the softening of divine presence in religion is not the same as claiming God's absence. There is nothing secular about disarming the idea of God; indeed, disarmament is an approach to religion that can be extremely passionate. Theological disarmament both produces and is the product of a religious disposition that places peace above other values, as does the rabbi who chooses peace over truth saying, "all manner of lying is prohibited, except it be to make peace between one and his neighbor." A theologically disarmed Judaism is a prayer for peace. It beckons to us, in the words of the psalmist, to "pray for the peace of Jerusalem." This is not only a prayer for peace *in* Jerusalem. It is a prayer for the peace *of* Jerusalem.

A theologically disarmed religion emerges when one transcends the dimension of explicit and open ritual practice. Religion is also an implicit imaginative understanding of faith that courses through the veins of religious experience, animating it from within. This inner imagination—more private and individual than the legalistic Judaism I practice collectively with other Jews—has a universal or even cosmic aspiration.[1] It is dreamy, hopeful, expectant, passionate, and open-ended. It sees itself in consort with the faiths of all nations and all creeds in the world and waits—perhaps naïvely—for the fulfillment of a promise that might never have been made and, if made, might never have been understood. It is a religion of prayer and attentive readiness, filled with countless moments of unrequited anticipation.

Inner reflective faith is subtle; it feeds delicately on metaphors, paradoxes, and oxymorons. Prophetic reports of it are often broken, aphoristic, and enigmatic. The texts of such reports tend to stop and start, never quite flowing, the words never quite fitting together. To whom did the Lord God say, "Let there be light"? (Genesis 1:1). How could the voice of revelation— the origin of the law at Sinai—be a voice that *answered* Moses? (Exodus 19:19). The prophetic words *seem* to point at something foundational, something solid and certain for religion to stand on. But how solid can they be when the ground they signify shifts, perpetually eluding those who reach for it? It seems hidden like a bewitched secret that disappears whenever it is whispered—always mutely and only into deaf ears.

Perhaps we could say that inner religion is an introduction to religion, a never-ending solipsism always leading *toward* something without ever arriving at its destination. My inner religion is like a path I follow toward the practice of Judaism. The path is irrevocably caught up in its own introductory nature, always leading toward its end and never breaking free of its journeying. It is a relentless prayer that yearns for Judaism but cannot fully survive entry into it.

This unanswered prayer draws ironic attention to the gap between the elusive foundation of faith and the religious practices that rely on it. It reminds us that religious practice relies on faith's foundation only by looking away from it. The gap commands us to remember the delicacy of religion and to protect it. When the delicate and vulnerable fragility of faith is forgotten or cast aside, religion easily arms itself like an automated tactical weapon. Almost of its own accord, it drags the name of Adonay-Elohim ominously to war.

The name of God is fearful in action; it runs eagerly to battle, wreaking havoc and destruction. Urban II barely uttered the words "Deus Vult," scarcely mumbled the name of God, and the world was plunged into *tohu* and bloodshed. Tolkien saw that it takes the flames of Mordor—the source of power itself—to destroy a power too great for humans to wield safely. It takes the name of God to extinguish the name of God. Peace is a prayer.

Mindfulness of the sacred delicate gap that divides the dream of God from explicit religion disarms the name of Adonay-Elohim and protects it from itself. Disarmed, I propose, the name of God is Shalom, "as it is written [Judges 6:24]: And called it Adonay-Shalom." It is this name and the gentle mindfulness of where it resides that stands for the "peace of Jerusalem."

This peace is a paradox. It is a setting in which the fire of Gabriel and the water of Michael do not oppose each other "for the Holy One blessed be He has made peace between them." Shalom is the name of the messianic promise that cannot come true in a world we know, a dream that concludes our prayers but resides outside of them, outside of our imaginations. It is a great surprise stored up nowhere we can know and promised us by a God we cannot fathom. Peace is an aspect of God through which we apprehend the created world—a broken and mysterious form of revelation—not merely a political situation. It is a *name* of God.

In an era of Jewish war—war I have been to and come back from—my religious rethinking began with wondering about what religion would be if the God of all creation were peace. What kind of service does Adonay-Shalom require? What are his commandments? What is the meaning of Rabbi Jehoshua's Israel to the people of peace who live in the promised land of Shalom?

Creating Language: Genesis

> *In the beginning God created the heaven and the earth. Now the earth was unformed and void, and darkness was upon the face of the deep; and the spirit of God hovered over the face of the waters. And God said: "Let there be light." And there was light. And God saw the light that it was good; and God divided the light from the darkness. And God called the light Day, and the darkness He called Night. And there was evening and there was morning, one day.*
>
> —Genesis 1:1–5

In the beginning, Elohim-Shalom first created the story of creation and gave it to a voice. The voice told the story to Moses, who passed it on to Israel. But no one, not even Moses, could understand the story. The story seemed to explain everything (creation), but it also did not, since creation remains a mystery. By speaking and yet not explaining everything, the articulation of creation in the narrative undermines from the outset our sense of revelation's purpose. God is not in full view. He is not the speaker of the narrative. The voice is not his; it is perhaps that of a vocal child of the creation that divided day from night, ever concealing as much as it reveals. This voice is the *creating language* that narrates the story and through the story coaxes the rest of the world into existence. It is a creature of speech that is not God but which, as Maimonides insists, God used to tell/not tell us about the created world.

> After you have advanced thus far, and truly comprehended that God exists without having the attribute of existence and that He is one without having the attribute of unity, I do not think that I need to explain to you the inadmissibility of the attribute of speech in reference to God. Speech is attributed to Him insofar as the word [*alkol*, voice] ascribed to Him was created.[2]

Maimonides' negative theology is heavily at play in this passage. The "advance" he describes is more of a retreat—away from the shackles of misconception. His "truthful comprehension" is an acceptance of noncomprehension. Thus, the voice that utters *creating language* is a creature of creation both that points—linguistically—to God and that protects God from the speech of human beings. It speaks in the text, giving us words such as "In the beginning" and "Elohim," all the while denying the very existence of divine speech. The created voice dazzles humanity with the blinding light of linguistic clarity—explaining everything and nothing—dividing the light from the darkness, preventing the light from illuminating the dark. The darkness is the silence that stands outside of language, the darkness that must remain (that cannot but remain)—as Wittgenstein insisted in his enigmatic finale to the *Tractatus*—enshrouded in complete silence.[3] Surely it would be a mistake to assume that Maimonides' purpose is to deny God's ability to speak. He seems more concerned with denying—or at least severely limiting—*our* speech about God. He reminds us to ask, "What do *we* know?" before we speak of God. We speak of God because we are compelled to praise him—how could we know his name and never utter it? But we ask, "What do we know?" to remember that we ought not speak of him. After all, what do we really know?

Creating Language: Babel

> *And the whole earth was of one language and of one speech.*
> *And it came to pass, as they journeyed east, that they found*
> *a plain in the land of Shinar; and they dwelt there. And they*
> *said one to another: "Come, let us make brick, and burn*
> *them thoroughly." And they had brick for stone, and slime*
> *had they for mortar. And they said: "Come, let us build us*
> *a city, and a tower, with its top in heaven, and let us make*
> *us a name; lest we be scattered abroad upon the face of the*
> *whole earth." And the LORD came down to see the city and*
> *the tower, which the children of men built. And the LORD*
> *said: "Behold, they are one people, and they have all one*
> *language; and this is what they begin to do; and now noth-*
> *ing will be withheld from them, which they purpose to do.*
> *Come, let us go down, and there confound their language,*
> *that they may not understand one another's speech." So the*
> *LORD scattered them abroad from thence upon the face of*
> *all the earth; and they left off to build the city. Therefore was*
> *the name of it called Babel; because the LORD did there con-*
> *found the language of all the earth; and from thence did the*
> *LORD scatter them abroad upon the face of all the earth.*
>
> —Genesis 11:1–9

Creating language pushes the idea of God beyond the category of human language, replacing certainty with mystery, hubris with humility, science with prayer. Creating language is the language that was spoken in a void to a void,

Yehi Or (Let there be light). The words seem to hail from something older than all human knowledge, but as we read and understand them we know they only illuminate the existing forms of life—the light we know inside the created world.

The Babel story tells us that God created human languages in self-defense; he created the languages that confounded the children of Shinar. God, who resides outside of language and about whom we can safely say nothing, created both the language that separates light from darkness in the created world and the confounded languages that stand guard, protecting *him* from the presumptuousness of humanity. Language is thus both the medium of creation and the mother of confusion created by God to prevent humanity from building "a single name"—an architectural monster of human construction, an artificially inseminated tree of knowledge.

The languages of Babel protect God, unhitching his name (the signifier) from the silent signified. Human language (Babel/babble)[4] is saturated with double entendre, pun, irony, oxymoron, translation (a leaky bucket at the best of times), enigma, paradox, and confusion.[5] Babel is the sentinel that keeps humankind away from the tip of the tower. Babel prevents humanity from grounding its uncertainties in irrefutable claims (claims that the voice of the Bible calls "names"—the names of God) about the heavens. In God's name, nothing can be said because, after Babel, God's name is Yahweh, Elohim, El Shaddai, Adonay, Hashem, Deus, Jesus, Allah, Atman, Theos, Bog, Jumala, Kami, Dumnezeu, Dominus, Dainichi, Jah, Gud, Om, Brahma, Akal Purakh, Satnam—and Shalom.[6] All the names of Babel can be used by those who believe in him to address the creator of all the names of God, to call to him, to beg him to come. But, after Babel, not one of them—neither truth, kindness, mercy, nor justice—can be used to build a tower, to conquer the heavens, "to make a name for themselves" to replace *the name* that holds all of humanity tyrannically at the point of one single loaded gun.[7]

Let us imagine that the names of God are like the different colors of the spectrum. When uttered together at once, would they not be as silent as light is colorless? The names point only at each other, refer only to each other, and point away—apophatically—from the silence that hovers beyond the tower's tip. This is the theology of peace, a coming together of opposing forces. Peace is the impossible culmination of all God's presences on earth. But, as distant and enigmatic as this peace is, the voice created by Adonay-Shalom still speaks through the created languages of Babel to men, saying, "Thou shall not build." By muffling and scrambling the presumptuous propositions that would resound through the palaces of heaven, the voice of creating language deconstructs and disarms the names men scratch in blood on banners and drag to war. In silence, Adonay-Shalom breathes, "Peace."

Shinar and Athens

"Let us build a city." He will come down to us and we will ascend to heaven and if not, we will declare war on Him. Despite this He left them alone and said to them "do as you will."

—Midrash Tanhuma, Genesis 18

And now look again, and see what will naturally follow if the prisoners are released and disabused of their error. At first, when any of them is liberated and compelled suddenly to stand up and turn his neck round and walk and look towards the light, he will suffer sharp pains; the glare will distress him, and he will be unable to see the realities of which in his former state he had seen the shadows; and then conceive someone saying to him, that what he saw before was an illusion, but that now, when he is approaching nearer to being and his eye is turned towards more real existence, he has a clearer vision, what will be his reply? And you may further imagine that his instructor is pointing to the objects as they pass and requiring him to name them, will he not be perplexed? Will he not fancy that the shadows, which he formerly saw are truer than the objects which are now shown to him?

. . . And if he is compelled to look straight at the light, will he not have a pain in his eyes, which will make him turn away to take refuge in the objects of vision which he can see, and which he will conceive to be in reality clearer than the things which are now being shown to him?

. . . And suppose once more, that he is reluctantly dragged up a steep and rugged ascent, and held fast until he is forced into the presence of the sun himself, is he not likely to be pained and irritated? When he approaches the light his eyes will be dazzled, and he will not be able to see anything at all of what are now called realities.

. . . He will require to grow accustomed to the sight of the upper world. And first he will see the shadows best, next the

reflections of men and other objects in the water, and then
the objects themselves; then he will gaze upon the light of the
moon and the stars and the spangled heaven; and he will see
the sky and the stars by night better than the sun or the light
of the sun by day.

... Last of all he will be able to see the sun, and not mere
reflections of him in the water, but he will see him in his own
proper place, and not in another; and he will contemplate
him as he is.

—PLATO, "The Allegory of the Cave," The Republic

The fantasies of Athens are the frustrations of Shinar. The people of the great city are afraid of dispersion. They are afraid of confusion, of not really knowing what's going on, of not understanding, of not remembering. They stand in the rain on the cold, paved, cobbled, dark, and poverty-stricken streets of the city and all they see are details—thick details they can't make any sense of. They see myriad moving parts with flashing lights and screeching sounds but no engine, no machine, no coherent purposes. They gaze up at the silent heavens from the bustling streets of the towerless city like an angry Alzheimer's patient: irritable, depressed, and hurting, peering defiantly into the eyes of the caregiver who claims to know better. "What do you mean I can't cook my own dinner, give myself a bath, go visit my grandmother after school, expect a fresh letter from my dead husband? What do you mean? What *right* do you have to tell me what to do and what not to do?" With a few pinches of self-justification, the frustration turns to indignation, the indignation to outrage, and the outrage to violence. There is no open acceptance of self-doubt, only violent denial. Before you know it, the frail, weak, veiny hand of the sweet old lady lashes out to scratch the caregiver's eyes. We can't bear the thought of what we do not know.

From the foot of the tower, the world is a maze of details that the people of Shinar and Athens are unable to grasp, arrange, order, and control. They can't take it all in from down there on the sidewalk. To them, being "scattered" is a humiliation; misunderstanding and non-understanding are unendurable and shameful chinks in their armor of pride. The gift of creation is not articulate enough for them. They want out, they want to see it from above and beyond. They want to tear their way across the serene firmament on rockets and missiles that light up the sky. They build a tower to disrupt the patronizing, beckoning, taunting serenity of the heavens. Even if it burns their eyes to do it, they will soar up and up till they come face to face with the sun, till they can see the stars and the spangled heaven by a light better and more dazzling than the lights created for—given with love to—the city below.

The people of Shinar and Athens build a great tower and drape a noisy flag around its waist. It reads "Metaphysics." They clamber up the tower, climbing and climbing all the way to the view at its tip. Someone, perhaps the last to leave the city, left a signpost behind at the bottom of the great stairway. On it, he scribbled a skyward-pointing arrow and the words "This way up—if you dare!"

So what *did* they do wrong? The question is so often repeated because the division of the world into languages doesn't feel like a punishment. We do not experience idioms, the inconvenience of interpreters, subtitles, and editions in translation in the same way that laboring mothers and farmers experience the pains of childbirth and harvest. We entertain the possibility that the tower is nothing more than a pathetic architectural/intellectual phallus with no hope of ever penetrating anywhere. What did God care? The children are climbing a treadmill, sweating away for nothing, waving their arms (limbs and weapons) in the air. So what?

In Athens, the aspiration for limitless translatability was noble. This aspiration is the counterintuition that Socrates bequeathed to Plato. Socrates taught that valuable knowledge in this world is only to be found in the "forms" that hide outside of the world. Wisdom depends on the realization that the sensory world is only a world of "shadows" while "reality" lies beyond and above the apparent. It might hurt your eyes to see in the true light of the sun, it might isolate you from your friends, but it will free you from prison. It will make your tragic life worth living. Freedom (from the prison)—liberty and enlightenment—are the redemptive gods both Greek and modern metaphysics serve. In the allegory, the prisoner is not content to contemplate the sunlight. Socrates describes a man who is compelled to get up on his feet and leave the cave. For him, philosophy is not a field of mere interest; it is his religion. He doesn't move because he is curious. He endures the pain of moving in order to save his soul. His aspiration leads to action—religious practice.

What makes him climb? What makes him suffer the scorching of his eyes? He climbs for the same reason Adam and Eve covered their bodies after tasting the fruit of knowledge: realization and shame. He realizes he is a prisoner—as they realized they were naked—and he feels ashamed. The shame cuts into his flesh. First, the shackles begin to hurt, and then they begin to offend. Soon, the offense turns to indignation, the indignation to outrage, and the outrage to climbing. This is the climbing instinct of Athens, the building fetish of Shinar. The climbing/building instinct confounded by the God of the Bible is an expression of the same demand for a place in heaven that convinced Cain to slay his brother and that Tanhuma ("we will declare war on Him")—like today's anti-philosophers of religion—associated with the violence of dogmatism. "This way up—if you dare" is the war cry of Western philosophy. Metaphysics, so it would seem, is violent; the crime committed at Babel was—as Tanhuma suggests—"disturbing the heavenly peace." As Santiago Zabala puts it in his dazzling introduction to two essays on religion without metaphysics (by Richard Rorty and Gianni Vattimo): "Post-metaphysical thought fundamentally aims at an ontology of weakening that reduces the weight of the objective structures and the violence of dogmatism. The task of the philosopher today seems to be a reversal of the Platonic program: the philosopher now summons humans back to their historicity rather than to what is eternal."[8]

The partial similarity between the Greek impulse to leave the cave (or the Shinarian impulse to build a tower) and the biblical one to call out to God from within the confines of the created world (Genesis 4:26) underlines the ambivalence that surrounds the sin of Babel. The metaphysical impulse of the city folk is a good one. It is good to look up and beyond. But the heavens are not up for grabs and God is not about to evacuate his home; neither is he going to defend it violently. The conclusion beckons the realization that enlightened ethics (justice and truth) are no safeguard against destructive violence. God's response—in the story—is not a direct one; neither is it a punishment. His move is subtler; confounding language is an emblematic corrective measure that takes the teeth out of humanity's yearning for heavenly conquest. The staircase is built, built and left standing, but after God's intervention it is designed to lead nowhere, as in an Escher drawing. The confusion of language does not destroy the tower; it only ensures that the tower has no top, no single purpose, no casus belli. Language is humanity's mark of Cain. Concealed behind language, behind his name, Adonay-Shalom is protected from the violence that might ensue when the metaphysical propositions of men are confused for the name (or the house or even the furniture in the house) of God.

I read God's confounding the languages of humanity as an emblem of what is peaceful, Jewish, and biblical in linguistic-turn, poststructuralist, and deconstructionist anti-philosophy. If "Jewish" and "biblical" are too strong here as adjectives, then the suggestion that there might be a path *toward* Judaism that takes its first steps in deconstruction and language games will suffice.[9] The integration of this path into a recognizable and explicit practice of religion is the project of this book. It is the disarming path I propose Judaism may take when reconsidered in the name and divine aspect of Shalom. Perhaps by starting simultaneously at both ends, explicit practice and implicit faith might be coaxed to call out to one another. This is what I believe they do—with clear difficulty—in the biblical text. This difficulty—perhaps impossibility— is reflected in the Bible's own ambivalence and secrecy about its foundations, its prophetic genre, and its narrator's identity. If we place at one end the irenic idea that men *cannot* declare war in God's name because they can make no metaphysical propositions about his will, and at the other the notion of explicit commandment as received through the foundations of prophecy and interpretation, our challenge will be to find how these two poles might come closer to each other, close enough for us to still call the result Judaism.

Religion and Religiosity

> Religiosity *is man's sense of wonder and adoration, an ever anew becoming, an ever anew articulation and formulation of his feeling that, transcending his conditioned being yet bursting from its very core, there is something that is unconditioned. Religiosity is his longing to establish a living communion with the unconditioned, his will to realize the unconditioned through his action, transposing it into the world of man. . . . Religion is the sum total of the customs and teachings articulated and formulated by the religiosity of a certain epoch in a people's life; its prescriptions and dogmas are rigidly determined and handed down as unalterably binding to all future generations, without regard for their newly developed religiosity, which seeks new forms. . . . But once religious rites and dogmas have become so rigid that religiosity cannot move them or no longer wants to comply with them, religion becomes uncreative and therefore untrue.*

> —MARTIN BUBER, "Jewish Religiosity"

Explicit religion—Buber's I-It religion—relies unwittingly on created language to tell it which articulated customs and rituals to keep. The voice that speaks in the Bible is understood as the hegemonic voice of God. The text gives testimony to the presence of a source that accounts for and explains the foundations of being, truth, law, and justice. Revelation sets the endless cycle of interpretation rolling like a bowling ball, all the while regulating its path, keeping it headed toward the pins, preventing it from spinning off into a gutter that leads nowhere. Thereafter, political systems—checks and balances of power and authority—determine what is and what is not a bowling pin, which path is and which is not a bowling lane. Once the ball is in motion, the mystery of the source matters a little less. It is authority—to interpret that which is "no longer in heaven"—that counts. From authority, debates and disagreements ensue; these are the wars of words that religious liberals believe they can handle.

But liberalism is no antidote for fundamentalism. Where liberals celebrate pluralism—multiple bowling lanes with pins of varied shapes, colors, and sizes—fundamentalists see a single target and a single path leading to it. But the difference between them is just a matter of degree. To an explicitly religious reader of either variety, "I am what I am" constitutes an answer to a question asked. Asked and answered (locked and loaded). The question arises, as it were, self-evidently from the natural curiosity of a conscious mortal experiencing a spatially and temporally situated linguistic encounter with an articulate and seemingly nameless being. "What is your name?" is almost the only polite thing to ask. "I am" is an awkwardly enigmatic, perhaps slightly rude, answer. But that is precisely what it is, an answer. Now you have your answer, *idach zil gmor* (go figure what it means). What the answer means and how many meanings it has is, once again, just a matter of degree.

In religion, prophecy is understood as divine statement, law as divine will, God as both a giver and a speaker of words. However mysterious and unfathomable its methods of reception and transmission are, prophecy involves the entry of God into history. God—at least initially—authors the law. Revelation is an event. It pierces through the mysterious crust of the heavens and can be witnessed—perhaps even simply (i.e., with normally adjusted human senses) and en masse—from within the confines of nature and history. However awkward, however complex and difficult it is to parse and use, "I am what I am" (I will be what I will be; *Aheye asher Aheye*) is as tangible a name as Jacob's limp is the physiological result of an injury. Perhaps someone needs to deem you especially worthy (it always helps to be in the right place at the right time), but revelation is—literally—*revelation*. Something secret is told—revealed. In this event of telling resides the metaphysical essence of what is sacred.

An implicit reading of faith that is grounded in religiosity (Buber's I-Thou) follows a different impulse. It has no essences. No statements. Only questions. Its aspirations are counterintuitive and its outcomes—when articulated—seem forced, impractical, and perhaps even impossible. Such is Buber's quest for a "life in communion with the unconditioned." But the conception of religiosity I propose to develop in this discussion—while no less open-ended—is slightly different from Buber's. In my use of the terms, religiosity (or implicit religion) coexists only paradoxically with religion. The impulse of religiosity follows a path that simultaneously leads away from and toward religion. This is the path that I refer to as an *advanced introduction* to religion.

I have chosen this term—*advanced introduction*—because it connotes a journey backward, a return from afar (a place of advancement) to a point of departure: a walk back across enemy lines. To Buber, the notion of advanced introduction might perhaps connote something mystical: a new beginning that follows the discovery of a secret essence.[10] Like a math professor in a university telling his students to forget all they learned in high school, Buber might think of an advanced introduction as a course in religion that elucidates the mystical or prophetic foundations (religiosity) that religion relies on. But advanced introduction is an oxymoron, a paradox that thwarts the refreshing and reinvigoration of religion by religiosity, even as it suggests it. Rather, implicit religiosity problematizes explicit religion. It does not replace it and it certainly does not help to account for its foundations. It disturbs more than it explains. As I understand the relationship between implicit and explicit faith: explicit religion relies on answers to questions it can never dare to ask, while implicit religiosity hopelessly and endlessly asks questions it knows it can never answer. Thus, religion and religiosity can never meet.

The path I propose to follow reinvigorates explicit religion but not by injecting any secret nectar into its roots. My path starts with a parting (and "every parting is a little death")[11] from the metaphysical assumptions upon which religion seems to rest. The route travels away from a philosophy of religion (the roots of religion in the Greek sense), stripping explicit religion of the very metaphysical assumptions that seem to present themselves at its core. This is a path that has been carefully walked and mapped out by many others. My purpose is not to blaze a trail so much as to recharacterize its point of departure and add a new destination at its end. The point of departure is, for me, a philosophy of explicit religion that is capable of justifying war; the objective is to return to explicit religion in peace. The initial point of departure is perhaps a quest for a secret store of divine power. Historically, we might attribute this quest to the frustrations of an exilic era of enforced powerlessness. The goal is to return to a religion sufficiently self-doubting, and hence peaceful, that it may serve today as the religion of Israel, Jerusalem, and Zion. This is the journey of theological disarmament: "May it be Your will that I step forward in peace, that You lead me in peace, that You bring me to my destination in peace and return me to my home in peace. Amen."

CHAPTER 4

Deconstruction and the Prophetic Voice

>—*[O]f him there is nothing said that might hold*
>—*Save his name [sauf son nom]*
>—*Save the name [sauf le nom] which names nothing that holds, not even a gottheit, nothing whose withdrawal [dérobement] does not carry away every phase that tries to measure itself against him. "God" "is" the name of the bottomless collapse, of this endless desertification of language.*
>
>*As if it was necessary to save [sauver] the name and to save everything except [fors] the name, save the name [sauf le nom] as if it was necessary to lose the name in order to save what bears the name or that towards which one is borne across the name.*
>
>—JACQUES DERRIDA, "Sauf Le Nom (Post-Scriptum)"

Saving the Name

The image of the warring prophet is a familiar one. He is easy to picture, mounted on his warhorse, sacred scrolls in hand, screaming the holy word as he leads kings, princes, and commoners to killing and dying in the name of God. His words ignite the passion of an eternal, messianic zeal. His certitude and conviction brush aside reservation, doubt, deliberation, and—perhaps most hazardously—the possibility of inaction. Prophecy, so it seems, can be treacherous.

I have already conceded that implicit religion, relying on methods of deconstruction—resisting dogma in favor of almost boundless flexibility—is perhaps a little harder to recognize as "Judaism" than the explicit religiosity that builds rabbinic interpretation on top of biblical prophecy like two bricks in a tower.[1] For fear of remaining useless—stranded on the other side of a rainbow[2]—it will be necessary later to articulate a crucial role for explicit Jewish religiosity. But since dismantling the weapons of war is my first task, I begin with the atom bomb of religion's arsenal—prophetic/messianic certitude.

In articulating a peaceful (theologically disarmed) notion of prophecy, it is necessary to remain mindful of the fact that biblical prophets spoke of war as much as they did of peace. In other words, prophetically informed sermons for peace on earth are inadequate to the task of disarming prophecy of its destructive potential. The irenic meaning of prophecy that I propose must reside in the very fabric of the prophetic genre rather than in the specific content of any particular prophetic message. In characterizing this genre, I hope to reconcile a quietist (almost silent) notion of God with the noise and violence that are often found in the textual content of biblical prophecy (and post-biblical messianism).

The reconciliation of prophecy with the tacit denial of divine speech that I propose lies paradoxically and impossibly within an explicitly wordy biblical tradition. What I wish to deny here is neither God's ability to speak nor the divinity of the Bible's origin. Perhaps denial is too emphatic a term since this particular "denial" is more of a humble acceptance of the ways in which language limits the human capacity to apprehend an unlimited God. Language thus protects God and his name. It is his place of hiding—a place where he is and is not. In Derrida's words, the name of God, or the word, "save[s] what bears the name or that towards which one is borne across the name." It is the passionately religious practice of saving the name that is described here. This is, perhaps, the exemplary practice of implicit religion. Perhaps it is this attitude toward God's concealment that allows us to leave him in peace.

I will present my phenomenology of biblical prophecy alongside a disclosure of the connection that I see between the *postmodern* and the *prophetic* voices. While the biblical readings I will offer in my chapter "Messianic Peace" do capture something that is organically Jewish, I wish to confess here that I could not have conceived them without Wittgenstein, Derrida, Jean-Luc Marion, Vattimo, Rorty, Caputo, Zabala, Taylor, Kearney, and many others who dedicated more of their energies to Western philosophy than to the interpretation of biblical or rabbinic texts. My admiration of these writers is underlined by an appreciation of the irenic—that is to say, valuable for peacemaking—quality of their work.[3] For reasons that transcend the purpose of offering plausible biblical readings, I have chosen to characterize what I call the *prophetic voice* following on the heels of those who, in Richard Kearney's words, "strive to overcome the metaphysical God of pure act and ask the question: what kind of divinity comes after metaphysics?"[4] I believe that the answer is: the God of the Bible.

As relevant and appropriate as it no doubt is to approach the biblical God from within the assumptions of a currently compelling linguistic philosophy, it is equally important to be able to say in good faith, as Kearney does:

> My basic wager is that this God is much closer than the old deity of metaphysics and scholasticism to the God of desire and promise who, in diverse scriptural narratives, calls out from burning bushes, makes pledges and covenants, burns with longing in the song of songs, cries in the wilderness, whispers in caves, comforts those oppressed in darkness, and prefers orphans, widows and strangers to the mighty and the proud.[5]

In other words, as a reader who finds postmodern skepticism both more convincing and less belligerent than both Hellenistic and modernist metaphysics, I recognize that a relevant reading of biblical prophecy—a reading that responds to contemporary trends of intellect and conscience—must still remain plausible and authentic for those (myself included) who continue to cherish the sanctity of the biblical text.

Wittgenstein's Prophetic Voice

> *What is a prophet like? Wittgenstein is the nearest to a prophet I have ever known. He is a man who is like a tower, who stands high and unattached, leaning on no one. He has his own feet. He fears no man. "Nothing can hurt me!" But other men fear him. And why? . . . They fear his judgment.*
>
> —OETS BOUWSMA, Wittgenstein: Conversations 1949–1951[6]

After the war in Lebanon, I chose a picture of Wittgenstein as the wallpaper for my computer-screen desktop. My son helped me to find it on the internet and—again with his assistance—I managed to download it. It is a well-known picture of the middle-aged Ludwig in a tweed jacket, with ruffled shirt and no tie, looking off to the side. But, in the copy we found, there is a twist: a mirror image of Wittgenstein is juxtaposed to the original. Though the two Wittgensteins are looking at each other, the nearer eye is also—at least partially—straying in the direction of the camera. The effect is chilling; a small slice of Wittgenstein's formidable gaze is twice diverted toward the observer.

I chose this picture because I wanted Wittgenstein's penetrating eye (and its mirror twin) to be the first thing to see me every time I dared to sit down and write. Wittgenstein's look reminds me of his curious idea that it takes special courage *not* to write. This is one of Wittgenstein's more interesting confessions. By his own standards (and arguably by these alone), "courage" is something that this most persistent of writers seems not to have had. Now, I only have to switch on my computer and I am a coward in his eyes—caught in the sheepish act of writing.

Thoughts of Wittgenstein accompanied me throughout the war in Lebanon. It is curious perhaps that I thought of him so much. Wittgenstein was no great champion of peace. But during the war, neither was I. Wittgenstein was in my mind almost constantly while we were stationed in Metulla. He was with me during the long night marches. He featured prolifically in pretend lectures (they were almost prayers) that I uttered, muttered, and mumbled under my breath to pretend audiences of pretend students during the long, dark, fear-filled nights that stretched out between Zar'it, Raj-a-Min, Sham'ah, and Ras-Bayada. Thinking of Wittgenstein somehow reminded me that I was not really a soldier.

I do not remember ever before being so moved by the sheer effort of another man, so impassioned, inspired, and ashamed by his powers of concentration. I imagined with yearning what it must have been like in those long, solitary, impoverished hours in Skjolden, where his mind was "on fire" as he wrote.[7] This turn of phrase stirred me when I first read it, kindling a strange fascination. (Perhaps it reminded me of something similar my father wrote about his state of mind when, at the age of sixty-five, he finally sat down to spend the last five years of his life writing the poetry and autobiographical prose he so loved after a career spent in geriatric medicine.) When I was in Lebanon, the image of Wittgenstein formulating the compact propositions of the *Tractatus* with his mind on (under) fire as he served on active duty in the First World War was an especially exquisite thought to savor.

On a number of occasions, Wittgenstein hinted at his prophetic ambition.[8] Strikingly, it was his sense of failure that he considered prophetic. Prophecy in the Wittgensteinian sense seems tragically doomed to fail. Prophecy demands the accomplishment of the impossible. Prophecy is speech that hangs precariously on language's outermost rim. The prophet works relentlessly to speak the ineffable word of God, but ultimately cannot succeed. He carries the word of God like water in his mouth. He cannot speak without spilling. Thus spoke the Lord to Isaiah, "Go, and tell this people: Hear ye indeed, but understand not. Make the heart of this people fat, and make their ears heavy, And shut their eyes; Lest they, seeing with their eyes, and hearing with their ears, and understanding with their heart, return and be healed" (Isaiah 6:9–10). Preach the impossible to the people. Tell those who will not understand. Thunder the word into ears that God has stopped. Pour judgment into throats that cannot swallow. Shine light into eyes God has blinded—"till when? *Ad Matay?*" Isaiah asks—until the world is in ruin.

"I destroy, I destroy, I destroy," said Wittgenstein. "And I will prepare destroyers against thee," Jeremiah screamed (22:7). Destruction is the recurring chorus of prophecy. Man can no more hear of his own destruction than he can imagine his own death. The voice of Jeremiah speaks impossibly of imminent destruction—he poured out words of wrath on those who would never comprehend them. Prophecy is a tragedy—it stirs the hearts only of those who have yearned for it. In the notebooks published under the title *Culture and Value,* Wittgenstein wrote of the "obscure language of prophecy comprehensible to very few indeed."[9] The few are perhaps only those whose minds have been on fire—the rare few who have been nearly mad.

Prophets are like fish bent on flying. Burdened with the ineffable, they relentlessly return to their hopeless task. Wittgenstein wrote, "My whole tendency and I believe the tendency of all men who ever tried to write or talk ethics or religion was to run against the boundaries of language. This running up against the walls of our cage is perfectly, absolutely hopeless."[10] Hopelessness is the experience of prophets (and philosophers) whose concerns lie beyond language. If philosophy is ever to atone for the terrible confusion it has caused, it must learn to live within the walls of the cage. Otherwise, philosophy (and prophecy) becomes a never-ending expedition to the grave of Moses. Ultimately, Wittgenstein's fastidious devotion to language's mechanisms claimed his obsessive attention just as the neglect of the poor enraged Isaiah, Amos, and Micah. This is a comparison that requires further explication.

Language and the poor share the same cage: both are tangible expressions of a reality and can be spoken of clearly. Wittgenstein's ladder—his metaphor for the nonmetaphysical world to which language is confined— is the object of all his philosophy. Despite the shifts and changes in his characterization of the correlation between language and reality, his object remained the same, as did his insistence that beyond the ladder there is only silence. Something more can—perhaps—be seen from the ladder's tip, so to speak. But it is always out of reach—beyond ownership. So why climb the ladder? Perhaps Sir Edmund was right, "because it is there" or, in more Wittgensteinian form, because its existence can be stated clearly. Herein lies the greatest moral accomplishment of Wittgenstein's work. Wittgenstein brought to twentieth-century philosophy the meticulous observation of *what is there,* finding value in noticing what is in the world, in seeing the world for what it is and not for where it leads. This is the shift from *telling* to *showing,* from explaining to observing that is so central to Wittgenstein's way of doing philosophy:

> 6.371 The whole modern conception of the world is founded on the illusion that the so-called laws of nature are the explanation of natural phenomena.

> 6.372 Thus people today stop at the laws of nature, treating them as something inviolable, just as God and Fate were treated in past ages.[11]

The fault of metaphysics is shared by modernist science and religion. It is the fault of those who would explain what—strictly speaking—they could not. Wittgenstein wrote, "The philosopher's treatment of a question is like the treatment of an illness."[12] Metaphysics is the illness, the source of the confusion that Wittgenstein set out to dispel. His achievement, therefore, is in what he prevents. His work is apophatic; it moves forward only by moving backward. The work of the Wittgensteinian prophet can never be more than the suppressing and dismantling of error, the drawing of attention away from faulty abstractions to the impoverished concrete reality. The prophet's role is to disturb and disrupt erroneous pretenses, but neither to erect nor construct their alternatives. He makes room for God; he does not bring him.

Wittgenstein's attitude toward the concreteness of language is prophetic because it echoes the moral preaching of the prophets. The prophets do not see metaphysical or conceptualized strife. They see the reality of the poor. The poor—like mechanisms of language—are in front of us. We can speak of them without abstract generalizations. The prophets insist that we acknowledge and notice them. Their presence generates our moral duty to confine ourselves to the tangible demands that their needs place upon us. We are claimed by the plight of the poor, not by the idea of poverty. There is no room for ultimate morals or justice just as there is no point in establishing propositions in ultimate terms of meaning. The world claims us because it is in front of us.

As a practicing religious Jew, it had been my custom to conceive of certain thinkers (certain books) as my backdoor, my trap door, my release valve from the confines of a religious dogma to which I remained obligated. Before the war in Lebanon, Wittgenstein served me better as a Christ and a Buddha—far better than he ever could as a Moses. I read him in the same way as I read the New Testament, Augustine, the Philokalia, Nagarjuna, the Dalai Lama, and the Upanishads. I habitually read Wittgenstein as if I were

---

a pilgrim visiting a foreign land. But this particular return home from this particular war pilgrimage with a souvenir of peace in my mouth brought "Wittgenstein the Jew" to light for me. For the first time, a Jewish rendition of Wittgenstein became a live option. I contemplated comparing Wittgenstein with Heschel. I could now read him—as it were—*at home*.

But I have never really felt comfortable with Wittgenstein as a Jew. His admiration for Otto Weininger is one of many indications that he never felt too comfortable with the idea either.[13] Perhaps his anti-Hellenism might help make the case. Perhaps Wittgenstein is the prophet of Hanukkah. The story of Judah the Maccabee's struggle was continued more peacefully by Ludwig the Jew. Wittgenstein sought to shut down the distractions with which Greek philosophy assaulted humanity—by changing the subject. He wrote a Talmudic tractate on linguistics to keep the Greeks out. "Philosophy," he wrote, "is an instrument whose only use is against philosophers."[14] Wittgenstein thought of philosophy as a practice. "Philosophy is not a theory but an activity." He begins with examples and then deduces principles. He *looks*. This is how rabbinic texts work. Study is a practice over which one recites a blessing as one does over the donning of *tephillin* and the sanctification of the Sabbath. The Wittgensteinian practice of philosophy is to rail against the untenable propositions that masquerade as great secrets. Secrets dazzle us, distract us with false curiosities, and prevent us from ever seeing the world that presents itself in open view. "A picture holding us captive is Wittgenstein's image of the predicament he is trying to pry us out of."[15]

Ranjit Chatterjee's *Wittgenstein and Judaism: A Triumph of Concealment* insists that Wittgenstein's habit of recommending Weininger's pernicious book to all his friends was a ruse—a test, a way of showing European readers how vile they look in the murky mirror of *Sex and Character*. Chatterjee argues, "the pointing function of all Wittgenstein's work was towards the Jewish tradition." He recognizes that there are no concrete statements to this effect to be found in Wittgenstein's writings. His effort is, therefore, both creatively interpretive and self-consciously demure. In the spirit of his subject, Chatterjee is content merely to point at Wittgenstein pointing at Judaism. He means to open up a compelling possibility, not to shut another one down. Chatterjee argues that, on the final analysis, Wittgenstein remains a puzzle. But, he suggests—perhaps a little more eagerly—puzzles and enigmas are a Jewish genre. Chatterjee's submission is that Wittgenstein, like Maimonides, "wanted to leave behind a puzzle of some profundity, whose solution only leads to more puzzles."[16] Like Maimonides, perhaps like Nachmanides, Isaac Luria, Abraham Abulafia, Abraham Ibn Ezra, Nachman of Breslov, and many others who do not really feature in Chatterjee's text, Wittgenstein, with his enigmas of concealment, is perhaps revealing/concealing the trademarks of a Jewish thinker.

Wittgenstein's triumph of concealment is therefore multilayered. According to Chatterjee, he concealed not only his Jewish ancestry but also his intellectual Judaism. The simple truth about his family's Jewish lineage seems to have been something of a secret for him too. To Fania Pascal, Wittgenstein's Jewishness was nothing more than an accident of birth. It meant nothing to anyone with a deeper understanding of "Jewish identity" than that possessed by the authors of the Nuremberg Laws. And yet, it is the secret of his Jewishness that Chatterjee identifies as the primary substance of the confessions Wittgenstein made to his friends in 1936.[17]

Ray Monk insists that these "confessions" are vital to the composition of the *Philosophical Investigations*. The act of confession accounts for Wittgenstein's success in formulating his ideas. *Philosophical Investigations* is a personal confession, the result of rigorous self-scrutiny. As he worked, Wittgenstein sought to dismantle his pride. He dug deep into his soul, reaching past his own capacities for self-deception. This "was terribly hard work," he wrote, but crucial to his philosophical accomplishment. "If anyone is unwilling to descend into himself, because this is too painful, he will remain superficial in his writing."[18] Chatterjee urges us to consider that Wittgenstein's soul-searching uncovered the awful truth of his philosophical Judaism—a Judaism characterized by hiding, by the ghettoizing of the soul. Concealment is Jewish.

Taking the *Philosophical Investigations* personally seems to emerge from Monk's account as the primary requisite for making any sense of the book, and I tend to agree. But, perhaps, it is not so much the concealment of Wittgenstein's Judaism that we should be looking for, but the suggestion that understanding revelation as concealment can be taken plausibly as a Jewish idea. Wittgenstein's work seeks to reveal what is out in the open (like ordinary language and the poor) in order to conceal or protect what must remain enshrouded in silence (mysticism and divine truth). Clearly, the effort of concealment was not made solely to protect the truth about his family; perhaps it was made to exclude God from human hostilities toward the nature, purpose, and intention of his divine existence.

The idea of Wittgenstein's philosophical Jewishness emerges when he is compared with Abraham Joshua Heschel's reading of the prophets. Heschel beautifully articulates the parallel between prophetic and non-Hellenistic philosophical morality. Heschel saw the significance of the prophets "not only in what they said but in what they were."[19] The genius of the prophet lies in his capacity for compromise with language. Steering away from the sublime and elegant mansions of the mind to sanctify the slums where the poor and needy call for help is the prophet's best strategy. He finds his way back from experiences that defy verbalization by articulating the most concrete of concerns. Heschel continues:

> A student of philosophy who turns from the discourses of the great metaphysicians to the orations of the prophets may feel as if he were going from the realm of the sublime to an area of trivialities. Instead of dealing with the timeless issues of being and becoming, of matter and form, of definitions and demonstrations, he is thrown into orations about widows and orphans.[20]

There is an unintended parallel with Wittgenstein here. Heschel downsizes the philosophical presumption of the prophet. The prophet is claimed and outraged by the concrete experience of suffering he observes. He is engaged by the poor and mystified by their plight. It is the experience of humility in the face of mystery that makes space for compassion. Humility is also—and in the same way—the mother of tolerance and peace.

> I suggest that the most significant basis for the meeting of men of different religious traditions is the level of fear and trembling, of humility and contrition, where our individual moments of faith are mere waves in the endless ocean of mankind's reaching out for God, where all formulations and articulations appear as understatements, where our souls are swept away by the awareness of the urgency of answering God's commandment, while stripped of pretension and conceit we sense the tragic insufficiency of human faith.[21]

A prophet is a person who remains radically open to the possibility of surprise. He has the least sentiment for dogma and his attention is most focused on the other—the completely Other (*tout autre*) as well as all others. This radical resistance to dogmatism is a lesson in humility that tempers our claims to speak in God's name and forces our ears to remain sharp, sensitive to the voices of those around us whose words and feelings stir our souls and move our sense of justice. As we listen to them, we pray for them and wish to live in peace with them. It is this humble concern for the Other (humble before the mystery of God and his surprises)—and not metaphysics and ideology—that moves the prophet to take moral action. In other words, the prophetic voice articulates biblical ethics in the form of a "sub" system (what Buber called *Ich-Du,* I-Thou) and not a "meta" system (*Ich-Es,* I-It).[22] The prophet is moved by a detail and not by an idea—by a person, not a principle. The subsystem that recognizes our own inadequacy reminds us how little we really know of God and how undeterred or unthreatened we must be by the possibility that we are getting it wrong again and again. Humility urges us (weakly) to engage in a constant process of rethinking and reassessing when faced by the claims of others.

This subsystem lies at the heart of Heschel's notion of prophetic "pathos." The prophet is attentive to God. He presents himself before God to answer God's insatiable need for revelation. He tries to contain and embody an aspect of the unlimited capacity of the divine for conflicting and paradoxical emotional impulses. Fury and love, mercy and vengeance all meet in the prophecies, though no single prophet can contain them all at once. Yet, as Heschel insists, the prophet is claimed by his subjective relationship with God. He answers the divine call to serve a divine need. He gains no mastery of meta-principles nor any full knowledge of a greater or higher law. He is radically undogmatic and endlessly sensitive. His notion of God is one of a divinity to be served and protected. God is not an oracle of ultimate knowledge or unflinching ideological purpose. The relationship is gentle and compassionate. It is an act of mutual kindness and empathy. It is not and cannot become grounds for the human declaration of war in God's name.

Wittgenstein and the Peaceful Future of Religion

Richard Rorty dubbed Wittgenstein the "ancestor of the 'linguistic turn'" in a collection of essays devoted to philosophical method.[23] The centrality of Wittgenstein's contribution (along with that of Heidegger and Dewey) to twentieth-century philosophy is a recurrent theme in Rorty's work. See, for example, the opening passage of his *Philosophy and the Mirror of Nature*:

> Philosophers usually think of their discipline as one which discusses perennial, eternal problems—problems which arise as soon as one reflects. Some of these concern ... the legitimation of claims to know, and are crystallized in questions concerning the "foundations" of knowledge. To discover these foundations is to discover something about the mind, and conversely. Philosophy as a discipline thus sees itself as the attempt to underwrite or debunk claims to knowledge made by science, morality, art, or religion. . . . Philosophy can be foundational in respect to the rest of culture because culture is the assemblage of claims to knowledge.[24]

Rorty continues:

> It is against this background that we should see the work of the three most important philosophers of our [twentieth] century—

Wittgenstein, Heidegger, and Dewey. Each tried in his early years to find a new way of making philosophy "foundational"—a new way of formulating an ultimate context for thought. . . . Each of the three came to see his earlier effort as self-deceptive, as an attempt to retain a certain conception of philosophy after the notions needed to flesh out that conception (the seventeenth-century notions of knowledge and mind) had been discarded. Each of the three, in his later work broke free of the Kantian conception of philosophy as foundational, and spent his time warning us against those very temptations to which he himself had once succumbed. Thus their later work is therapeutic rather than constructive, edifying rather than systematic, designed to make the reader question his own motives for philosophizing rather than to supply him with a new philosophical program.[25]

Rorty's choice word here is "usually": "Philosophers usually think." Wittgenstein, Dewey, and Heidegger are the three most important philosophers of the twentieth century because their work is unusual, extraordinary, and responsible for a significant shift *away* from the foundations of secularism. What is most interesting here is perhaps only "here" between the lines. All the same, it is striking to observe the metaphors Rorty uses, as his discussion unfolds, to portray "usual" philosophy as warlike.[26] He begins with a brief mention of Husserl and Russell:

At the beginning of our century, this claim [that science had defeated religion] was reaffirmed by philosophers (notably Russell and Husserl) who were concerned to keep philosophy "rigorous" and "scientific." But there was a note of desperation in their voices, for by this time the triumph of the secular over the claims of religion was almost complete. Thus the philosopher could no longer see himself as in the intellectual avant-garde, or as protecting men against the forces of superstition.[27]

This brief picture of Russell and Husserl is something of a caricature. Rorty depicts them as the last standing soldiers who relentlessly continue fighting a battle that has already been won. Ironically (perhaps even stupidly), it seems as if Russell and Husserl were still struggling to perfect the arguments of secularism well after "the triumph of the secular over the claims of religion was almost complete." If this triumph is awarded to Kant and Hobbes and the battle *is* already over, it seems as if Wittgenstein was beating a more peaceful retreat.

Whether or not this military theme is of conscious importance to Rorty in *Philosophy and the Mirror of Nature*, it is echoed elsewhere in his work.

For example, it appears in the context of a discussion that Rorty shared with Santiago Zabala and Gianni Vattimo about the future of religion.[28] In this discussion, secularism was recast or given a new tune, one that can be played in harmony with religion. The secularism that followed Kant was rooted in his claim to demystify and crystallize the foundations of human knowledge, describing the mind as knower (or mediator of knowledge) and assembling the fundaments of knowledge into broad, general theories of representation that challenge the validity of religious claims about revelation. Rorty points out that secularism for Wittgenstein is therapeutic. Wittgenstein secularizes secularism. Hence, in "usual" philosophy, secularism discredits religion's attempts to lay claim to foundational knowledge. After Wittgenstein and the linguistic turn, secularism ironically discredits the presumptions of philosophy to undercut religion. Secularization debunks *both* religion and philosophy when either one makes claims to foundational knowledge. But a disarmed notion of secularism can make its (perhaps ironic, perhaps ambivalent, but never cynical) peace with religion. This realignment cuts both religion and philosophy from their foundations in a way that echoes Derrida's religion without religion, messianism without messianism.[29] The paradox of Derrida's formulation is perhaps clearer put as "*r*eligion without *R*eligion, *m*essianism without *M*essianism" (the uppercase suggesting something concrete and specific and the lowercase alluding to a generality). Derrida intimates that there can be general—William James would call them "personal"—religious or messianic structures in philosophy that do not comply with the institutionalized (organized) structures and narratives stipulated by specific religious doctrines. Secularization no longer refers to a turning away from the mysteries of religion. It is only reticent about those who would solve (resolve or dissolve) them. Understood in this way, secularizing is akin to deconstruction, theological disarmament, or "saving the name." (Might I suggest the more Jewish "sanctifying the name"?) Secularism has a place in a religious program as a dismantler of violence and a prayer for peace. Santiago Zabala warns, "Whatever future awaits us will depend on the capacity of culture to annul all the reasons for conflict and to assume the program of secularization as its task. Thanks to this program it is much more difficult today to resort to religion in order to legitimize political positions or 'just' wars."[30]

Zabala is not rejecting religion. He suggests that the linguistic turn is really a turning back toward something that would perhaps have remained natural to religiosity had religion not been drawn into combat over competing propositions about justice and God. The shift that moves philosophy away from the "absolute" ushers in a new conceptualization of religion; it is not an annulment of faith. *Secularization* now refers to a cooling down of the tone, a lowering of expectations, a making of room for mystique, and a resistance to universally valid propositions. In Zabala's words:

> Thought must abandon all objective, universal, and apodictic foundational claims in order to prevent Christianity, allied with metaphysics in the search for first principles, from making room for violence. Hermeneutics has been the friendliest philosophy towards religion because of its critique of the idea of truth as conformity between propositions and objects. From the point of view of the return of religiosity, the prominence of hermeneutics in contemporary culture seems to indicate, much more than in any previous epoch, that the road to salvation does not pass through description and knowledge, but through interpretation and edification.[31]

Zabala is underlining the soteriological value of hermeneutics and interpretation by aligning them with religion. Hermeneutics and religion build their friendship on a shared critique of propositional truth, a critique that Zabala sees as crucial to religion's natural or desired purpose. The practice of philosophy is no longer geared toward truth. Like religion, philosophy now seeks only to educate and edify. There is no foundation to be sought, no final satisfying outcome to be revealed, only an endless journey toward the uncertain possibility of salvation. Though Zabala is not specifically referring to Wittgenstein, his alignment of hermeneutic philosophy and religion echoes one of the closing passages in the *Tractatus*:

> The correct method in philosophy would really be the following: to say nothing except what can be said, i.e., propositions of natural science—i.e., something that has nothing to do with philosophy— and then, whenever someone else wanted to say something metaphysical, to demonstrate to him that he had failed to give a meaning to certain signs in his propositions. Although it would not be satisfying to the other person—he would not have the feeling that we were teaching him philosophy.[32]

The interaction of the philosopher and the speaker here is ironic. The philosopher is the educator, but his role is to keep the student away from philosophy. The outcome of this is unlikely to satisfy the student—it offers little, demanding humility and the lowering of expectations. But it is the only practice that is strictly correct. Anything else requires faith: *Je ne sais pas, il faut croire.* Faith is not something we know about the world but the acceptance of what we cannot (perhaps are not allowed) to know. It is a peaceful affirmation of trust, an acceptance of the world as echoed in the Hebrew "Amen." I'm in.

The Future of Religion presents the linguistic turn as an opportunity for making peace between the passionately faithful and the unrepentantly secular. Rorty retracts his previous association of secularism with atheism, suggesting that—in its new meaning—"atheist" is a rough synonym for anti-clerical. He continues, "I now wish that I had used the latter term on the occasions when I have used the former to characterize my own view. For anti-clericalism is a political point of view, not an epistemological or a metaphysical one."[33] Rorty is more careful about condemning religion as irrational. His political objections acknowledge the irrationality and the inhibiting limitations of secularism. Religion and philosophy are inhibited, commanded by their ignorance not to be too sure, to assume the picture is a fragment. The religious quality of this inhibition is prophetic in nature. The deconstruction of metaphysics elicits an almost prophetic negative commandment—an unutterable "thou shall not"—that reaches us from beyond language and from outside understanding. Philosophical religion and organized religion appear to meet not in what they know and say but in what they are commanded not to say. I'm in.

Derrida's Prophetic Voice: Messianism without Messianism

> *We cannot forget that the distinction between the messianic and the concrete messianisms is always a political distinction for Derrida, one that spells the difference between war and peace, the war that Christianity has waged relentlessly on Judaism, and all the wars among the determinate messianisms. This is perhaps the point of this distinction in the first place. For the history of Western politics, and of the relations between the West and the Middle East is and has been, from time immemorial, a history of wars waged in the name of the several messianisms, the incessant battle to take Mount Moriah. The concrete messianisms have always meant war, while the meaning of the messianic is, or should be shalom, pax.*
>
> —JOHN D. CAPUTO, *The Prayers and Tears of Jacques Derrida*

From time immemorial, wars have been waged over peace. Wars have raged over competing visions of peace—visions defiled by dissent and disagreement about peace. Concrete messiahs and prophets, whose words have been set in stone, habitually adorn sacred monuments to everlasting peace. But these are monuments worshipped in the shrines of warriors. Valiant soldiers go down on one knee before them to pray for a peaceful return from the killing field. "Lead me away in peace and return me to my home in peace," they say—but theirs is a prayer for victory and honor. Not for peace. Peace requires a meeker disposition.

The concretized Isaiah promises wolves lying with lambs on a day that *will* come. It is a day of exclamation—a concrete day of future certainty. On *that* day, there *will* be peace. On *that* day, all the enemies of God *will* be vanquished. The nations of the earth will unite with the praise of the one and only God on their lips. They will acquiesce together at the foothills of Moriah and pay homage to the triumphant few who have spoken in his name all along. This is a familiar messianic promise. But whose is it to make good?

This promise has given comfort to generations of powerless and toothless exiles who bore the brunt of hatred and persecution, scattered around the world, stuffed into gas chambers, torn away from their homeland, from their seat at the table, and from their place on the stage. It now invigorates their triumphant hopes for a better future—a future whose present they now see taking shape before their fleshy eyes.

It has given equal comfort to lords, barons, knights, and popes whose compassionate fear of damnation and ruin for a world soaked in sin spurs them to preach their truth to tortured infidels and savages. The same dreams send suicide bombers to their deaths and to the waiting arms of celestial virgins. This is the dream that beckons to Jews, Christians, and Muslims, who all fancy themselves as the lamb and each other as the wolf. But concretizations such as these leave no room for wondering, little space for doubts, no cracks in the monument for the quiet mystery of God to seep through. They make no allowances for *différance.*

Perhaps the most famous misspelling in modern philosophy: *différance* is a word that technology has just forced me to write twice. The beautiful irony of the word strikes me afresh as Microsoft Word's auto-correct function resists my deliberate attempt at (mis)spelling it. No sooner do I type the letters *ance* than "difference" (with an *e*) glares back at me from my computer screen. I persist and persevere, delete and rewrite, emphatically make my point—but the damsel "difference" has a powerful champion in technology. As I finally vanquish the independent will of my computer, a new monument to difference appears: a little red squiggle that reminds me of the difference/*différance* between difference and *différance.* The two words are inextricably tied. Always and forever, the one will connote the other.

John Caputo suggests that, throughout his career, Jacques Derrida saved up a secret for his readers. Even his earliest works on grammatology and deconstruction prepare us for the secret of his religion—a religion without Religion. This is the secret Derrida repeatedly insisted that nobody understood. Not even Georgette, his mother, who prayed and wept over the infant Jacques like Monica over Augustine, could understand his religion.[34] "The omnipresence to me of what I call God in my absolved, absolutely private language being neither that of an eyewitness nor that of a voice does anything other than talking to me without saying anything, nor a transcendent law."[35]

Derrida's religion is a religion of *différance* and deconstruction. It is a religion whose practice is the constant interrogation of the words that exist only after creation. It is the religion of tireless, vigilant resistance to convention and posterity—a religion that demands perpetual receptiveness to the incoming possibility of something impossible. Deconstruction keeps vigilant watch over the unturned stone, preventing all who come near from engraving their words in it. Deconstruction turns the stone over and over, greasing and oiling it to keep its surface slippery, to keep words from sticking to it long enough to conceal/reveal the illusion of their impermanence. Deconstruction is not a technique of literary analysis nor an elaborate word game. It is a calling. Nothing is unsusceptible to it. It is a moral duty. Were it otherwise, Derrida's critics would be right. There would be no point to it all. Without its moral force, deconstruction would be nothing more than smarts and trickery, pointless cleverness. To be honest, it is hard to know if I have taken sides with Derrida himself or with the compassionate readings of John Caputo whose rendition of Derrida's later work touched my soul and made room for me to accept and take home the experience of being touched by an inexplicable (blue) hand. Caputo reconstructs the entirety of Derrida's work after discovering the great surprise that Derrida saved up for the end of his oeuvre. Finally and ultimately, Derrida reveals in the books he wrote near his death that deconstruction is a prayer for the impossible to come. *Viens.* Deconstruction is the repeated statement of willingness to accept the impossible. *Oui. Oui.*

Is nothing unsusceptible to deconstruction? What of the simplest of equations, the most axiomatic of conclusions? Take, for example, 2 = 2. What theological value can be found in questioning something so self-evident? These are some of the thoughts that rumbled through my mind in the pretend lectures I delivered to no one during the interminable nights I spent—trying to stay awake and vigilant—in Lebanon. The *statement* of the equation underlines the metaphor that is at play. The metaphor seems to insist that the equality of the two 2s somehow dissolves the obvious difference between the two numerical signs positioned at different places on the page before you. Deconstruction calls attention to the possibility that their equivalence is merely a metaphor. The metaphor itself—the need to reduce two separate and distinctive 2s with a statement of equivalence—underlines the possibility of their difference. Name the word that is not a metaphor and you transcend the limits of language. Such a name cannot exist. Such conjecture leads to nothing more certain than the possibility of the impossible. Each and every word in a language corresponds to its referent only up to the point where the *différance* between the word and its referent is recalled. The word here and the object there remind us that the metaphor established by language exists only in language. The forced combination of the word and its meaning only remind us of the imperfections of language—of how perilously the word clings to its meaning. Word and meaning combine and conspire to make sense of the desert chaos—*khôra*—on which they stand. Deconstruction reminds us of an ancient world—a world before technology—that can always return to topple the towers of "babble."

So what, then, of the most daring metaphor of all: *Adonay Hu HaElohim* (It is YHWH who is the [true] God)?[36]

> The name of God for Derrida is not the name of a universal, panoptical witness to his most hidden thoughts and deed[s], a party to his innermost interiority. . . . Nor is God the name of the Law, or the voice of conscience, or of the transcendent creator of heaven and earth, the first cause, etc. God is not a metaphysical or a moral foundation, the ground of being or the author of moral law. . . . the name of God is not the name of some "theological" being or object. "God" is given only in praying and weeping; . . . we would say for him here that "God" is given not in theological analysis but in religious experience, in a certain passion for the impossible.[37]

Who would dare condense the mystery of God into something so mere as a word? What word—however hidden and secret, great and magnanimous —could ever compress the being of God into a human utterance? The name of God is good only for prayer. Call out to him. Scream his names in the dark, but dare not name him. Naming is failing.

Derrida's religion is without orthodoxy, free of law and free of the limitations that the imperfections of language impose on all we can claim to say or know. The claiming itself is an act of violence, a crucifixion and a deicide that crushes the sands of *khôra* into mortar, blocking the path of the incoming impossibility, of something beyond humanity. The declarative and propositional use of God's name to compress the great surprise that an unpredictable messianic future might have in store is a denial of all that might be sacred in the mystery of God. Derrida saves God from the fate of being reduced to the words of human beings. Deconstruction is a tireless onslaught against the heathens who would dare parcel and package God into something they think they can understand and control. If knowledge is articulation, then we cannot dare to know anything absolute. No articulation is final enough, no picture detailed enough, no *mot* that is *juste* enough to clinch the mystery of the impossible. Derrida's religion rests upon the tacit denial of theology. It is a religion of atheists, of those radically unsatisfied with the feeble reports of scientists. Derrida's faith is the faith of the prophet who stands stranded on a cliff's top, waiting for the absolute surprise that will never come, for the promise that is forever a promise of something to come in a future that is *tout autre.*

I feel strangely torn between my post-Wittgensteinian, post-Derridian path to the implicit side of Judaism and my awareness that the community of Jews that surrounds me thinks of theological realism as essential to the religious meaning of Jewish law. It seems to me that the very suggestion that God is anything other than a supreme (speaking, commanding, warring) "being" is heard by many as a liberal heresy. At the same time, the dream of a silent, peaceful God has no place in the theology of liberals who, I fear, might find both the religious passion this image evokes and the enshrouding of God in mystery that it entails a little alarming. In my view, the deconstruction and disarmament of metaphysical notions of God is an authentic form of Jewish religious service. Though Jacques Derrida was a self-professed atheist, I believe, like John Caputo, that deconstruction touches the heart of Jewish prophecy, law, and prayer. On this account, Derrida's work (and on Ranjit Chatterjee's account, Wittgenstein's work) emerges as biblically informed.

CHAPTER 5

Messianic Peace

Then Judah came near unto Him, and said: "Oh my Lord, let thy servant, I pray thee, speak in my Lord's eyes, and let not thine anger burn against thy servant for thou art even as Pharaoh."

—Genesis 44:18

Thus the word of the Lord came to me: Now, son of man, take a single stick, and write on it: Judah *and those Israelites who are associated with him. Then take another stick and write on it:* Joseph *[the stick of Ephraim] and all the house of Israel associated with him. Then join the two sticks together, so that they form one stick in your hand. When your countrymen ask you, "Will you not tell us what you mean by all this?," answer them: Thus says the Lord God: I will take the stick of Joseph, which is in the hand of Ephraim, and of the tribes of Israel associated with him, and I will join to it the stick of Judah, making them a single stick; they shall be one in my hand. The sticks on which you write you shall hold up before them to see. Tell them: Thus speaks the Lord God: I will take the Israelites from among the nations to which they have come, and gather them from all sides to bring them back to their land. I will make them one nation upon the land, in the mountains of Israel, and there shall be one prince for them all. Never again shall they be two nations, and never again shall they be divided into two kingdoms. No longer shall they defile themselves with their idols, their abominations, and all their transgressions. I will deliver them from all their sins of apostasy, and cleanse them so that they may be my people and I may be their God. My servant*

David shall be prince over them, and there shall be one shep-
herd for them all; they shall live by my statutes and care-
fully observe my decrees. They shall live on the land, which I
gave to my servant Jacob, the land where their fathers lived;
they shall live on it forever, they, and their children, and
their children's children, with my servant David their prince
forever. I will make with them a covenant of peace; it shall
be an everlasting covenant with them, and I will multiply
them, and put my sanctuary among them forever. My dwell-
ing shall be with them; I will be their God, and they shall be
my people. Thus the nations shall know that it is I, the Lord,
who makes Israel holy, when my sanctuary shall be set up
among them forever.

—Ezekiel 37:15–28

The Coming Near of the Messiahs

The disarming of prophecy is our project in the discussion that follows, as is making the case that prophecy disarmed is a Jewish thing. The notion of a silent and peaceful God runs against the grain of the biblical stage where God is forever making star appearances in a speaking part. It seems hopeless even to attempt to pacify the voice of "a Man of War whose name is God" (Exodus 15) in the reading of prophetic texts. Indeed, if the voice of God is there to be muffled, why is it there at all? Why is the God of the Bible not as silent and as distant—safely distant—as the linguistic-turn anti-philosophers and hermeneuts need him to be for their comfort? Why does he appear to be so *other* from the *tout autre* of Emmanuel Levinas and Derrida, so thunder-ous and noisy next to the silence of Wittgenstein? If, as Kearney suggests, God is a possibility (*posse*)—in the sense of something beyond comprehension that is reified only by our paradoxical belief in the possible incoming of the presently unimaginable—why is he so present (*esse*) in the biblical narrative? If this silent God's name is—or at least can be—Shalom, why has he created such vivid and violent words as the command to sacrifice Isaac, the drowning of Egypt, and the curses of Deuteronomy? Why is this gentle, silent God so jealous and destructive? If God is peaceful, why does he command the exter-mination of Amalek? Why is it not a scandal that Adonay-Shalom chose one nation above all others and sent it to war over—of all things—a promise?

Can Derrida's gently irenic messianism without Messianism be reconciled with more orthodox readings of biblical prophecy? Do visions of the utopian future deconstruct themselves? What would be the religious meaning of such self-obstructive forms of expression? And are the deconstructive features of the biblical text sufficiently self-presenting and indispensable as to define the very nature of biblical prophecy as concealment? What about all of these questions? What do they conceal? Can my religion suffer such deconstructive articulations of faith?

The explicit Talmudic tradition speaks of two archetypal messiahs—the messiah of David hails from the house of Judah and the messiah of Ephraim comes from the house of Joseph. Jews have yearned for the messianic incoming of prosperity since the days of Ezekiel. As a child I learned to sing the words of Maimonides' *Ani Ma'amin*—"I believe with perfect faith in the coming of the Messiah even though he tarries"—to sweet and saddened melodies, so different from the triumphant marches that are sometimes sung today. Those melodies are a clue, a clue to an organic, unrelenting, messianic hopelessness.

Abraham Isaac Hakohen Kook—one of the leading rabbinical thinkers of the twentieth century and the premier ideologue of religious Zionism—in his famous "Eulogy in Jerusalem" went so far as to proclaim Theodor Herzl to be "Messiah—the son of Joseph." This was a posthumous award, a metaphorical tribute, but one easily misconstrued. After he spoke, concretization set in. The prophetic time bomb started ticking, and Zionism donned the messiah's cloak when Rabbi Kook's son (Rabbi Zvi Yehuda Hakohen Kook) interpreted his father's words as a spur to military conquest—as messianism *with* Messianism.

In Abraham Kook's rendition of the tradition, the messiah from the house of Joseph is a political messiah. He builds the roads, the schools, the hospitals, the prisons, the government offices, the national water and sewage carriers, and monuments that the Davidic messiah will imbue with greater spiritual meaning. He reclaims the sacred territory pledged and promised by the eternal God of Israel to his chosen people, establishes its legal and democratic governance, and makes ready for the future-present. Like a house-proud hostess standing expectantly at the door with table set and floors squeaky clean, he prepares the body of Israel for the incoming of its soul, "Thus the nations shall know that it is I, the Lord, who makes Israel holy, when my sanctuary shall be set up among them forever."

The disciples of Rabbi Kook demystified the messianic age, concretizing it in their brand of religious Zionism, dragging Judaism with them into fierce ideological conflict. In their form of Zionism, the lowly donkey that timorously awaits the messiah's coming grew steel wings. A jet engine, supersonic speed, a night-vision navigational system, and side-winding missiles were all attached to the donkey's back. A shimmering blue and white F-16 was prepared to fly the messiah safely home. For ground transportation, heavy iron tanks were arranged, complete with cannons. Chariots of gunfire—Merkava[1] tanks—were prepared for conveying so precious a guest. I have seen tanks and warplanes on military bases, standing ready, pristine and clean, waiting for him to come. I have seen them on the move, covered in dust at the entrances to villages and settlements, protecting those who cleave to the land with unflinching conviction, waiting for him to come. I have seen them in Lebanon, floundering and burnt out, splattered in blood like the chariot of Jehoshaphat, king of Judah (1 Kings 22), backing up in the dark, crushing the skulls of evacuated houses and unseen soldier-boys trying to catch a moment's rest in the dust—all waiting still, in breathless anticipation, for him to come. Rabbi Kook's ill-fated metaphor recast the words of Ezekiel as the script for the unfolding of a predictable future-present. With Jerusalem reunited and the enemies of Israel vanquished by the hand of God, all is ready—all has for some time now been ready—for him to come. *Viens!*

But Rabbi Kook's metaphor was embedded somewhat more hesitantly in his mournful eulogy than many of his disciples cared to notice. The two messiahs have a painful and paradoxically conflicting shared history. As the Talmud insists, the messiah of Joseph must die before the messiah of David can come. His death is troubling, not triumphant. It is the stuff of aching eulogies. It represents a politics unfulfilled and incomplete. The two messiahs never meet, yet their missions can only be complete when they do. Alas, the destiny of Joseph and Judah is one of near misses. It is never stable. Judah comes near, but he never quite reaches Joseph. Like the lovers of the Song of Songs, Joseph and Judah share an unrequited love. Judah and Joseph are forever driven asunder. Rabbi Kook's eulogy is full of fear for the future.

Vayigash elav Yehudah vayomer: And Judah approached him and said, "Let me speak with you, for you are like Pharaoh" (Genesis 44:18): Let me confess to you my darkest sin and beg you not to compel me to sin again, to stir up the blood that the ground has swallowed and rekindle the flames of anguish that consume my father's soul with grief. My brother is lost. His body was torn, his blood spilt. Indeed, the stain still burns the back of my hand. Tsaphnat Pa'aneach,[2] I beseech you to help me. I can no longer ask Joseph for his forgiveness nor can I repair our broken brotherhood. The years of suffering that Israel (my father) has endured can never be erased. The blood smear will never wash away. Now, only one of Rachel's sons remains. How can I return to my father without him?

Year after year in the endless cycle of Torah reading, Judah stands naïvely before "him" (the unnamed Joseph), begging compassion from a man he knows only as Tsaphnat Pa'aneach. Even after Joseph reveals himself to his brothers, Judah is still standing there ensconced in Genesis 44:18 for eternity—locked in the enduring memory of sacred text and cyclical time.[3] Each time the text is read and reread, their broken brotherhood lives on in pursuit of healing while the unstoppable dramatic irony of their situation forever pushes them apart. Time after time, they close half the distance between them, but Joseph and Judah can never meet. Judah talks to this Egyptian stranger with an intimacy that he could never dare in the conscious presence of his murdered brother:

> And Joseph could no longer restrain himself before all them that stood before him, and he cried: "Cause every man to go out from me." And there stood no man with him, while Joseph made himself known unto his brethren. And he wept aloud. . . . And his brethren could not answer him for they were affrighted by his presence. And Joseph said unto his brethren, "Come near to me, I pray you." And they came near. And he said, "I am Joseph your brother, whom ye sold unto Egypt. And now be not grieved, nor angry with yourselves, that ye sold me hither, for God did send me." (Genesis 45:1–6)

How could Judah fully reunite with a brother whose first candid words were, "I am Joseph your brother, whom ye sold unto Egypt"? How could he make amends to Joseph who listened so deceitfully to his brother's fraudulent confession—to a myth Judah had perhaps come to believe—knowing all along that it was a lie? Now, Joseph calls the brothers to come near. There is a brief moment of relief as the imposing Egyptian mask of Tsaphnat Pa'aneach is removed. Adrenalin and blood flow through the body as the reader anticipates full disclosure and a thrilling reunion. The forbidding formality of Egyptian etiquette subsides for a moment as Joseph clears the room, making ready for his confession. "Does my father live?" The comforting familiarity of Joseph's Hebrew falls on Judah's ears like a forgotten melody—it stirs up frightful memories that now swarm irrepressibly to the surface. Concealed remonstrations torment the bursting souls of Judah and Joseph as they realize together that they are both deceived deceivers. Nothing can put an end to their timeless cycle of reconciliation. Its ironies are as painful as the crimes it comes to erase. "Now—after so deliberate a charade—you dare ask after your father? Where have you been all this time?" Their reconciliation is an eternal monument to their insatiable need for forgiveness. Their fragmentary narrative of reunion insists over and again that the alliance between them is never complete. Now Joseph calls his brothers to approach, but they cannot come. His brethren could not answer him. "I am Joseph your brother, whom ye sold unto Egypt." I forgive you. But, I want you to remember that it is I alone who can forgive you. Dare not forgive yourselves! Only I can tell you not to be grieved, because only I truly know why you should grieve. You think you can tell Tsaphnat Pa'aneach that wild animals tore Joseph to shreds? But I know better. "I am Joseph your brother, whom ye sold unto Egypt." Now, accept my forgiveness. Your awful crime was the design of God. His plans for me were greater than you could ever have known. You were but pawns in the unfolding of my legend. The narrative of partial conciliation only underlines the *différance* that can never be erased. The cure irrepressibly recalls the sickness. The fraternity of Judah and Joseph remains shattered.

In the eyes of Joseph, Judah takes his place with the other instruments of his destiny. He is like the wife of Potiphar, the prison guard, the baker, and the butler—all of whom transgressed to work the will of God on earth, to turn the wheel of Joseph's fortune. Judah's destiny is not at issue. His claim to the throne is of no importance. Joseph wants to forgive and make *his* triumphant peace, the peace of Joseph. He recalls the dreams of his childhood as he sees his brothers grovel on the ground before him. Justice has been done. Now, he is ready for peace. But Judah knows better. Each year, he returns to close a little more of the distance. He supplicates. He forgives himself. He grovels. He makes amends because he knows that one day he will be king. *VayigaSH elaV YehudaH:* And Judah approached him. The last letters of each word in the Hebrew phrase combine to spell ShaVeH, meaning "equal"; Judah the slave stands before Joseph the king and says, "I am your equal. I too am king."[4] The time will come when I will have my justice and make my peace. The peace of Judah will triumph. Two kings. Two peaces. This is not reconciliation but conflict.

Nothing demonstrates the destiny that drives Judah and Joseph asunder more poignantly than the prophecy of Ezekiel 37 (quoted above). Nothing disrupts the narrative of natural rapprochement more starkly than Ezekiel's redress to the miraculous. Peace between Judah and Joseph will take an act of God. Joseph and Judah's unforetold future—the future covenant is scored in a prophetic key—is a song that resonates only with the *tout autre*. Ezekiel's vision tells us more of what cannot be said now than of what will come in the unforeseeable and impossible future. It insists that Judah and Joseph remain forever locked in their struggling embrace (like Israel's struggle with the angel whose name he could never know) until God comes. It reminds us that Israel is broken, scarred, penitent, and in need of forgiveness that can never be given. It insists that we stand guard against those who deny impossibilities, who dare wipe out the *différance* that recalls the sin in the forgiveness— which brings Judah back to Joseph time and time again. The tragic brokenness of their rapprochement (forever re-approaching—*Va[yigash]* and, and,

and—year after year after year) keeps the concrete prospect of messianisms at an impossible distance. It takes a miracle to bring peace, and miracles cannot be seized. Ezekiel's vision reminds us that the messiah will come on a broken-backed donkey, not a steed. In the words of the psalmist, "A horse is a vain thing for salvation. Behold the eye of the Lord is toward them that fear Him, toward them that wait for His mercy to deliver their soul from death, and to keep them alive in famine" (Psalm 33:17–19). The people must wait patiently for their redemption even though it can never come.

The unanswerable prophetic prayer for the messiah to come is altogether different from the triumphalist calls to action with which messianism is concretized. The peace of Ezekiel is neither that of Joseph nor that of Judah. It is the covenant of God—*Brit Shalom*—that paradoxically contains the peace both of Judah and of Joseph.[5] It unites all their dreams and those of all other unrequited messiahs and uncrowned kings.[6] *Shalom* is described by Ezekiel apophatically. He disturbs and dismantles political visions of it, obstructing the designs of those who would resort to God and prophetic promises in order to secure it for themselves. In the covenant that Ezekiel promises, *shalom* is a mystery that lies beyond the limits of language's descriptive powers. Rather than actually telling us about *shalom* in propositional terms, this prophetic narrative protects and conceals—blocking our view of anything we might declare a concrete political monument to eternal peace. Such images describe nothing other than victories posited as God's will by the eye of the beholder. The prophetic voice—the disruptive, deconstructive, self-obstructing, stammering voice that insists on the impossibility of natural reconciliation between Judah and Joseph—comes to display the impossibility of speaking unilaterally of eternal *shalom*. The passion with which the prophet speaks flows from his tragic appreciation of the prophetic task as an impossible one: no one can speak with human words of a rapprochement that erases the memory of the conflict it resolves. Such a union of opposites cannot be in the world that we know. This revelation comes to conceal whatever lies beyond the name of *peace* and to protect it from becoming the ultimate cause of all wars. The mysterious setting of *Brit Shalom* in Ezekiel's future *tout autre* disrupts, deconstructs, and disarms the messianic ambitions of men who kill time and again in the name of politics, submitting humanity to the terrifying economics of calculated sacrifices. It leaves the world broken and unfulfilled, clinging with enduring patience to a name in a text. Messianic peace is nothing when it is not world-changingly *everything*—*tikkun olam*. For now the meaning of Ezekiel's *Brit Shalom* is that it is nobody's war cry. For now the meaning of Ezekiel's *Brit Shalom* is that *Ani Ma'amin—I believe—* should be sung soulfully.

The messiah is forever coming—*Ani Ma'amin*—but never arriving. We wait for him to come. For all we know, the promise does not exist. It is something we can never know and never expect. It usurps our dreams of triumph, forcing us to wait quietly, skeptical of impostors. Ezekiel points us away from all types of liberal negotiations—achieved in the shadow of a looming sword or Leviathan force. Such "agreements" can never erase the fault lines (like the wrinkles of Yugoslavia) they forcibly join together. As Ezekiel silences triumphant marches and anthems, he also points an index finger in the direction of their alternative. In the unheroic darkness sits a peaceful, timid quorum that waits with eager anticipation and sings a more somber tune. As Ezekiel disarms our dreams, disrupts our plans, and extinguishes our violent ambitions, he urges us to make room in our deepest hopes for *shalom*. Peace is a prayer for the incoming impossible—the *shalom* that no violence of ours can hurry, the *shalom* that we can only wait for peacefully. Even though he tarries, I will wait for him. *Ani Ma'amin.*

Koheleth and Shiloh

> *Judah, thee shall thy brethren praise. Thy hand shall be on the neck of thine enemies. Thy father's sons shall bow down before thee. Judah is a lion's whelp. From the prey, my son, thou art gone up. He stooped down. He couched as a lion, and as a lioness; who shall rouse him up? The scepter shall not depart from Judah, nor the ruler's staff from between his feet, until the coming of Shiloh. And unto him shall the obedience of the peoples be. Binding his foal unto the vine. And his ass's colt unto the choice vine. He washeth his garments in wine and his vesture in the blood of grapes. His eyes shall be red with wine and his teeth white with milk.*
>
> —Genesis 49:8–12

The messianic line, the line (lion) of David, the loin of Judah and Boaz is ill conceived. It is a line that straddles the forbidden flesh of sacred whores with covered eyes (Genesis 38) and flirts precariously on the threshing floor with a forbidden Moabite princess (Ruth 3). It is a line that the zealous Pinchas might well have gouged with his spear. The hereditary pride of Israel, the messianic lion, the slayer of Goliath is the object of a princess's contempt (2 Samuel 6) and the iniquitous usurper of another man's wife (2 Samuel 11). The blood line is splattered with drunken stupors, incestuous unions (2 Samuel 13), sliced-up bodies (Judges 19), violated laws, and sneaking seductions—all of which the biblical narrative belabors just enough to make sure we never confuse the man for the myth, the king for the messiah, the present for the future, the future-present for the future-miraculous.

The prophetic voice that narrates in the Bible does not seem to allow the Davidic line its moment of glory for fear of its metamorphosis into an object of profanity. The word *king* points away from the messiah. The messiah king is only the messiah king, not the messiah. David starts off a very long wait whose end is unforeseeable. He is the pinnacle of political achievement, but one fatefully preordained, doomed, and destined to lead only to calamity, destruction, and exile. In the same vein, Solomon's wisdom is undercut by his stupidity, his royal grandeur by the unruly circumstances of his birth. The wisest of men sins so obviously, so stupidly, with hubris and excess. The greatest builder of all is the attributed author of the Bible's most consistent treatise on deconstruction. The greatest accomplishment, so he tells us, is naught:

> I made me great works, I builded me houses; I planted me vineyards; I made me gardens and parks.... So I was great and increased more than all that were before me in Jerusalem. In all this my wisdom stood me in good stead.... Then I looked on all the works that my hand had wrought, and on the labor that I had labored to do and behold all was vanity and a striving after the wind and there was no profit under the sun. (Ecclesiastes 2)

All is vanity. "Better a handful of quietness than both hands full of labor and striving after the wind." There are ends that can only be reached through inaction and benign acceptance of imperfection. In this state of mind, there is a glimmer of hope that humanity may cultivate the art of pure anticipation and learn to wait patiently for Shiloh to come. "The scepter shall not depart from Judah, nor the ruler's staff from between his feet, until the coming of Shiloh." But when he does, depart they shall, and Joseph and Judah (and all who fight to inherit their legacy) will make their peace.

The Explicit and Implicit Prophetic Voice

> *And Jacob was left alone; and there wrestled a man with him until the breaking of the day. And when he saw that he prevailed not against him he touched the hollow of his thigh and the hollow of Jacob's thigh was strained as he wrestled with him. And he said, "let me go for the day breaketh." And he said, "I will not let thee go except thou bless me." And he*

said unto him, "What is thy name?" And he said, "Jacob."
And he said, "Thy name shall no more be called Jacob, but
Israel for thou has striven with God and with men, and hast
prevailed." And Jacob asked him and said, "Tell me, I pray
thee, thy name." And he said, "Wherefore is it that thou dost
ask after my name?" And he blessed him there. And Jacob
called the name of the place Peniel, "for I have seen God face
to face, and my life is preserved."

—Genesis 32:25–31

And Moses said unto God, "Behold when I come unto the
children of Israel and shall say unto them: the God of thy
fathers hath sent me unto you; and they shall say to me:
What is His name? What shall I say unto them?" And God
said unto Moses: "I am that I am"; and He said: "Thus shalt
thou say unto the children of Israel, I am hath sent me
unto you."

—Exodus 3:13–15

My post-Derridian portrayal of the messianic should not be confused with an insistence on naïve or entirely passive utopianism. Again, the point is not simply to undermine or deconstruct the realism that might be attached to messianic prophecies and future-future promises. Rather, it is to insist that the primary effect of the way in which these promises are stitched into the fabric of the biblical text is to dictate the ethics of how we wait for promises to come true. I maintain that the reunion of Judah and Joseph in Ezekiel's vision of *Brit Shalom* is formidably impossible in the world as we know it. This impossibility means that the messianic vision, rather than fueling our flight toward the end of history, quenches or weakens our impulse to drive history toward any kind of ultimate end. It slows us down, forcing us to question our certitude and our resolve to act. In Gianni Vattimo's phraseology,[7] "it weakens thought." While we may rest assured in our religious conviction that ultimate things truly matter, we must acknowledge that our view of them is necessarily obstructed. Put as an aphorism: Our obstructed view of ultimate ends inhibits our capacity to justify questionable means of achieving them. Not only do ends *not* justify means, they undermine and disarm justification itself.

This is what I believe Derrida means by messianism without Messianism. Similarly, from this perspective, prophetic accounts of divinely commissioned or ultimate holy wars (such as the conquest of Jericho, the annihilation of Amalek, and the apocalyptic showdown of Gog and Magog) obstruct and undermine our certitude about the ethics of warfare and violence. The biblical treatment of war is no different in this respect from its treatment of messianism. The effect of prophetic (biblical) narratives dedicated to war and to portrayals of God as a god of war is to articulate an implicit (or, in Caputo's terms, "a general and not specific") notion of *war without War*. The wars that we wait for peacefully—just like the messianic peace that we wait for quietly—weaken (rather than set a precedent for) the ethical foundations we construct to justify the wars we make on our own. Despite explicit appearances, God—and, by way of extension, everything in the Bible (and, as we learned from the story of Babel, everything in language)—defies absolute or specific translation into human politics.

Despite explicit appearances, biblical narratives never make complete irreducible sense; but they still give the impression that they do. The appearance (or the impression) of translatability is crucial to the relationship between the text's explicit or constructed meaning and its disillusioned, implicit, or deconstructed meaning. In other words, the combination of illusion and disillusion is an indispensable feature of the prophetic genre. The impossibility of translating from the prophetic to the concrete is thickened by the illusion of translatability and then again by the perpetual experience of disillusion that a closer reading—insisting on a degree of reference that might meet Wittgenstein's standards for a "correct method"—necessarily yields. It is hard to imagine sitting with Wittgenstein to read a prophetic text without stumbling on something that he would say "failed to give a meaning to certain signs in [its] propositions." Stephen Geller refers to this failure as the "sacred enigma" of the biblical text.[8] The prophetic encounter disarms the human impulse to call sacred things by their names, to master them. The limping Jacob asks after the angel's name and the stammering Moses begs to know whom he may say spoke with him, but neither one is answered with anything more than a sacred enigma.[9] The enigma undermines the whole impression created by the text. Once the narrative reaches its confounding climax, the reader can only wonder if Jacob ever struggled with anyone ("Jacob was left alone") or whether Moses's bush ever burned. Once the narrative reaches its climax, the reader can only wonder if anything happened at all.

The compound of the explicit and the implicit, the exoteric and the esoteric, is the paradox that characterizes the prophetic voice. It is sound and silence, revelation and concealment. The paradox interferes with the semantic flow of the biblical text, disrupting the narrative in places where the Bible seems to talk—as it were, self-consciously—about the nature of revelation.

Revelation and Silence

And as he lay and slept under a juniper tree, behold, then an angel touched him, and said unto him, Arise and eat. And he looked, and, behold, there was a cake baking on the coals, and a cruse of water at his head. And he did eat and drink, and laid him down again. And the angel of the LORD came again the second time, and touched him, and said, Arise and eat; because the journey is too great for thee. And he arose, and did eat and drink, and went in the strength of that meat forty days and forty nights unto Horeb the mount of God. And he came thither unto a cave, and lodged there; and, behold, the word of the LORD came to him, and he said unto him, What doest thou here, Elijah? And he said, I have been very jealous for the LORD God of hosts: for the children of Israel have forsaken thy covenant, thrown down thine altars, and slain thy prophets with the sword; and I, even I only, am left; and they seek my life, to take it away. And he said, Go forth, and stand upon the mount before the LORD. And, behold, the LORD passed by, and a great and strong wind rent the mountains, and brake in pieces the rocks before the LORD; but the LORD was not in the wind; and after the wind an earthquake; but the LORD was not in the earthquake. And after the earthquake a fire; but the LORD was not in the fire; and after the fire a still small voice. And it was so, when Elijah heard it, that he wrapped his face in his mantle, and went out, and stood in the entering in of the cave. And, behold, there came a voice unto him.

—1 Kings 19

The epiphany at Sinai has confounded readers and exegetes for centuries. God delivers the foundation stone of law, justice, and ethics to the people of Israel in a shattered and confusing text whose pieces will not fit together. And yet, they do. The dogma of explicit religion rests on the reification of Sinai. The hermeneutically sophisticated interpretive rabbinic project, so it would seem, derives its source from the unquestionable factuality of revelation to all who stood to hear it. Our notion of the prophetic voice rests on the plausibility of that explicit experience. But, in my understanding of revelation, the exoteric is only one of the axes of the paradox. The impression of explicit revelation is never erased by its deconstruction. It is always present, an accomplice to the act of concealment. We teach explicit revelation to our children. At first, we tell them that accepting it is religion. But it is also there to be transcended, even as it endures. It is our primary suspect for religious interrogation, our first perilous clue to the puzzle of God. God gave the Torah to the people of Israel at Sinai: "I believe with perfect faith that the entire Torah that we now have is that which was given to Moses" (Maimonides' eighth principle of Jewish faith). But, like the grain on a piece of wood, the biblical text here can be stroked both ways: one way to smooth it down into coherent sense, the other to pick up its bristles and edges, one way to solve the puzzle, the other to show its insolvability.

Benjamin Sommer's essay "Revelation at Sinai in the Hebrew Bible and in Jewish Theology"[10] is bristly and edgy in the sense that it sets out to disturb the semantic flow of the Exodus narrative. It is a wonderful display of thickly descriptive Bible scholarship complexly intertwined with religious sensitivity, communal concern, and theological daring. Given the significant overlap between his thesis and the point I am making, an extensive account of Sommer's argument is warranted.

The essay begins with an interrogation of the coherence of Exodus 19. In Sommer's view, "The chapter defies a coherent sequential reading. More than any other passage in the Pentateuch, it is full of ambiguities, gaps, strange repetitions, and apparent contradictions, as many scholars (one thinks especially of Toeg, Greenberg, and Brevard Childs) have shown."[11] Interestingly, he repeatedly acknowledges the plausibility of the hegemonic or orthodox account of the narrative that sanctions an explicit and public revelation at Sinai. However, the main thrust of his thesis runs against this grain. He insists that the passage is incoherent because it is impossible to sort out the narrative details contained in the text. It is just not clear what the people of Israel experienced, where, and when. He continues:

> These texts present a bewildering aggregate of verses describing Moses' ascents and descents on the mountain. Moses seems not to be located at the right place when the Ten Commandments are given: God tells him to ascend the mountain and then reascend with Aaron (Exodus 19:24) whereupon he descends (19:25); but before he reascends the theophany occurs (20:1). Similarly, we may ask, where is God located before and during the theophany? According to Exodus 19:3 God is on the mountain several days before the theophany itself, but according to 19:11, God descends to the mountain immediately prior to the theophany (in agreement with 19:18);

in 19:20 YHWH comes down to the summit again. (Other biblical texts incidentally describe God as speaking from heaven, not from the mountain; see Exodus 20:19, Deuteronomy 4:26, and possibly Exodus 24:10. The tension between these verses is reflected in Nehemiah 9:13, "you came down on Mount Sinai and spoke to them from the heaven.")[12]

Paying deferent attention to what I have called an explicit understanding of revelation, he suggests:

> These oddities can be resolved after a fashion, through harmonistic exegesis, but their presence already intimates either that the extraordinary event chapter 19 describes was witnessed through a fog or that the narrative of that event could not be articulated in human words. As Greenberg has noted, one senses that the text combines many different recollections of this essentially un-reportable event. Nevertheless, regarding the aural and visual experience, these verses from Exodus 19 seem fairly clear. The theophany was accompanied by, or consisted of, loud noises and radiant sights: we read of smoke, fire, the mountain shaking, a loud horn.[13]

It is the disrupted flow of the narrative (and not the incomprehensibility of the event) that carries special theological significance. The conflicting accounts that cloud our view of what happened on Sinai comprise a biblical statement about the mysterious nature of revelation. They amount to much more than a tangle of historical reports that needs straightening out. The pivotal moment of confusion or complexity surrounds the scene portrayed in Exodus 20:15–19. The Israelites were frightened by the experience of direct revelation and asked Moses to approach God and put a stop to it. But it is not clear when this conversation between Moses and the people took place. Three significantly different options emerge from the text:

> Either the people heard the Ten Commandments (either a noise or an unbearable sound) and could not stand it OR they only heard part of the Ten Commandments. . . . A third possibility exists: the events of Exodus 20:15–19 follow temporally on Exodus 19:19 or 19:25 so that the people did not hear any of the Ten Commandments at all. The people's fear may have resulted from the extraordinary seismic events (as Nachmanides noticed, the people do not say to Moses in 20:16, "Let not God speak to us any more, lest we die," but simply, "Let not God speak to us lest we die"). . . . Three answers emerge as possible regarding the . . . question [How much of the Ten Commandments did the people hear?]: they heard all of the Ten Commandments

(if we understand the textual location of Exodus 20:15–19 in the redacted Book of Exodus as reflecting temporal sequence), they heard some of them (if we understand Exodus 20:15–19 as occurring during the revelation), or they heard none of them (if we understand Exodus 20:15–19 as preceding the revelation).[14]

This threefold schematic reading of the Exodus narrative yields three corresponding possibilities in the text. While the first represents the explicit axis, the other two options (the first partially and the second more radically) undermine the notion of explicit or articulate revelation. Sommer deduces that the ambiguity of this passage is deliberate. But to what end?

Drawing on Deuteronomy's account of the revelation at Sinai and then on rabbinic and midrashic literature, Sommer divides readings of Exodus 19 into two opposing camps. The "maximalist" (explicit) reading insists that the people of Israel heard God speak.[15] The "minimalist" reading places the complaint to Moses in the midst of the revelation, confining the experience of direct revelation to the first two commandments alone.[16] However, the full complexity of the text, Sommer suggests, is captured by the more radical minimalist position attributed to Nachmanides. Sommer continues, "Later minimalist commentary limited the verbal content of the revelation experienced by the nation even more."[17] Several centuries later:

> The Hasidic rebbe Naftali Zvi Horowitz of Ropshitz (died 1827) quotes his teacher Menachem Mendel of Rymanov (died 1815) as presenting an especially fascinating understanding of the revelation at Sinai. "It was possible that we heard from the mouth of the Holy One blessed be He, only the letter *aleph* of *anokhi*—that is, the first letter of the first word ('I') of the first commandment." This statement has gained fame for its paradox: the consonant *aleph* is silent. . . . at Sinai Israel heard nothing, but it did experience a revelation, a wordless, inarticulate signification of God's commanding presence.[18]

Menachem Mendel seems to understand the epiphany in radically implicit terms. He silences the revelation, minimizing it to the scope of an *aleph*.[19] This mysterious silence conceals the hidden and singular mystery of God's speech, embedding it in an enigmatic narrative that points beyond and outside the language of the text. As radical as this reading is, Sommer believes it has a biblical precedent in 1 Kings 19. The silent voice—*qol demama*—that emerges from the thunder and lightning at Sinai is "echoed" in the story of Elijah. After stirring up the wrath of Queen Jezebel on Mt. Carmel, Elijah flees to Sinai. It is here (in a passage that consciously recalls the language of

Exodus 19) that Elijah searches for God. Like a detective returning to the scene of a crime in search of clues, Elijah returns to Sinai to reexperience the epiphany. "And, behold, the LORD passed by, and a great and strong wind rent the mountains, and brake in pieces the rocks before the LORD; but the LORD was not in the wind; and after the wind an earthquake; but the LORD was not in the earthquake. And after the earthquake a fire; but the LORD was not in the fire; and after the fire a still small voice." Elijah learns that God is neither wind nor fire, but a *qol demama dakka,* an enigmatic phrase that Sommer captures beautifully in translation, "a sound of thin utter silence." He continues, "This passage modifies earlier Israelite conceptions of the theophany. . . . In so doing, the text also contests, or at least refines, the portrayal of the event that had taken place at Sinai centuries earlier. YHWH's manifestation is not a matter of loud noises. . . . Rather, God becomes known through a sound (*qol*) of silence (*demama*)."[20]

While the passage in 1 Kings 19 is perhaps the strongest biblical comment about silent revelation, it is not the only one.[21] Moreover, the idea of silent revelation reverberates throughout the Bible through the enigma of God's name—YHWH—which, Sommer points out, "consists entirely of sounds that are barely sounds at all." The name of God is a name with no sound whose correct pronunciation is not known and whose enunciation (were it known) is strictly forbidden. God, so it seems, has locked himself away behind a silent word and thrown away the key.

It is this complex notion of revelation and silence that Sommer believes is suggested by the confusing incoherence of the narrative in Exodus 19. In one especially stark formulation of his thesis, Sommer suggests that the silent *aleph* is all we know of the "written law" while the biblical text as we know it is "oral law." To soften the radical edge of this reading, he cites a remarkable number of midrashic and medieval Jewish commentators who expressed similar or related points of view.[22]

I surmise that all of this appeals to Sommer because it elegantly resolves the inner conflict that many religious academics feel when it comes to evaluating the question of the Bible's authorship. Sommer secularizes the secularism of critical biblical scholarship, dissolving the potential conflict between the question of the text's divinity and its sanctity or religious meaning. Instead, he follows Heschel in emphasizing the sacred value of Jews working collectively through the medium of tradition toward a fuller understanding of the heavenly Torah itself. The starting point of this journey is the text we have, and the fail-safe that ensures we do not defile its sanctity is the collective and communal commitment to mine it for its deeper meaning. In this conclusion Sommer, like Heschel, emerges as a scholar assuming the role of a communal leader who is seeking to enhance the religious lives of his readers. This is an unusual move for a Bible scholar, but one that I very much appreciate and applaud. However (and here is where I begin to disagree), in so doing, Sommer seems not to have despaired entirely of the Socratic premise that language can lead to metaphysics. In his view, the silent *aleph*—of which the entire biblical text is but an interpretation—is a signpost saying "Start climbing here!"

Despite his radically gentle version of the silent epiphany, Sommer's view is that the national collective can still nurse its hopes of mastering the heavenly Torah. Jews united may still claim to wield the word of God. With such a conclusion, Sommer is perhaps not taking the silence of the *aleph* as seriously as Wittgenstein's closing remarks in the *Tractatus* would have insisted. He is less intimidated than I would urge him to be by the spinning fiery sword that still blocks the path to Eden. He even goes so far as to express his position in Kantian terms when he says, "the only Torah we can know is a phenomenon, a product of perception and interpretation, but this Torah reflects a noumenon that is at once real and unrealizable."[23]

But even without adopting the stricter regime of absolute, whisper-free silence and intractable impossibility that Wittgenstein and Derrida would impose, this effort does a great deal to assist the contention that prophecy disarmed of its explicit strength is nonetheless a plausibly Jewish thing. The biblical and exegetical credentials of such a radically minimalist reading are well established in Sommer's paper (as they are in several chapters of Heschel's *Heavenly Torah as Refracted through the Generations*),[24] and for that I am most appreciative. However, I believe that there is a more radical conclusion to be drawn, one that sits more comfortably with the "utter-ness" of the thin silence. But this can only be appreciated when the minimalist reading proposed by Sommer is placed next to the maximalist reading in full glaring paradox. When the maximalist understanding of revelation is recognized as one that continues to endure in the normative reading of the text, the tantalizing paradox of epiphany and concealment emerges as an inescapable feature of the Sinai story.

Prophetic Reluctance

And Moses said unto the Lord, "O Lord, I am not a man of words, neither heretofore, nor since Thou hast spoken unto Thy servant; for I am slow of speech and of a slow tongue." And the Lord said unto him, "who hath made man's mouth,

or who maketh a man dumb, or deaf, or seeing or blind? Is
it not I, the Lord?"

—Exodus 4:10–12

On February 12, 2008, the day after a senior Hezbollah member, Imad Mughniyeh, was blown up in Damascus, an Israeli newspaper reported a brief telephone conversation between the deputy defense minister of Israel and the bereaved father of one of Mughniyeh's victims. According to this slightly melodramatic report, the politician uttered only three words on the phone, *El Nekamot Adonay!* (The Lord is a God of vengeance!).

Prophecy is less declarative than politics. The nearly helpless plea of the psalmist who turns to God for vengeance says nothing about God's willingness to actually avenge him. I have been saying those three words every day in morning prayers for years. At times, they have comforted a sting of shame or vindicated me in a moment of defiance. But to me, all that means is that God can be prayed to for vengeance. Counterterrorist foreign services might need to assassinate lethally dangerous people in order to protect innocent civilians from harm. But they dare not answer prayers. They dare not speak so boldly of their actions as those of a god of vengeance. Bold pronunciations that account for genocide, famine, and climatic calamities have nothing to do with prophecy. Prophets speak reluctantly. They do not run to the nearest microphone. They vomit the fire that burns in their bones, lying in the gutters of the city's murky streets. Jeremiah says, "I cannot speak for I am a child." Amos says, "I was no prophet, neither was I a prophet's son; but I was a herdsman and a dresser of sycamore trees" (Amos 7:10). Leave me to my trees and animals. Why do you thrust these words upon me and light an insufferable fire in my bones? Moses said to the Lord, "O Lord, I am not a man of words." The prophet is slow of speech, self-consciously unconvincing, disarmed of political rhetoric.

But God reassured Jeremiah, "Say not: I am a child." I am with you. I shall forever protect your speech, "and whatsoever I shall command thee thou shalt speak." The Lord touches Jeremiah's mouth. He feeds a honey-sweet scroll into the mouth of Ezekiel; the angel scorches the mouth of Isaiah with a burning coal. The prophet needs no speechwriters; he need not agonize over what my father called "enticing titles" and "lucid phrase making." His mouth has been touched. He knows nothing of what Annie Dillard describes as "the precarious materiality of the writing life":

> How fondly I recall thinking, in the old days, that to write you
> needed paper, pen, and a lap. How appalled I was to discover that,

in order to write so much as a sonnet, you need a warehouse. You can easily get so confused writing a thirty-page chapter that in order to make an outline for the second draft, you have to rent a hall. I have often "written" with the mechanical aid of a twenty-foot conference table. You lay your pages along the table's edge and pace out the work. You walk along the rows; you weed bits, move bits and dig out bits, bent over the rows with full hands like a gardener. After a couple of hours, you have taken an exceedingly dull nine-mile hike. You go home and soak your feet.[25]

I can identify with every line, but the prophet knows none of these tribulations. He has no blocks. Words pour out of his soul like vomit. The prophet's writing is a tragedy because he also knows no satisfaction from it. Who would return to his own vomit other than a foolish dog? (Proverbs 26:11). The prophet will not "worship the work of his own hands, that which his own fingers have made" (Isaiah 2:8). He is not proud of himself for "The Lord alone will be exalted." God is with the words of the prophet. And yet, Jeremiah remonstrates, "O Lord, Thou has enticed me, and I was enticed, Thou hast overcome me, and hast prevailed; I am become a laughing-stock all the day, Everyone mocketh me" (Jeremiah 20:7). This is not a man who celebrates the genius of his muse. Admittedly, Jeremiah's unsatisfactory role is to warn ominously of imminent disaster, but even Moses, the bearer of good tidings, is no more satisfied: "Lord, wherefore has Thou dealt ill with this people? Why is it that Thou hast sent me? For since I came to Pharaoh to speak in Thy name, he hath dealt ill with this people; neither hast Thou delivered Thy people at all" (Exodus 5:22–23). And again, "Erase me from the book that Thou hast written" (Exodus 32:32). Jeremiah is not mocked simply because his message is unpopular. He is mocked because he is a messenger of God. Prophetic speech, whether threatening or comforting, commanding or forgiving, is never applauded.

Ezekiel is sent to speak to the people of Israel whose language is intelligible to him. But, God continues, "Surely, if I sent thee to speak to many peoples of an unintelligible speech and a slow tongue, they would hearken unto thee. But the house of Israel will not consent to hearken unto thee for they consent not to hearken unto Me; for all the house of Israel are of a hard forehead and of a stiff heart . . . fear them not" (Ezekiel 3:4–9). God stiffens the heart and hardens the forehead. Prophecy stiffens the heart and hardens the forehead too. Prophecy cannot be borne by the people. Understanding prophecy will always entail misunderstanding—until the impossible happens.

Prophets are the reluctant representatives of an impossible idea. They are an explicit distraction from an implicit silence. The God they represent is inescapably incomprehensible. So, prophets are fodder for mockery. Only when God comes "shall thou not see the fierce people . . . of a deep speech that thou canst not perceive, of a stammering tongue that thou canst not understand" (Isaiah 33). Only when the impossible happens, can *différance* be eliminated from language and sin finally be forgiven. Then, "Thine eyes shall see Jerusalem a peaceful habitation" (Isaiah 33). Prophets are reluctant, perhaps even ashamed, because they promise an impossible vision of peace.

Prophetic Politics and Peace

And a little child shall lead them. . . . They shall not hurt or destroy in my holy mountain for the earth shall be full of the knowledge of the Lord as the waters cover the sea.

—Isaiah 11

The prophetic notion of peace is most fully articulated in the opening chapters of Isaiah, which culminate in his celebrated account of wolves dwelling with lambs, leopards lying down with kids, and the calf and the young lion fatling together. Isaiah's vision is not a manifesto that human power can set about concretizing in political reality. No policy can resolve the noncontemplative and unconscious enmities that pervade nature. The effect of Isaiah's metaphor pushes peace outside the realm of the natural and beyond the aspirations of humanity. Isaiah's vision follows a portrayal of a world ruled by children. The wolf, the lion, the cow, and the kid are subjects of a juvenile regime: "and a little child shall lead them." Peace is not only beyond the reaches of political power, it is concealed behind an opaque parody of politics. Peace will emerge as a critique of the evils that (as Hegel insisted) have been inherent to humanity and politics.[26] In this sense, peace is antipolitical as in Isaiah's portrayal of it, which interrogates and deconstructs explicit politics.

The deconstructive motif of childlike government is carefully and repeatedly interwoven with Isaiah's vision of an ultimate peace. It is introduced overtly for the first time in the third chapter—"and I will give children to be their princes and babes shall rule over them"—but the reference to the princes who must relinquish their power to children looks back to the theme that, in effect, opens the book—God's displeasure with the corruption of Jerusalem. The city of Jerusalem represents the political world whose attention has been distracted from God.

The prophet wails, "Children I have reared and have brought up and they have rebelled against me." God holds Jerusalem and its politics to account for this rebellion. While every ox knows its master, Israel believes that it has come of age. Jerusalem has lost sight of the source of its bounty and prosperity. It no longer follows the subtle clues that lead to God. Ideals have become concretized as policies and no longer signal a consciousness of God. Jerusalem is distracted and intoxicated by its own power. Without implicit attentiveness to the mystery of God, the practices of explicit religion are repulsive. "To what purpose is the multitude of your sacrifices? It is an offering of abomination unto Me" (Isaiah 1:11).

Jerusalem has become an obstacle to faith and must now be removed. The city is laid to waste so that God may once again emerge. God's loathing for the politics of Jerusalem is integral to the prophet's critique of empty religious practices. *Learn to do well, seek justice, give justice to the fatherless, plead for the widow.* Be claimed by the plight of the individual instead of building a body politic that will swallow up God's individuality into its impersonal economy and call for sacrifices in his name. Political society, as Agamben put it in *Homo Sacer,* "politicizes life," i.e., it attaches price tags to life and death. It constructs an economy of sacrifice and builds mechanisms empowered to "consent" to the sacrifices society must make in its own (general) interests. A Jerusalem of princes and kings is one that will tolerate these calculated sacrifices, but the prophetic consciousness cannot endure them. Look away from government and face the individual! Respond directly to the plight of the poor and the widow! Agamben writes:

> In the final analysis, however, humanitarian organizations—which today are more and more supported by international commissions— can only grasp human life in the figure of bare or sacred life, and therefore, despite themselves, maintain a secret solidarity with the very powers they ought to fight. It takes only a glance at the recent publicity campaigns to gather funds for refugees from Rwanda to realize that here human life is exclusively considered as sacred life— which is to say, as life that can be killed but not sacrificed—and that only as such is it made into the object of aid and protection.[27]

The disadvantaged citizen, like the refugee, is victimized by political society where humanitarianism and politics may separate to such a degree as to establish a clandestine coalition between the governments that bear responsibility for human crises and the humanitarian organizations that seek to alleviate them. The political system has a vested interest in victimizing the underprivileged even as it helps them. Humanitarian politics allow for the little old lady whose hospital bed was stuck in the corridor because there was no room in the ward, in order to help elect the politician who promises a reform in health care. Similarly, U.S. bombers can drop "humanitarian" food parcels on the innocent victims of the bombs the same planes dropped only hours before. In attempting to clean up the political, the humanitarian agenda ends up assisting it and perpetuating its violence. The checkpoint-watch women, who stand at military roadblocks throughout Judea and Samaria protesting the military occupation, inevitably and paradoxically maintain the very occupation they seek to protest. By their monitoring of the soldiers, attention is distracted from the unnecessary cruelties that the roadblocks themselves impose because the checkpoint-watch women are there to make sure that the conduct of the military personnel at each roadblock is impeccable. In Agamben's words, "our age is the one in which a holiday weekend produces more victims on Europe's highways than a war campaign, but to speak of a 'sacredness of the highway railing' is obviously only an antiphrastic definition."[28] Agamben is seeking a way out of politics through theology.

Prophecy offers a very specific view of political theology. The God of the prophets is not a humanitarian. Prophetic theology cannot be reduced to worldly politics. The prophetic voice remains, like Moses on Mt. Nebo, on the border of politics and yet unable to enter the land. Prophets cannot tolerate the suffering of the poor, who pay the price of belonging to a political system that promises to guarantee their welfare. The I-It relationship between the poor and the conceptualization of a charitable society offers no protection to those responsible for poverty. But it does not hold them to account either. The prophet moves away from politics and simply demands, *Relieve the oppressed!*

Prophetic expressions of reticence toward politics underscore an implicit critique of the Davidic monarchy. Isaiah envisages God as king: "And it shall come to pass in the end of days that the mountain of the Lord's house shall be established as the top of mountains." The stories of the book of Kings dismantle and expose the flaws in the Davidic vision. The kings who ruled by divine appointment offered no way out from the corruptions of a political society and from its inherent idolatry. Even the greatest kings are disturbingly flawed. Though David's royal palace stood symbolically in the shadows of Moriah, the Temple remained unbuilt because David was a man of war. The palace balcony that stretched out above the sacred city was symbolically stained by the immodest iniquity that bred Solomon. Solomon, though he built the Temple, did so only after dedicating his energies to the construction of a greater palace than his father's for himself. In stark contrast to the history of the Davidic legacy, Isaiah's prophecy insists that in the end of days the mountain will never serve the interests of men and their political ends. It shall be emptied of human hubris, "and the haughtiness of men shall be bowed down, and the Lord alone shall be exalted in that day." There is no space in

Isaiah's "political theology" for the political. There is only theology. God will emerge at the expense of Jerusalem. The city must be broken so that God can draw attention back to himself. "Cease ye from man in whose nostrils is a breath, for how little is he to be accounted." And what Hegel called the "individuality of politics"—the trait that breeds inevitable and ceaseless conflict—will end when *all* the nations flow toward Zion to hear the word of the Lord. When government is transferred away from mechanisms and structures that serve the interests of a society of men, then "they shall beat their swords into plowshares and their spears into pruning-hooks, nation shall not lift up a sword against nation, neither shall they learn war any more."

Isaiah's vision of peace is not just anti-political. It is an impossible one for human hands to mold. The prophetic genre is devoid of concrete realism, rich in metaphor, paradox, impossible images, and broken language. No more concrete a portrayal than the dry bones and burning chariot of Ezekiel, Isaiah's vision of peace should be read as an ideal, a prayer that God will emerge and purge revelation of its concealing quality. The prophet prays for God to come (*viens!*) and draw our interest back to pondering the mystery of his transcendent incomprehensibility. No human or political project can resolve the contradictions and conflicts of narrow interests that must be contained for this kind of peace to be achieved. The prophet's vision of peace coincides with an unimaginable redemption that comes only when the governance of human society is free from human baseness.

"For behold the Lord of Hosts doth take away Jerusalem from Judah." Isaiah's vision involves more than the critique of monarchy. His carnivalesque inversion of human government expresses not only the dismantling of human power; it parodies monarchy and government by exposing their ultimate dependence. When human vulnerability is fully exposed, the hubris of kings, prime ministers, and presidents is the raw material of satire. So Isaiah describes a Jerusalem ruled by children and babes. Society is neither better nor worse off for its change in human leadership. Children behave insolently toward their elders. But to the prophet, it is of no matter because society is already manifestly upside down. Isaiah flattens the social hierarchy of Jerusalem and empties the political city of its meaning. God's presence wipes away the distinctions between the base and the honorable, the powerful and the weak. "There but for the grace of God go I," proclaimed the truly devout John Bradford. When human beings fix their attention on God, the differences between all wise, foolish, powerful, and weak men, women, and children feel trivial.

A conventional reading of Isaiah 3 might suggest that the motif of a government ruled by children is a punishment for social injustice. What I am suggesting is that the portrayal of society as upside down tells us little if anything of God's actions and intentions. Prophecy can at best describe inadequately the experience of the person who has faced God's presence. Isaiah emerges from the divine encounters as a stranger to the world. His portrayal of an inverted Jerusalem is a prophetic critique of politics. He deconstructs and parodies the normative, highly structured political society and rails against it for daring to believe in its own value. Social injustice is not a sin of those who act alone. It is a mirror image of Israel's collective inattention to God, an inevitable sickness that plagues irreverent human society. Societies, like people, are much of a muchness. The difference between a polis led by (even a just and noble) prince and one led by insolent children is simply a trivial matter of degree. When the prophet describes the callous and indifferent behavior of the people who "oppress one another . . . for a man shall take hold of his brother for the house of his father," he is intimating that all human cities—even Jerusalem—are ultimately the same as Sodom and Gomorrah.

"The show of their countenance doth witness against them." The medieval biblical commentator Rashi reads this verse as an echo of Deuteronomy 16:19: "thou shalt not respect persons." The allusion continues the prophetic deconstruction of political society: the supposed distinctions between people of different social ranks and standings count for nothing. The rule of men is no different from that of women or children—"As for my people a babe is their master and women rule over them"—and the wealthy are no more entitled to their wealth than the poor since "the spoil of the poor is in your houses. What mean ye that crush my people and grind the face of the poor? Because the daughters of Zion are haughty and walk with stretched-forth necks and wanton eyes." Society is caught up in a series of contradictions and paradoxes that cannot be untangled. The rich are rich with the money of the poor. The wealth of one person is unavoidably responsible for the starvation and poverty of another. The illusion of all-knowing power is built on ignorance, human vulnerability, and suffering. Valor is effeminate and age childish. All of the differences that social hierarchies are built upon are trivial in comparison to God.

In conveying this idea, the prophet uses the daughters of Zion as a metaphor for all of Jerusalem. God wants their attention, but they look elsewhere with their wanton eyes. God resolves to dismantle their pride. "And the Lord will lay bare their secret parts. In that day the Lord will take away the bravery of their anklets, and the fillets, and the crescents, the pendants and the bracelets and the veils . . . and instead of curled hair baldness" (Isaiah 3:17). The extended metaphor portrays Israel as a whore who is laid bare and stripped of her jewels like a *sotah* (woman accused of adultery). But her shame is not simply a punishment. Her susceptibility to being shamed shows that her former glory was only an illusion that can be undone. The wondrous monuments to the permanence of human achievement, the Parthenon, the Lighthouse in Alexandria, the Roman Forum, the Reichstag, the World Trade Center, the Pentagon, and the Temple in Jerusalem will all come tumbling down. They are objects of frivolous adoration and unsound complacence, plagued with the mortal flaws of the societies that built them.

While it has often been observed that Isaiah's portrayal of the destruction of Judah follows his accusations of social injustice, less attention has been paid to the relationship between this portrayal and the visions of peace that follow it. Rather than analyzing destruction as a punishment for injustice, I propose a reading in reverse. The implication of the visions of peace that follow Isaiah's portrayal of a flawed and senseless human politics replete with injustice, corruption, manipulation, and victimization is that peace—in all its paradoxical impossibility—is ultimately the politics of God.

God repeatedly uses war to punish Israel's pride: "And he looked for justice, but behold violence." When Israel concentrates upon its national pride, its national plight is war. The people of Jerusalem go into captivity because "they regard not the work of the Lord. The men shall fall by the sword and thy mighty in the war. And her gates shall sit and mourn; and utterly bereft she shall sit upon the ground." Jerusalem's ultimate downfall is war. Indeed, in chapter 5 of Isaiah, war emerges as the tool that God wields most disastrously to expose the powerlessness of Israel. War reduces Jerusalem to the poverty and powerlessness that are its natural state. "And He carried away all the princes, and all the mighty men of valor, even ten thousand captives, and all the craftsmen and the smiths; none remained save the poorest sort of the people of the land" (2 Kings 24:14). Israel is a nation of slaves or, as Ezekiel described it, a female child rejected at birth wallowing in her own blood with none to care for her save the Lord (Ezekiel 16:5–7).

When God summons the nations against Israel, they serve him expertly:

> None shall be weary nor stumble amongst them; None shall slumber or sleep; Neither shall the girdle of their loins be loosed, Nor the latchet of their shoes be broken. Whose arrows are sharp, And all their bows bent; Their horses hoofs shall be counted like flint, And their wheels like a whirlwind. Their roaring shall be like a lion, they shall roar like young lions, yea they shall roar. And lay hold of their prey and carry it away safe, And there shall be none to deliver. . . . And if one look unto the land, Behold darkness and distress And the light is darkened in the skies thereof. (Isaiah 5:27)

But war is also the context in which the prophet introduces his vision of peace. War and peace are not in the hands of humanity. Peace comes when human beings are powerless and desperate because this is when they remember to turn to God. Peace is the prayer of the humble. Thus, in the chapters that follow, the effeminate and decimated Jerusalem returns to God. Devoid of hubris and pretenses, broken and powerless, "seven women shall take hold of one man. . . . in that day the growth of the Lord be beautiful and glorious" (Isaiah 4:1). Jerusalem finally relinquishes its quest for self-rule, and without politics it becomes holy and dependent like the children who (should have) clung to God in the desert of Sinai:

> And it shall come to pass, that he that is left in Zion and he that remaineth in Jerusalem, shall be called holy when the Lord shall have washed away the filth of the daughters of Zion, and shall have purged the blood of Jerusalem . . . by the spirit of judgment and by the spirit of destruction. And the Lord will create over the whole habitation of Mt. Zion and over her assemblies, a cloud and smoke by day, and the shining of flaming fire by night. (Isaiah 4:5)

Though the stories of Exodus and Numbers set no such precedent, the desert here connotes an apolitical or prepolitical Israel in which total dependence generates total attention on God. God now appears among the feminized posttraumatic survivors of Jerusalem as a cloud of smoke by day and fire by night. The sacred mount now becomes a holy refuge. "And there shall be a pavilion for a shadow in the daytime from the heat, and for refuge and for a covert from storm and from rain" (Isaiah 4:6).

The metaphor of the child now takes on a new meaning. Rather than symbolizing the true weakness that hubris conceals, a new child is born with a fresh start and a chance to bring peace to Israel"

> For a child is born unto us and the government is upon his shoulder and his name is called *Pele joez el gibbor Abi ad Sar Shalom* [wonderful in counsel is God the mighty, the everlasting Father, the ruler of peace]. That the government may be increased, and of peace there be no end upon the throne of David, and upon his kingdom. To establish it and to uphold it through justice and through righteousness for henceforth, even forever. The zeal of the Lord of hosts doth perform this. (Isaiah 9:6)

The gentle child who leads the other broken children back to God brings everlasting peace to Israel. This son of the house of David is not a king. He stands for God's kingdom and for the divine rule of peace. "And a little child shall lead them. . . . They shall not hurt or destroy in my holy mountain for the earth shall be full of the knowledge of the Lord as the waters cover the sea."

The Political Theology of Peace

In order to find things beautiful that are manufactured by men uninspired by God, it would be necessary for us to have understood with our whole soul that these men themselves are only matter, capable of obedience without knowledge. For anyone who has arrived at this point, absolutely everything below here is perfectly beautiful. In everything that exists, in everything that comes about he discerns the mechanism of necessity and he appreciates in necessity the infinite sweetness of obedience. . . . As soon as we feel this obedience with our whole being, we see God.

—SIMONE WEIL, "The Love of God and Affliction"

Peace is part of an implicit prophetic vision that cannot become political with anything less than the greatest caution. By framing prophecies of peace in messianic time, the prophets leave Jewish history with the legacy of anticipating the impossible. The full-blown political irony that has preceded the portrayal of the child messiah in Isaiah confirms the inference that messianism and triumphalism must never go hand in hand in the world of possibility. As we saw with Judah and Joseph in Ezekiel 37, the portrayal of Judean triumphalism over Assyria, Egypt, Pathros, Cush, Ephraim, Edom, and Moab that is loaded into verses 10–16 of chapter 11 in Isaiah is postponed to the end of days. All of this can only take place in a world where wolves lie with lambs, i.e., in an impossible future that is not consistent with the world as we know it in the present. Finally, in the day when the flaws of politics can be escaped, the slippery limitations of language will be defied and revelation will shed its cloak of concealment. "And in that day shall ye say: Give thanks unto the Lord, proclaim His name. Declare His doings among the peoples." But what in the meantime? Are we destined to an inevitable cycle of corruption, war, and injustice? Does prophecy offer us nothing of contemporary use?

In part, it would seem, there are no optimistic answers to these questions. But even without completely changing the world, faith does have a redemptive role in it. Religion can be a terrible force of destruction, but it need not be. My purpose in emphasizing the impossibility of the prophets' visions of peace has not been to dishearten, but to dismantle the potential for violence that the abuse of prophetic visions has engendered throughout the history of monotheism. The prophetic perspective is not so much a point of view as it is a statement about how points of view are to be located in a world-view. As such, my reading of prophecy is consistent with Rav Kook's notion of "the unification of the opposites,"[29] which brings history to its messianic culmination in universal peace and which, in the meantime, requires a radical capacity for accepting the world as it is. Prophetic self-consciousness about the limitations of language and about the fallibility of human understanding reminds the reader that what is being revealed in prophetic texts is only a fraction of what the language itself conceals. Thus, any understanding and all conflicting understandings of prophecy are only a fraction of the unity of opposites, which no conventional or human observer of history can grasp.

Simone Weil refused baptism all her life. She felt that she needed to stay outside the limits of institutionalized or explicit religion. She also seems to have felt herself perpetually unworthy of baptism. Were it not for this strange decision on her part—a decision that her mentor, Father Perrin, tried very hard to talk her out of—she would have been canonized by the Vatican as a saint. During the latter years of her short life, she received mystical revelations almost daily as she recited the "Pater Noster" with extraordinary devotion. Seeing God meant, for her, a total acceptance of the limitations of mortal life in contrast with God. The full and sweet beauty of the world is seen when the illusions and the distractions that present themselves explicitly to the natural observer are understood for what they are. In Weil's "The Love of God and Affliction" (as in prophetic literature), affliction is one of the keys to noticing the cracks in the illusion. Affliction is agonizing. It draws the soul under, driving nails of agony through it. But this suffering has the power to turn the gaze of human beings toward heaven and in so doing to draw their attention to the "blind mechanism" or the "mechanism of necessity" that confines natural things—whether living or inanimate—to their own tragic paths. She frequently uses the metaphor of gravity to illustrate this binding. Things fall. In falling, they are what Weil calls "obedient without knowledge." Human beings cannot break out of the cycle of their own "mechanisms of necessity" unless they look to God. They are pulled through life by "gravity." This is the idea that is captured in Psalms 148: "for He commanded and they were created. He hath established them for ever and ever; He hath made a decree, which shall not be transgressed." All they can do, from wherever they are, is recognize the inevitable limitations of their existence in the world and turn their gaze toward God in praise.

Before moving on to the conclusion of Weil's argument, it is worth considering the implications of mechanisms of necessity for the way we understand good and evil, virtue and crime. When we perform an act of evil, we do so within nature. As such, we cannot rebel against God; we can just fall into a particular part of our own (created) gravitational path that is there in nature. Evil is part of creation. More significantly for Weil (and this now is the climax), affliction is an opportunity for observing the mechanism from close up. When we observe this and gaze at God from the confines of gravity, we see the world as God's creation and attain (albeit apophatically, i.e., by recognizing the nature of the world) a fuller sense of his presence.

The Wittgensteinian/Derridian attitude toward language that I have adopted sees language as a worldly mechanism that confines humanity. In the same way that Weil looks beyond the confines of the mechanism at God, the deconstructive or broken quality of prophecy is what gives the prophet his authenticity. Prophecy is predicated upon a complex paradoxical relationship between the explicit and the implicit, the revealed and the concealed, the general and the specific. When one recognizes that the exoteric meanings of prophetic texts are simultaneously obstructed, undermined, deconstructed, and resituated by the implicit and mysterious impossibility of comprehending in "normal" language the most abnormal of human experiences (i.e., prophetic experience), the potentially destructive human passion for complete expression in this world is restrained. The exoteric voice is one in which language is not devoid of meaning while the implicit voice insists that meaning is without essence, precarious and reversible. Put differently, following on Wittgenstein, Derrida, Kearney, and others, I have come to believe that the poetry of prophetic texts is no more or less than a glorious display of the religious energy that is released when humanity comes to terms with its flawed mortality in the face of God. This is the great secret that Derrida saw when he insisted on awaiting—yearning and weeping—the possibility of the truly impossible.

The semantic incoherence of the broken biblical texts is a spectacle of human limitation. Prophecy is enigmatic and beautiful. It moves the soul to face the incomprehensible as it stands precariously on the precipice of an abyss. Prophecy speaks of God by failing to capture him in words. In its comprehensible and successful communications, the exoteric dimension of prophecy gives us only footprints, faded and indecipherable images to cherish. It gives us inverted clues that steer us away from idolatry and corruption. However, its perpetual failure to expose essences and to grant access to the secrets of heaven reminds us of the message of Babel: the heavens are not ours to conquer. They are concealed in silence behind a curtain of language. The attention to God that prophets preach guards us from becoming intoxicated with our own worth. It teaches us to be claimed by those who need our compassion. Down here, in the slums, the prophetic message is loud and clear. We finally understand that we all share the same plight of our common humanity. "At this point," Weil puts it, "absolutely everything below is perfectly beautiful."

Prophecy reveals and conceals. It bequeaths to us an awareness of God, but not knowledge or mastery of God. In this sense, prophecy is to be read or sung bivocally. The tune is filled with explicit (though incomplete) representations of God and his will while the harmony (and the two can never be sounded separately) implies an apophatic reversal of language's function in sacred texts. The endless cycle of construction and deconstruction, of drawing near and falling away that this bivocalism sets into motion engenders the experience of religious life as one that combines mystery and uncertainty with steadfast, secure faith.

Prophecy seeks to ensure faith in God while undermining claims to knowledge of God. No sacred claims can be made for systems of government or for political ideologies—not even the most philanthropic and benevolent ones. They are all ordinary in the same way as language is ordinary. Prophecy is as apt to mislead its readers up a metaphysical path as is philosophy. But both ultimately leave the world as it is. They can only point at what lies beyond in resigned and peaceful silence. As Williams puts it:

> The "world" is a place where it is barely possible to speak without making things more difficult and destructive; the commonwealth of God is a place where speech is restored, in praise, in patience. . . . this is not about any kind of despairing silence, being silent because there is nothing to say or know or because you're always going to be misunderstood. It is more an *expectant* quiet, the quiet before the dawn, when we don't want to say anything too quickly for fear of spoiling what's uncovered for us as the light comes.[30]

In this sense, the peaceful message of prophecy is twofold. Some prophecies point toward the idea that an impossibly perfect society is one that lives in universal peace. These prophecies teach us to dream of peace, to pray for peace, to allow desire for peace (along with a love of justice, charity, etc.), to pin our attention and our hopes on God. But, at the same time, the generic structure of prophecy, which contains *all* of its specific content (and not only its messages of peace), warns against attempting to bring peace, justice, and faith into the world by the use of human force. Prophecy and the infinity of free will impose a quietist damper upon human dabbling in history. Prophetic visions of peace guide our steps from afar, while the linguistic flaws of the prophetic genre hinder and quench the enthusiasm with which we might convert our idealism into holy war. The paradoxical combination of reckless idealism with the suspicion that this experience of prophecy produces engenders a religious consciousness that commands us to act slowly—more slowly than the Israeli government did on the day it declared war against Hezbollah. It reminds us that, as long as our dreams and purposes are political, our interests in peace will be political and necessarily flawed. This is the deeper meaning of *prophetic peace*. Beyond the specific content of any and all prophecies, the religious soul stirred by reading prophecy prefers to wait expectantly and quietly for the dawn to break. Prophetic faith implies that before and even while we act, we must also remain peacefully attentive to God—able to stop in our tracks and put down our weapons, saying, as Abraham did, *Hineni*—Here I am. Faith inhibits violence and hotheaded action. By teaching faith and expectant humility, prophecy is ultimately *about* peace.

CHAPTER 6

The Rabbinic Voice

Our language can be seen as an ancient city, a maze of little streets and squares, of old and new houses, and of houses with additions from various periods; and this surrounded by a multitude of new boroughs with straight regular streets and uniform houses.

—LUDWIG WITTGENSTEIN, *Philosophical Investigations*

Touring the Mansion

Rabbinic literature is like a huge mansion of variously decorated chambers in which it is easy to get completely lost. As you wander around the chambers, you notice that some of their ancient decorations still suit current tastes and styles while others do not. Looking at the various guidebooks and histories available, you can see that periodic rearrangements have been made to the decor to draw public attention at different times to one item or another. Current tastes place the emphasis on those furnishings that, despite their years, still appear to be in good working order. Today, liberal readers of the rabbinic tradition tend to emphasize those passages that teach social justice, pluralism, tolerance of and respect for the Other, charity for the poor, respect for parents and teachers, civil rights and obligations, the importance of compromise, entitlement to rest, modesty, humility, diligence, law and order, compassion for animals, attention to the needs of strangers, acceptance of and dialogue with other religions, and, more recently added perhaps, respect for the environment and mystical spirituality. All of these are given pride of place in publications and conversations about Jewish ethics and contemporary Jewish values. The list, of course, goes on and on, and anyone who has followed my argument thus far might justifiably expect me to complete it with a mention of peace.

However, the mansion has other, less pleasing furnishings too. There are service corridors, storerooms, laundry rooms, and basements (maybe even a dungeon or two) in which we have stored the cast-off furniture and dirty linen of days gone by—items for which (some might believe) we have no further use. To wit, we do not know what to do with disturbing (and apparently obsolete) ideas such as the relentless and unforgiving persecution and annihilation of idolaters; excruciating capital, corporal, and collective punishments; the trial of allegedly treacherous women by humiliating ordeals; animal sacrifice; holy war; patrilineal inheritance; preferential treatment of the first-born son; men's possession of women; slavery; the categorization of homosexuality as an abomination; and so on. Classical, medieval, and early modern Jewish practices have added to the list such laws and customs as the habitual ritual cursing of Christians, oligarchy, religious intolerance, the brutal sacrifices of children, asceticism, polygamy, the exclusion of women from synagogue ritual and Torah study, and so on. (My list is illustrative and by no means exhaustive.) And so, we keep returning to such passages as the *sotah* (the woman accused of adultery), the *eshet yephat to'ar* (the beautiful woman captive), the *ben sorer umoreh* (the rebellious child), the *eved Cna'ani* (the Canaanite slave), trying to discover how we might digest, sublimate, or perhaps even conceal them. In certain cases—such as the rebellious child whose biblically ordered execution by stoning is virtually erased in the Talmud[1]—rabbinic interpretation chimes happily in tune with contemporary values. When this happens, we celebrate the rabbis' ethical sensitivity. But, this is not always possible and, when it is, the celebration is perhaps misplaced.

The Mishnah says, "Regarding one who says while praying: You are so compassionate and gracious that Your mercy extends to the bird's nest . . . we silence him." The Talmud asks, "What is the reason that we silence him?" Rabbi Yose Bar Zevida answers, "Because he renders the commandments of the Holy One, Blessed be He, into acts of mercy while in truth they are nothing other than decrees [*gezerot*]" (Talmud Berachot 33b). The use of the foreboding word *gezerot* to describe the supposedly compassionate commandment of *shiluach heken*[2] (sending the mother away from the nest) stands out in this passage. While Rabbi Yose Bar Zevida's position seems less extreme in context (i.e., as part of a discussion about appropriate prayer), his warning against simplifying the connection between prophetic law and ethics still rings very clear.

The attempt to align religious law with post-Enlightenment ethics has had a complex and ambiguous impact on modern Judaism. Despite its many merits and accomplishments, post-Enlightenment liberalism has had a disintegrative or perhaps even destructive effect on modern Jewish life. Most poignant to our concerns, liberalism has entrenched the conviction among many modern Jews that the *living* resources of the tradition are only those that have a place on public display in the wings of the mansion that are open to visitors. The problem here emerges when space in the front rooms and display cabinets is deemed scarce—and when much of what is there can affect the public policies of a Jewish state; the struggle over what Judaism "stands for" has led to a social rift that has come, on occasion, alarmingly close to civil war. Peace depends on making more space in the public light for the mansion's less fashionable chambers.

Dirty Laundry

> *Both Purim and the Book of Esther . . . are subjects that have impelled both apologists and anti-Semites to show their true colors, as they have impelled me to show mine. . . . Others [among my readers] may be upset that I am packing so much dirty laundry between the covers of an academic book instead of leaving it to fade on the pages of soon-to-be-forgotten newspapers or consigning it to the dreary darkness of the microfilm room. But in doing so I am following in the path of many worthy predecessors, including the biblical author of the Book of Esther.*
>
> —ELLIOTT HOROWITZ, *Reckless Rites: Purim and the Legacy of Jewish Violence*

The chief rabbi of Safed addressed his followers in a flyer distributed among the congregants of synagogues throughout Israel in the fall of 2007. He called upon them to demand a policy of revenge for Palestinian terrorism. In his view, Jews who are committed to the Torah must press the "evil" secular government to exact cruel and bitter revenge on the Palestinians. "We must be as cruel to them as they are to us, so that they will fall on their faces and beg us to stop." In his view, the spineless government of Israel is not "Jewish enough" to understand the ethics of revenge. "[So] great is revenge that it is mentioned betwixt two mentions of the name of God, *El Nekamot Hashem.*" "Liberals" and "leftists" cannot and must not dictate what Jewish values are, the rabbi warns. "Don't let those whose Judaism will soon fritter away deter your commitment to the values of the Torah. The Torah calls for revenge. It might not be politically correct but it is an eternal truth and we should call it by its real name: Judaism believes in revenge! Revenge! Revenge!"

How is one to respond to such hatred directed against both Palestinians and Jews? How can one live in peace with it? Rather than conclude (as many have before me) that religion is an obstacle to peace, I take an alternative view of things. As disturbing and counterintuitive as this may sound in a book dedicated to peace, I suggest that such beliefs as those of the rabbi from Safed have an authentic—and even irenic—role to play within the Jewish legal tradition. My point is made clearer when we consider the liberal alternative to it. I do not, for example, share Jaroslav Pelikan's view that we can "rely upon the tradition to vindicate us . . . by how it manages to accord with our own deepest intuitions and highest aspirations (intuitions and aspirations which . . . are themselves imbedded in the tradition)."[3] I do not agree because it seems clear that traditions, by their very nature, contain political incorrectness and ugliness subscribed to by the most tenacious of adherents. Pelikan falls short because he assumes that there will always be a consensus of values, an agreement about what is and is not ugly, and that the tradition can be both liberalized and authentically spoken for by its representatives. A genuine articulation of faith in a tradition cannot afford such homogenization of its complexities. What is more, an irenic notion of faith will always be incomplete without acknowledging the (often intolerable) variety of beliefs and believers that any religion contains.[4] To become peaceful, traditions need to readjust to the idea of washing their dirty linen in public.

In my discussion of revelation, I proposed a reading of prophetic texts that draws upon deconstruction and weak theology. My vision of prophetic peace is imbedded in the prophetic genre and not in any one of its singular messages (including its peaceful ones). In my treatment of the rabbinic voice, my approach is similar. I will attempt to reconstruct the hermeneutical principles of rabbinic literature in non-essentialist or nonmetaphysical, philosophically weak terms. My object will be to dismantle or perhaps overwhelm "the reason/revelation duo"[5] that dominates conventional understandings of the rabbinic project. I will do this with the overt purpose of disarming claims to certainty about the truth of rabbinic law, supplementing these with a notion of religious—even prophetic—passion for the impossible. As in the case of prophecy, I will seek to demonstrate how even the most violent of rabbinic messages (the dirty linen) might be absorbed into a vision of peace when the truth claims of the genre are relocated. Put simply, I believe that rabbinic law is quietly humble about the mystery of God, not triumphantly intoxicated with certainty about its own versions of either truth or ethics. In this, it shares with prophecy its peaceful heart.

A Short Note on Relativism

Today, having a clear faith based on the Creed of the Church is often labeled as fundamentalism. . . . We are building a dictatorship of relativism that does not recognize anything as definitive and whose ultimate goal consists solely of one's ego and desires.

—Joseph Ratzinger (Pope Benedict XVI),
"Homily Pro Eligando Romano Pontifice"

Ultimately, modernity threatens religion with its hermeneutical and methodological presumptions more than it ever could with its (often dubious) ethics. The distaste of the modern palate for the rough textures of tradition, though often expressed in ethical terms, is as much a result of the censorship imposed by empirical historical criticism—which claims the right to distinguish admissible from non-admissible classical texts—as it is of ethics. This scholarly process has been responsible for a great deal of intellectual conflict, as we sense when reading the metaphors that Pelikan uses to describe it:

> Historical study makes the authority of tradition relative rather than absolute, by exposing its participation in the ebb and flow of historical currents. In response, the *defenders* of tradition often manifested a *garrison* mentality, seeking to *demarcate* those areas into which historical research, with its relativizing criticism, was not to be permitted to *penetrate*.[6]

Historical study has a relativizing effect, but not only on the authority of tradition. In the long run, historical study has had a relativizing effect on the authority of history as well. It is crucial that we recognize the irony here. With the passage of time, the empirical methods of historical criticism have done more to undermine certainty than they have to establish criteria for evaluating the past on objective grounds. The quest for historical objectivity has exposed the subjectivity with which the criteria for objective analysis are determined. The Enlightenment notion of cumulative knowledge has been surpassed by one of switching trends, or paradigm shifts (which, in my view, provides contemporary religious thinkers with a tremendous opportunity for squaring rational or critical investigation with faith in new and promising ways). However, in response to high modernity, religious leaders have notably chosen to resist relativism even more vehemently. With significant justification, they perceive it as a threat to the integrity of conviction itself—whether religious or scientific.

In his final address as a cardinal, Joseph Ratzinger expressed his concern about those who have "been tossed about—flung from one extreme to another: from Marxism to Liberalism, even to Libertinism." In Ratzinger's view, the shifting sand on which scientific knowledge is now built has lowered the expectations among believers for clarity of creed in religion. "[H]ow many winds of doctrine have we known in recent decades, how many ways of thinking . . . ? Every day new sects spring up, and what St. Paul says about human deception and the trickery that strives to entice people into error comes true." In the interest of the church, Pope Benedict XVI seems to prefer an iron-fisted opponent who stands against religion from the outside to a deceptively gentle and flexible one that infiltrates it and works from within. In this preference, he feels wrongly accused of fundamentalism when the alternative, in his view, is no less tyrannical.[7]

In a world disillusioned with empirical standards, a proof is not a proof and a truth is not a truth. Most pressingly perhaps, a victory is no longer a victory; not even the overwhelming military victory in Iraq vanquished America's opponents there. Defeated or not, they continue fighting, wielding their weapons against the Leviathan force of the mighty. But for all the horror of terrorism and the flippancy of fads, there is a complexity to the tyranny of relativism that the pope and even the rabbi of Safed might still note with approval. The collapse of empiricism has indeed allowed for the legitimization of trends. It has perhaps reduced almost every cause—however grand and noble it might be—into a fashion. But trends and fashions—whether you are for them or against them, for a day or for a lifetime—have little more power than their capacity to command attention for a while. (One day, they dominate the agenda, and on the next they are forgotten.) What they lack is a formative impact on historical cultures. In the terms that are most critical for the Jewish—text-learning—community, trends do not lead to the elimination of texts from the bookshelf. The current shift of attitudes toward homosexuals—even within some Orthodox Jewish circles—is perhaps the most striking current Jewish example. While many religiously observant gays and lesbians have emerged from the closet, claiming active roles in synagogue life and even communal religious leadership, they have done nothing and do not seem to aspire to delete or even conceal the very texts that sent them to the closet in the first place.

My point is that, one way or another, whether you see ugliness to your left or to your right, while tastes and fashions shift and move around, "tossed here and there, carried about by every wind of doctrine," there must be room for dirty linen. A culture's capacity to accept (or "contain" in the expansive sense) the rough edges of its tradition is crucial to its ability to make peace.

The Tyranny of Explicit Law

> *Moses received the Torah at Sinai, and transmitted it to Joshua, and Joshua transmitted it to the Elders, and the Elders to the Prophets, and the Prophets transmitted it to the men of the Great Assembly. They said three things: Be moderate in judgment; and raise up many students; and make a fence around the Torah.*
>
> —Mishnah Avot 1:1

Now let us turn to the details of the halakha and to the primary weapon that must be disarmed in order to articulate an irenic notion of rabbinic law: the potential certitude and violence of explicit law.

Explicit law requires definitive practical action. Legal deliberations have outcomes. Law forces order and clarity on the conflicted chaos of the raw and shattered human world. At any given moment, there are courses of action to be followed and choices to be made. Some are better and some are worse. None are perfect, since the choices are always predicated on a human (and therefore partial) understanding of defiantly complex circumstances. Wisdom, learning, experience, and character can help. Judges (and we are all called upon to make judgments and choices) are forced time and time again by the necessities of life to settle for the best decisions possible and to pursue practical outcomes with integrity. But, by their very nature, choices, judgments, and decisions can never be absolute. Some point of view is always rejected or forbidden. Someone is always convicted or acquitted. Something is always cast aside or locked away. A single act of theft, murder, infidelity, or inattention redefines the entirety of a human being's life as completely as a lump of butter or a dollop of cream halakhically transforms a chicken soup. In any legal outcome, the part must always masquerade as the whole.

Jewish law relies (in part) upon the metaphorization of rabbinic halakha as an explicitly authoritarian legal system. It is by necessity as flawed and incomplete as any legal ruling. Law is limited by its need to reach decisions and by the confines of the categories it must use to determine outcomes. In practice, a vessel cannot be both pure and defiled; an act cannot be both permitted and forbidden. Similarly, the fierce blow of a truncheon—even one raised in fear, regret, or compassion—cannot both hurt and heal. While the system of explicit halakha is notoriously complex—offering multiple opinions for every form of action, exploring the minutiae of meaning and application for every legal category to the boundaries of reason and the limits of possibility—explicit halakha is ultimately geared toward reaching a legal outcome. It follows an impulse of canonization and codification, seeking to focus the energies of its deliberations into a single point of law.

One of the more prominent contemporary philosophers of halakha, Avi Sagi, put it like this, "According to the rabbinic tradition, the halakhic endeavor is 'God's word': 'God's word—that is halakha'" (Talmud Shabbat 138b).[8] The practical and implemented outcome of a human course of deliberation is understood as an explicit expression of God's will. This means that the halakha must live up to its own claim to offer instruction in God's name. *Deus Vult!* However, explicit halakha faces one fundamental challenge that Jewish scholars have been writing about incessantly for generations. Because of its supposed divine origins, it can barely endure its own inevitable imperfections.

The mechanism used by explicit halakhic thought to make truth claims about the word of God is based on rational interpretation. Revelation (understood in explicit terms) is handed over to a college of empowered interpreters whose resourcefulness, exemplary human qualities, and scholarship ensure the truthfulness of their rulings. By necessity, the explicit halakhic system carries the certainty of its rulings from the source of its divine instigation into the validity of its interpretive outcomes.

The foundation of this interpretive enterprise is built upon the book of Deuteronomy, where interpretation is placed firmly on top of prophetic revelation like two bricks in a tower. In Deuteronomy 16:18, Moses describes a legal system of courts where witnesses give testimony and judges rule. In this chapter, the law is authoritarian and unequivocal in its struggle against idolatry —a struggle that provides the context for many of the Bible's most violent injunctions.[9] But in Deuteronomy 17, the system of justice is expanded and mandated to confront a broader span of legal challenges:

> If there arise a matter too hard for thee in judgment between blood and blood, between plea and plea and between stroke and stroke, even matters of controversy within thy gates; then shalt thou arise, and get thee up unto the place which the Lord thy God shall choose. And thou shalt come unto the priests, the Levites, and unto the judge that shall be in those days; and thou shalt inquire; and they shall declare unto the sentence of judgment. And thou shalt do

according to the tenor of the sentence, which they shall declare unto thee.... thou shalt not turn aside from the sentence which they shall declare unto thee, to the right hand nor to the left.

Moses gives the judges, the Levites, and the priests the power to wield the word of God and rule on matters that encompass the full spectrum of Jewish law. They are authorized to rule in capital cases, to resolve controversies, and to minister before the Lord. Most poignantly, they are empowered to punish those who reject the authority of the court and deviate from the tenor of its sentence. Thus, a human institution with divine authority is established—a veritable time bomb and a potential source of unthinkable tyranny—and the Jewish tradition has much to be proud of in its history of handling this power. It is in this context that the tractate of Avot should be read. Arguably, the wise advice that the sages offer to judges is to ensure the safe handling of all this rabbinic power.

Avot acknowledges the potential dangers posed by the first Mishnah (see the epigraph to this section). Moses receives the words of God at Sinai and hands them on explicitly to Joshua, who then passes them to the elders and to the prophets until they reach the hands of the sages. The explicit nature of this process is underlined (whether emphatically or ironically) by the mention of the prophets in this list of passive recipients. The literary device of planting an incongruity or a surprise in a list is put here to wonderful effect. Reading the list, one stumbles across the mention of the prophets, thinking, "What are they doing here? Do they not receive revelation by another path?" This, of course, is precisely the point. The mention of the prophets ensures the demystification of the law's evolution beyond the point of its origin at Sinai. The uninterrupted consistency of the legal process bypasses subsequent prophetic revelations, making sure that the poetic and religiously evocative messages of the prophets are not allowed to touch the law. The prophets are effectively claimed as scholars and indeed as recipients of the tradition in that scholarly capacity alone. It would seem that rabbinic rule is complete; its demand for obedience is irrefutable and the potential of its disruption by the charismatic or the unruly is subdued.[10] In Avi Sagi's words:

> Its [the halakha's] source then is transcendent. Ascribing a divine source to halakha could have led to a human disposition of submission and subservience. Human beings are expected to submit to the will of the divine legislator, the sovereign of the universe. Absolute obedience is expected from God's children, impotent creatures facing the power and the authority of the divine.[11]

The explicit law, which is embraced by many (if not most) observant Jews today, views rabbinic rulings as inextricably connected to the word of God. The problem is that, left to its own devices, this religious orientation invests extraordinary power in the hands of men and is prone to breeding the kind of religious certitude that produces holy violence, vengeance, and religious tyranny. Ultimately, the potential for rabbinic holy violence is always there when the law is viewed in exclusively explicit terms. It is the domination achieved by explicit readers of the law that potentially leads to the kinds of halakhic fundamentalism that must be thoroughly disarmed for Judaism to function "safely" (and more fully) as the religion of the state of Israel. With all due respect to a long history of rabbinic restraint, once a gun is placed in a room where there are bullets, it takes more than a safety catch to prevent it from being fired.

The Liberal Attempt to Disarm Explicit Law

> *A story is told about R. Yohanan ben Beroka and R. Elazar ben Hisma who went to greet R. Yehoshua in Peki'in. He asked them: "what novel teaching was there at the house of study today?" They said to him: "We are your disciples and drink only from your water." He said to them, "even so, it is impossible for a study session to pass without some novel teaching."*
>
> —Talmud Hagiga 3b

Prior to introducing the implicit perspective from which I will propose a more irenic understanding of the halakha, I will discuss in some detail the liberal strategy of disarmament. In particular, I want to draw critical attention to liberalism's enduring commitment to the metaphysics that makes legal tyranny possible.[12]

Liberal readings of rabbinic literature seek to undermine or interrogate rabbinic authoritarianism from within—claiming the authenticity of rabbinic liberalism from the halakha's primary literary sources. Responding to the (fundamentalist) claims of those religious teachers in the Jewish world today who associate religious authenticity and "orthodoxy" with unquestioning obedience to rabbinic authority, liberal thinkers and scholars build the rabbinic religious disposition on the claim that foundational and canonic rabbinic texts themselves drive a wedge between religious obligation and submissive obedience. Liberal readings of classical rabbinic literature argue that the rabbinic project is authentically committed to progressive critical thinking and pluralism. Let us consider some examples.

In *Rational Rabbis,* Menachem Fisch makes what strikes me as a compelling case for rabbinic progressivism. The book is essentially an account of how rabbinic rationalism replaced the authority of mystical revelation in the exposition of Jewish law. While the "threat" of prophecy intruding upon the halakhic process was not an imminent one for the rabbis of the Mishnah and Talmud, Fisch shows how the halakhic system continued to struggle with the shackles of prophetic traditionalism in its attempt to establish a contemporaneous and evolving legal system. He identifies two ideological dispositions in rabbinic literature and dubs them "traditionalist" and "anti-traditionalist" schools of thought:

> For all traditionalists Torah-study is primarily conceived of as a matter of meticulous reception and transmission from one generation to the next of the one allegedly revealed binding meaning of the written Torah. Whatever halakhic discretion is granted to rabbinic authorities of each generation with respect to new questions, it pales for the traditionalist in comparison to the central and holy task of preserving, synthesizing, and passing on the great legacy of old.[13]

However, despite the traditionalist/anti-traditionalist duality, there is a significant imbalance between the respective importance of these two schools' impact upon the law. In Fisch's view, the traditionalists are "accomplices," playing a necessary but auxiliary role in the anti-traditionalist exposition of the law. Following the formula that Karl Popper developed to portray rational progress in science, Fisch suggests:

> Two different yet complementary traditions are required to ensure and perpetuate an ongoing rational inquiry. First, and obviously, the theories themselves need to be transmitted efficiently from one generation to the next, otherwise scientific work would be trivially terminated . . . but to avoid indoctrination, a second tradition—a critical tradition—is equally pertinent.[14]

The composition of rabbinic literature marks a concerted "educational" effort to initiate capable students into the practice of critical inquiry. In this sense, the Talmud is more of a logbook—a testimonial to the procedure of study—than a textbook of binding authority. The Talmud showcases the form of study that the rabbis identified as essential to the development of halakha.

In Fisch's words, "Had the redactors of the Bavli [Babylonian Talmud] wished to compile no more than an up-to-date, ordered and appropriately synthesized halakhic codex, they would probably have produced a very different kind of text."[15] Instead, they were theologically and indeed halakhically open-minded thinkers whose anti-traditionalist manifesto was "founded upon a sharp demarcation of divine and human authority." Fisch continues, "Where the dividing line runs [is] between word and meaning, between text and understanding, between *interpretandum* and *interpretans*. And, within the hermeneutic space allocated to humans, not only is the force of tradition ruled uncompelling, but the Almighty himself is refrained from interfering."[16]

Clearly, this conclusion references Rabbi Yehoshua's famous admonishment of God for interfering in the halakhic process, to which I will return later.[17] Fisch understands Rabbi Yehoshua's position as one that democratizes the methods by which the rabbinic law claims to be truthful. Significantly, he confesses that this facet of the rabbinic project was—to a great extent—unsuccessful. Few got the point of the exercise, and instead most have confused the generic complexity of the Talmud's interplay between traditionalist and anti-traditionalist voices for a largely traditionalist attitude toward explicit law. Rather than developing an impressive "cadre of keen anti-traditionalist trouble-shooters," the rabbinic plan "backfired, and the Bavli's traditionalist idiom appears to have contributed instead to a wholly unintended revival and reinstitution of a major traditionalist school of thought that would later come to dominate post-Talmudic culture."[18]

Following Popper's disintegration of the observationalist-inductivist account of science, Fisch proposes a notion of the halakha as an ongoing, ever-evolving, innovative human composition that appreciably dictates the will of God. Similarly, he promotes a critical-rationalist religious disposition in which the impulse to interrogate the tradition along multiple lines of questioning—rather than submissive obedience to its dicta—is the highest expression of religious commitment. In Fisch's vision, the rabbis position themselves at the junctures of historical change. The rabbinic voice is there to be sounded at the helm, where the law must confront the waves of history that crash against its bows. Clearly, this proposal is as much a manifesto for the present and future management of the halakha as it is an interpretation of its workings in the past. It allows for, or perhaps even demands, radical innovation and a willingness to rethink the troubling concerns of each generation. Seated on the fault lines of history, the "rational rabbis" are both qualified and authorized by the tradition to confront and absorb the legitimate claims of feminists, homosexuals, reformers, critical thinkers, and peacemakers as plaintiffs in the halakhic process.

Fisch recognizes that this method has failed to accomplish one very significant aspect of the rabbinic vision. The rational rabbis are, by ironic necessity, an intellectual elite open to discourse with only the most highly skilled partners. They are at a loss when confronted by the needs of the lay community whose members are often oblivious to the tradition's complexities. In order to successfully lead the wider community, the rational rabbis must fight an almost hopeless uphill battle to educate the masses. In order to follow their lead, knowledge and critical expertise are required to a degree that is usually attained only by the most capable of students. Whenever this is not possible, the rabbis have no choice but to establish a rule of law and to command obedience to their authority (in the same way, perhaps, as elected officials in a liberal democracy exercise power between elections). In realizing this vision—as Fisch admits—the rational rabbinate has a long history of failure. Ultimately, the wedge between religious obligation and submissive obedience crumbles, and the ugly, ignorant conservatism that this progressive project sought to dethrone is left tenaciously in place.

The clash between this vision of the halakhic ethos and its regressive results can easily lead to social conflict, mutual condescension, and side taking between the right and left wings. Figures such as the aforementioned chief rabbi of Safed might be classified among those in need of reeducation while forward-thinking religious leaders face the accusation of behaving like pilots on a plane with no economy-class seats and therefore no lay passengers. Beyond this sociopolitical problem, *Rational Rabbis* makes excessively bold epistemological claims about the capacity and the authority of the human intellect to determine the law of God. The metaphorization of the halakhic process as one built upon a commitment to scientific/legal exposition overstretches the line connecting rabbinic law to the theological context that gives it religious meaning. Consequently, it is hard for many religiously committed Jews to identify with rabbinic rationalism's religious sincerity.

A second example of a liberal articulation of the rabbinic tradition is Avi Sagi's *The Open Canon*. Sagi's book is a detailed and systematic exposition of classical and more recent rabbinic understandings of dissent and disagreement in halakhic literature. Starting with the rabbinic formulation "These and these are the words of the living God," Sagi explores the pervasive tradition of *makhloket* (dispute), giving an intriguing account of the rabbinic *makhloket* about the meaning of *makhloket*. Like Fisch, Sagi argues that the sages of rabbinic Judaism founded their religious consciousness on autonomy rather than on tyranny and obedience. But the thrust of his discussion is different. Sagi traces the answers given by halakhic thinkers to the question: To what extent can a legal system that is so full of disagreement and variety claim its rulings to be God's will?

Sagi provides a sophisticated and intricately structured taxonomy of the various strategies used by classical, premodern, and modern Orthodox rabbis to answer this question. He distinguishes between "monist," "pluralist," and "harmonic" outlooks. While each of these is divided into multiple subcategories, a monist point of view can be satisfactorily summed up as one that "assumes only one correct solution for every normative dilemma." Pluralism "acknowledges more than one option as possible," while the harmonic method allows "contradictory positions [to] enjoy equal status." The monist considers rejected legal options "false, invalid and illegitimate, while the pluralist does not." The pluralist allows for more than one option to be true (or to make a legitimate claim to truth). Finally, harmonists claim "that the halakha rests on a unified foundation that binds the gamut of contradictory views into one truth." As such, it is halakhic literature in its entirety (and not one or another individual opinion) that purports to be truthful. "These and these" emerge as the "words of the living God," while the individual opinion (the text cites a preference for Bet Hillel) carried out in practice is the "halakha."[19]

While the purpose of *The Open Canon* is broadly descriptive of all three models, it seems quite clear—in the final calculation—that Sagi is interested in promoting the pluralist model as the one that most effectively captures the authentic nature of the halakhic commitment to truth. It is in the multiplicity with which truth can be articulated that the human endeavor of rational discussion emerges as divinely inspired and religiously sincere. In Sagi's words, "Halakhic culture, unlike classical culture, not only recognized the existence of different truths but also ascribed deep religious value to this fact." The halakha expects its proponents to engage in the "creative appropriation of tradition," thus allowing for multiple interpretive attempts to emerge simultaneously as truth on the grounds that "God granted human beings the power to create and shape halakha according to their own understanding." Finally, when addressing the possibility that the human interpretive effort might yield tolerably false—rather than multiply truthful—results, Sagi insists:

> The picture is clear. We found no instances of typical toleration or even an approach close to toleration in halakhic tradition. We did not find attitudes of negation and contempt for rejected options and no one claimed them to be reprehensible deviations. Supporters of the accepted view were not required to practice self-restraint and refrain from action against the rejected option. We did find, however several versions of weak and strong pluralism.[20]

Liberal readings of explicit law are committed to the evolution and progress of halakha free from authoritarian dogmatism. By presenting classical rabbinic Judaism in pluralist and progressive terms, contemporary thinkers and scholars add historical authenticity to the liberal claim that a golden trail may be blazed between secularism (and estrangement from the tradition) and religious fundamentalism.[21] In contemporary (left-wing, religious, Zionist) terms, liberal orthodoxy proposes classical halakhic pluralism as a foundation for negotiating Jewish political disunity in religious, political, and communal affairs.[22]

The Limits of Halakhic Pluralism

> On that day R. Eliezer brought forward every imaginable argument, but they did not accept him. . . . He then said to them: "If the halakha agrees with me, let them prove it from the heavens" whereupon a heavenly voice issued forth and declared: "What have you against R. Eliezer, for the halakha agrees with him everywhere?" R. Yehoshua rose to his feet and declared: "It is not in heaven!" (Deut. 30:12). What does it mean, "It is not in heaven"? Said R. Yermia: "Since the Torah was given at Mount Sinai, we pay no heed to a heavenly voice for You have already written in the Torah at Mount Sinai 'to incline after a multitude'" (Exod. 23:2).
> —Talmud Baba Metzia 59b

These two examples—Sagi and Fisch—illustrate how liberal pluralist views of explicit halakha struggle against the dogmatic limits of the system. Yet, both Sagi and Fisch share the conviction that the halakha seeks—through interpretation or the assumption of rabbinic authority—to determine either the "original" or the "current" intentions of revelation in definitive terms. In other words, for both of them, a radical rejection of the tradition's authenticity and authority would not constitute a position that one might legitimately take within the walls of the traditional Bet Midrash (House of Study). While it is clear to anyone who opens almost any rabbinic text that halakhic literature is multivocal, when viewed in explicit terms it seems equally clear that freedom of interpretation is necessarily and self-avowedly limited. Thus, the halakhic system insists that legal precedents, once set (i.e., once established as complying with divine commandment), are extremely difficult to overturn. Similarly, certain bottom-line principles (such as the injunction against eating pork or lighting a fire on the Sabbath) are easily exploited to stay the fear that excessively liberal readings might allow contemporary reinterpretation to spin out of orbit. In other words, even the most liberal readers accept the premise that the integrity of the halakhic discourse is protected by the belief that the halakha has an intractable core. Reinterpretation cannot penetrate this core, and rabbinic injunction can and must be relied upon to defend it.

How the substance of this core is determined and how in practice the boundaries of legitimate dispute are drawn are not at all clear. Sagi, for example, is noticeably evasive about this question. Though he recognizes that "the rabbis are aware of the potential limits concerning legitimate halakhic options," a precise characterization of these bounds is placed outside the confines of his "open canon."[23] This is no small omission. The limits of halakhic pluralism are of crucial importance to any attempt to model an open and accepting modern Jewish society on halakhic precedent. As long as these are unclear, the risk is run of determining the boundaries of "legitimate" discourse according to problematic or perhaps even frivolous considerations. The dangers of this emerge quite clearly in one famous Talmudic passage.

The frequently cited debate over the ritual purity of Akhnai's oven (the context of the epigraph to this section) is embedded in a wider discussion about *ona'at devarim* (harmful or deceitful speech). When considered in context, I believe that this story should be read as a warning against the contamination of the halakha by the irresponsibly extreme and frivolous positions that tend to emerge when combatants face each other. According to this reading, neither the conduct of Rabbi Eliezer nor that of Rabbi Yehoshua represents a Talmudic ideal. The miracles that Rabbi Eliezer performs pose a menacing threat to the world of Torah study that the Talmud holds dear and therefore disqualify him as the hero of the story.[24] He should never have resorted to them and would not have done so had he not been provoked "in combat." The other rabbis' conduct is no better. They blatantly ignore Rabbi Eliezer throughout the entire discussion. Rabbi Eliezer's numerous attempts to make his case with rational arguments are simply brushed aside. Rabbi Eliezer is said to have rallied "every imaginable rational argument in the world" while the other rabbis—ad hominem—"did not accept them *from him*."[25] It is at this crucial point in the proceedings that the debate spirals out of control. Rabbi Eliezer threatens the destruction of food and water supplies by supernatural means, and the rabbis respond by joining ranks to oppose him. (I think it is anachronistic and inappropriate to read the rabbis' commitment to majority rule as a harbinger of modern liberal democracy. It seems to me more accurate to describe the rabbis' conduct as an exercise in what John Stuart Mill called "the tyranny of the majority.")[26]

As the debate reaches its climax, Rabbi Eliezer tears open the heavens to evoke direct divine intervention. A heavenly voice appears and vindicates his position. This is perhaps a short-lived moment of triumph for Rabbi Eliezer, but it is not even that for God. Immediately after the Talmud completes its account of Rabbi Yehoshua's infamous rejection of the heavenly voice's authority, a short story is told of a meeting between Rabbi Nathan and Elijah the prophet. As I understand Elijah's report, he relates how God watched the dispute deteriorate and, smiling wryly, he said, "My sons have defeated Me."[27] The story describes the defeat of God, not his acquiescence. "My sons have defeated Me."

The Talmudic story does not end here. It continues to relate how Rabbi Yehoshua and his disciples issued a ban on Rabbi Eliezer, publicly reversing all his previous rulings on matters of ritual purity. Vessels whose purity he had authorized were publicly shattered along with Rabbi Eliezer's scholarly reputation. The ban was a devastating blow to Rabbi Eliezer. When Rabbi Akiva informed him of it, the Talmud reports that "tears streamed from his eyes and that the world was then smitten." Like the humiliation of God, the destruction of the crops suggests the cosmological import of the clash. The Torah and those who study it, along with the crops and the harvest, have been wrenched out of God's hands and out of his protection. This is the calamity about which Moses warned the people of Israel, saying, "and then the Lord's anger be inflamed against you, and He shut up the heavens that there be no rain, and that the land yield not its fruit" (Deuteronomy 11:17).

Rabbi Yehoshua's anti-traditionalist position—"not in heaven"—is typically understood as emblematically humanist and pluralist. My purpose is not to disagree but to draw attention to the ways in which this story exposes the notorious incapacity of pluralists to confront their enemies. The pluralist model indeed makes room for multiple, varied, and even conflicting points of view. But it lacks the capacity to endure those who do not accept its rules of engagement—those (including God) whose dissent is understood as a threat to the autonomy of the pluralist discourse itself. As it collapses agonizingly into heart-wrenching calamity, the story so often cited to support liberal philosophies of halakha unleashes a bitter critique of humanist liberalism. According to my reading, the conflict between Rabbi Eliezer and Rabbi Yehoshua shows how easily a religious humanist can become violent when confronted with a religious fundamentalist. It suggests how inadequate humanist theory might be to the task of making peace with unvanquished enemies. It illustrates how dangerous comfort in numbers can be. Finally, it intimates how easily the facade of liberal civility can melt away when the limits of its patience are seriously tested.

The Implicit Rabbinic Voice

> *A story is told about R. Yochanan ben Zakkai, who was rid-ing on a donkey, while R. Eleazar ben Arakh walked behind him. R. Eleazar said to his master, "My master, teach me one lesson on the Merkavah."[28] His teacher replied, "Have not our sages taught that it is forbidden to teach one individual the mystery of the Merkavah, unless he is a scholar and can understand it independently?" R. Eleazar then said to him, "Do permit me to expound something on this subject." He answered, "Speak." As soon as Eleazar ben Arakh began to speak about the secret of the divine chariot, R. Yochanan descended from his donkey saying, "It is not proper that I shall hear about the glory of my Maker while riding on a donkey." They walked a while and then sat down beneath a tree, whereupon a fire descended from heaven and sur-rounded them. The ministering angels leapt before them with joy like guests at a wedding who rejoice with the groom. One angel spoke from within the fire saying, "Eleazar ben Arakh, it is exactly as you have explained it—you have revealed the secret of the Merkavah!" Instantly, all the trees opened their mouths and sang, as it is written, "Then all the trees of the forest will sing." (Psalms 96:12)*

> —Palestinian Talmud Hagiga 2:1, 77a[29]

I have spent most of my adult life identifying with a liberal approach to Orthodox Judaism, believing that liberalism might be the key to contain-ing the potential violence that religious law can produce when mixed with political or institutional power. After observing with concern the fury of my own "dovish" opposition to the protests of Israel's religious right against the Oslo process and the disengagement from Gaza, I became deeply distressed and dissatisfied with liberalism and the potential violence that *it* can produce when mixed with power. I was disturbed by my own incapacity to make peace and accept the beliefs of others—even when that so-called otherness actually referred to the vast majority of the religious camp of which I am ostensibly a member. Against the backdrop of these realizations, the fantasy that peaceful bridges can be built on a liberal middle ground between Israel and its enemies seems ever more elusive. Peace requires a radical, powerless openness and acceptance that liberal politics is too judgmental to supply. Peace requires an intensification of (rather than a dilution of) religious commitment and a conviction no less passionate than that of the settlers to the sanctity of the land. Peace requires the religious humility of Rabbi Yochanan, who descended from his donkey, and the passion for Torah that makes the trees sing.

My view is that this passionate combination of religious conviction and humility must be separated from apodictic epistemology and ethics. It cannot be built upon foundations of justice, certainty, or truth presumed universal only by their adherents. I favor an attitude built upon the humility that a passionate consciousness of transcendent mystery can bring.

The philosophical or theological heart of my critique of halakhic liberalism is that its capacity to prevent religious tyranny is limited, first and foremost, by the *explicit* understanding of revelation that it shares with fundamentalism.[30] Once the assumption that the word of God is exoterically accessible to human understanding is disrupted, it becomes much harder to demand and command obedience to rabbinic injunctions made in God's name. The liberal strategy admittedly diversifies the idea of truth and softens the encounter with rabbinic authority. But it also leaves metaphysical epistemologies intact. I propose supplementing the strong theology of explicit law with a softer or weaker one. As with prophetic language, rabbinic literature delicately combines explicit legal premises with self-deconstructing implicit critiques that expose the shortcomings (and dirty linen) of the halakha. It is these critiques that pave the way to a peaceful understanding of Jewish legalism.

In my discussion of prophecy, I suggested that an implicit understanding of revelation distances religious discourse from potentially violent understandings of divine truth. Implicit faith experiences revelation as paradoxical, confined by the limitations and inadequacies of language, bound to fail and to conceal as much as it reveals. The complex combination of apparently exoteric divine speech and implicit religious experience that is found in prophetic literature disarms the violent potential of prophecy by exposing its inescapable connection with religious mystery. This combination of revelation and mystery leaves prophetic texts intelligible and unintelligible at the same time. Prophetic language pulls the platform out from under the feet of the prophet; its esotericism undercuts the declarative force of its pronouncements but without rendering them meaningless. Rabbinic literature is similarly self-conscious and ambiguous in its use of language. As with the explicit dimensions of prophetic language, the metaphor of explicit rabbinic law is only one axis in a paradox. This axis is delicately intertwined with an oppositional impulse to expose the limitations of rabbinic law and deconstruct its absolute authority.

A complex interplay of explicit and implicit rabbinic thinking emerges in many places in rabbinic literature. Heschel describes this interplay as one of the critical characteristics of the rabbinic project. In his view, attention to the distinction between and balance of "halakha" and "agada" exposes the religious depth of rabbinic Judaism and counters the false impression that the rabbis were theologically naïve and excessively formalistic. In Heschel's words:

> Halakha represents the strength to shape one's life according to a fixed pattern; it is a form-giving force. Agada is the expression of man's ceaseless striving, which often defies all limitations. Halakha is the rationalization and schematization of living; it defines, specifies, sets measure and limit, placing life into an exact system. Agada deals with man's ineffable relations to God, to other men and to the world.[31]

Heschel's use of halakha and agada should not suggest that the rabbis express their explicit and implicit concerns in separate contexts or that each has its own tractates. On the contrary, the two are intricately intertwined. The two genres can naturally flow into one another on the same Talmudic page, while the subject matter of an agadic text is often intrinsically connected with a point (or a philosophy) of law. For example, here is the Talmudic passage that immediately precedes (and in my view defines) the frequently cited "These and these are the words of the living God":

> R. Aha bar Hanina said: It is revealed and known before Him Who spoke and the world came into being, that there was none in the generation of R. Meir like him; why then did they not fix the halakha according to his view? Because his colleagues could never fathom the depths of his reasoning. For he would assert that something unclean was clean and make it seem plausible, and he would assert that something clean was unclean and make it seem plausible. A boraitha taught: his name was not actually R. Meir rather Nehorai was his name. Why then was he called Meir? Because he made the eyes of the sages shine in the law. And similarly, Nehorai was not his name rather R. Nehemiah and others say R. Eliezer. Then why was he called Nehorai? Because he lit up the eyes of the sages in the law.[32]

This is an agadic passage that specifically reflects upon scholarly methods in legal deliberation. The complexity of this text comes into view when its various statements are considered in terms of the explicit and implicit assertions that the passage seems to make. Rabbi Aha begins by equating the general appreciation of Rabbi Meir's brilliance with what is revealed before—or known to—God. This expression of what "God knows" as a working definition for "common knowledge"—though not unique to this passage—is especially significant in this context. Rabbi Aha seems to draw Rabbi Meir's genius out into the open. And yet, the concept of what is known to God simultaneously draws common knowledge into the realm of mystery. What God knows is really a secret. Or, as Caputo put it, "'God knows what's going on!' we say with exasperation, by which we mean, 'who knows?' It's a secret!"[33]

This irony leads tellingly into the curious account of Rabbi Meir's teachings that follows. Rabbi Aha tells us that Rabbi Meir's teachings cannot be understood. This is something of a conundrum. What is obvious is that Rabbi Meir is like none other in his generation. But what he teaches is appreciated only as a mystery. The brilliance of his study is known because the self-contradictory method of his argumentation conjures up a rationally generated mystery that—ironically—no one understands. In theological terms, Rabbi Meir's articulation of conflicting legal premises through ingenious halakhic argumentation demonstrates his ability to generate endless paradoxical combinations of conflicting points of view through the manipulation of legal language. It is these incomprehensible combinations that the rabbis associated with the word of God. His seemingly exoteric teachings intertwined to create a puzzle—simultaneously concealing and revealing, explaining and deconstructing the law till it can no longer be contained in the human mind.

The paradox of clarification (revelation) and contradiction (concealment) that wins Rabbi Aha's admiration is the organizing theme of the rest of this passage. The two names that are offered for Rabbi Meir—Meir and Nehorai—both mean "light." But the unexplained and uncalled-for question about Rabbi Meir's *real* name suggests that something about him is shrouded in darkness. Similarly, the Talmud continues with Symniachos, "who could give forty-eight reasons for the cleanness of unclean things and then the same number of reasons for the uncleanness of clean things."[34] Though this description does not go into specific details, it is clearly referring to Symniachos's capacity in the rational, exoteric, explicit interpretation of the law. Within the context of conventional, rational legal discussion, Symniachos is able to construct contradictory and paradoxical arguments that confound the explicit impulse to arrive at a legal ruling. In so doing, he generates a conundrum. Again, as with Rabbi Meir, it is this puzzling outcome that the rabbis revere.

This passage as a whole seems to pit a *general* appreciation of explicit legal clarity against a *specific* approbation of those who confuse, complicate, entangle, and ultimately undermine the practical application of the law. It suggests that legal argumentation attains sublimity and transcendence when rational interpretive techniques are used to hinder singular implementation. It is in this context that the Talmud describes the appearance of a heavenly voice: These *and* these—combined—are the words that emerge as those of the living God.

The Hermeneutics of Prophetic Law

> *Rabbi Avdimi of Haifa said: Since the day the Temple was destroyed, prophecy was lost to the prophets and given to the* hakhamim *[sages]. But are the* hakhamim *not themselves prophets? He means to say: Although prophecy was lost to the prophets, it was not lost to the* hakhamim. *Amemar added: Indeed, a* hakham *is superior to a prophet.*
>
> —Talmud Bava Batra 12a–b[35]

The idea that prophetic law is mysteriously unfathomable, confounding, and contradictory is perhaps best exemplified by the biblical category of statutory law. The statutes, or *chukim,* are quite simply the laws that cannot be understood. Laws such as *shatnez* (the prohibition against mixing wool and linen in the same garment), *kilayim* (the forbidden interbreeding of plants or animals), *kashrut* (dietary laws), and most notably *para aduma* (the use of a red heifer's ashes to achieve ritual purity) are often believed to represent the halakha's fundamental and unflinching commitment to obedience. Though these laws have no explanation, we observe them because we are thus commanded. But the rabbinic rendition of this crucial legal phenomenon turns the obedience thesis on its head by supplementing it with an alternative. The rabbis argue that the *chukim* are mysterious not because they are unexplained but because deep exploration into them uncovers their incomprehensibility. Deeper study of these laws exposes their paradoxical and self-contradictory nature. This idea is expressed, for example, in the following midrash:

> This is what the Torah states: Who will bring pure from impure, not one (Job 14:4). Like Abraham who was born of Terach, Chizkiah from Achaz, Yoshiah from Amon, Mordechai from Shim'i, Israel from idolaters, the world to come from this world. Who has done this? Who commanded this? Who ordered this? Is this not the work of the Only One? A spot on a man's skin is impure. If the rash spreads to his entire body he is pure. Who has done this? Who commanded this? Who ordered this? Is this not the work of the Only One? A

woman whose child dies in her womb, if the midwife reaches in and touches the body she becomes impure for seven days while the mother is pure until the dead baby is delivered. If a man dies in a house the house is pure, when his body is removed it becomes impure. Who has done this? Who commanded this? Who ordered this? Is this not the work of the Only One? It was taught: those who are occupied with the red heifer from beginning to end make their clothes unclean. It itself (contrarily) purifies defiled garments. God said: I set a statute, I decreed a decree, and you cannot transgress my decree. (Midrash Bemidbar Rabba 19:1; my translation)

Each of the statutes described in this passage contains some kind of paradox. The red heifer both purifies and defiles. The impure mark of gonorrhea is purified by the spread of the disease. A dead body—generally understood as the ultimate source of ritual impurity—defiles the house or womb in which it is held but only after it has been removed. Despite the explicit statement about obedience that brings this passage to its conclusion, the overall effect is to call attention to the paradoxical—rather than the irrational or erratic—nature of divine commandment. Ultimately, through *chok* (law), man submits himself to being overwhelmed by the law's complexity. As he digs deeper into the law, he is overwhelmed by the glory of God and the mystery of his own humble origins: he remembers how purity originates in the impure, how Israel originated in idolatry. The marvel, the spectacle of these intricate contradictions evokes the composition of a prayer to be recited in the synagogue before the reading of Numbers 19:

We cannot speak of the force of Your wonder; we cannot articulate the depths of Your laws; we cannot fathom the logic of Your actions; we cannot decipher the depths of Your mysteries; we cannot explain Your hidden qualities; we cannot explore the secrets of Your riddles; we cannot fully praise Your glory; and we cannot reveal the secret of Your testimonial. What seems explicit is contradictory; what is revealed is concealed; what is explained is obscure; ... what is omitted is superfluous; what is forbidden is permitted; what seems black is white; ... what seems flexible is stringent.... from the prohibition of eating lard we learn that we may eat the fat of the heart, from [the prohibition of drinking] blood we learn that we may eat the blood in the spleen. From meat comes milk, from the forbidden mixture of wool and linen in clothes we make *tzitzit*; levirate marriages are made between a man and his brother's wife. ... From the impurity of menstrual blood we learn that the blood of a virgin is pure, from what is permitted we learn what is forbidden and from what is forbidden we learn what is permitted, from what is impure we learn purity and from what is pure we learn impurity. . . . So we cannot understand the secrets of Your Torah, distill clarity from the enigma of Your sayings . . . and therefore we must observe the mystery of Your Torah . . . and we cannot question the reasons for Your laws for they were given thus in a kiss and all the wise will appreciate this. (my translation)[36]

Like many medieval hymns, this text is replete with legal detail and learning. It is the product of a tremendous effort to fathom, to understand, to explore, and to make sense of statutory law. But the outcome of this effort is not explicit understanding. It is an implicit religious experience that attaches theological meaning to the mystifying experience of study. This perception of study is perhaps close to the approach of Judah Loew ben Bezalel (the Maharal) of Prague:

A dispute for God's sake prevails even when it involves opposites because He, may He be exalted and blessed, unites the two opposites. Although they are divided and opposed, from God's perspective they are nevertheless united since God, who is one, is the cause of both opposites. As the cause of both opposites, He Himself is unity because otherwise He would be the cause of only one of them. As if you were to say that He is the cause of fire and were to assume, God forbid, another cause for the opposite of fire, which is water. . . . Hence the controversy, which is for the sake of God: although the dispute is between intrinsic opposites that cannot coexist, for God, who is the cause of these opposites, both are one . . . because God is one and both are effected by the divine will as He wishes, may He be blessed.[37]

This passage from the Maharal is quoted by Sagi and used to illustrate what he calls a harmonistic position. According to Sagi, the great virtue of this approach is the richness of the theoretical construct it provides for containing humanly generated variety within a structure of monotheistic unity. But Sagi favors the account of the rabbinic project as pluralistic and not harmonistic because, to his mind, theoretical harmony is clearly not enough. According to the harmonistic position, the entirety of halakhic literature—with all its internal disagreements, contradictions, and paradoxes—is a mirror in which the immense complexity of divine law is reflected. But no single opinion qualifies as the "word of God." As Sagi puts it, this complexity is captured in the activity of the study house but not in the halakhic decision-making process (*pesika*). According to Sagi, despite being intriguing this position is something of a soft option: "A construction of the various positions showing them to be united and no longer in conflict is easy to establish while engaged in study, but poses a much harder challenge at the performative level."[38]

Sagi's critique of the impracticability of harmony is a significant deviation from the overwhelmingly epistemological thrust of his taxonomy. He has no complaints about the breadth or truthfulness of the Maharal's understanding of the law. But Sagi commendably wants more from the halakhic tradition than a shot at capturing an ultimately unattainable truth; Sagi wants the halakha to work when planted into the context of practical and contemporary (perhaps even extra-halakhic) disagreement. He wants it to produce a viable system and thus needs a definition of truth that can be used to mediate dissent in a pluralist, political Jewish society.

The Maharal, who lived in a very different historical climate, seems to have a different concern. His primary interest is not the negotiation of political or religious difference but the divinity of the law. In his view, the complexity of the law attests to its divinity because its unity—like God's—is a mystery. The underlying premise of the halakhic project, as he understands it, is that humanity can only duplicate the law's divinity by preventing the semblance of legal singularity (as demonstrable through rational interpretation) from standing for the singular will of God. Hence, the rabbinic voice is rife with the generation of excess and contradiction. It manufactures *chok*. In rabbinic disputation, the intellect is put to its most virtuosic use in the creation of conundrums and irreconcilable paradoxes that engender a second-order— or hermeneutically generated—"prophetic" combination of revelation and concealment. In this sense, the implicit project of rabbinic interpretation is geared toward duplicating the generic esoteric complexity of prophetic texts rather than toward the explication of their precise meaning in law. It is perhaps this capacity of the rabbis to duplicate prophetic complexity through their deft manipulation of language that provides the contexts for the many rabbinic statements that place rabbinic scholarship beyond and above prophecy.[39] Indeed, certain passages suggest that the prophetic insights gained through the use of rabbinic hermeneutics serve as the primary justification for the entire rabbinic project.[40]

When viewed in terms of the implicit religious purpose of halakhic argumentation, the manipulation of logic and language produces a body of literature that is perpetually deconstructive and puzzling. Ultimately, it offers an apophatic—backward—path away from singular claims about law, ethics, and justice. The implicit rabbinic voice confounds arrogant delusions about the scholarly acquisition of immutable or divine truth, undermines the scholar's sense of his power as a legislator of divine law, and leads him to display his fallibility before God. It disarms the potential zealotry that emerges when legislators of religious law believe that they are the executors of his will.

Is there a way in which this approach to the law can operate effectively in a performative or political situation? Can it stand the test of negotiating conflict?[41]

If we accept the idea that the implicit dimension of the halakha disarms the tyranny of law by inhibiting rabbinic scholars from arriving with certainty at explicit claims about the truth, the explicit purposes of rabbinic study can now be supplemented with implicit alternatives. An implicit investigation into the halakha leads to an encounter with transcendent law. This is an experience that both engenders and requires religious humility. This humility then becomes a crucial aspect of the irenic quality of rabbinic law and its capacity to serve as a model for negotiating peace.

The Practice of Torah Study and the Acquisition of Humility

> *Because of what reason did Bet Hillel merit to fix the halakha according to their view? Because they were easy and forbearing.*
>
> —Talmud Eruvin 13b

Contemporary concerns with the truth claims of the halakha are a reflection of an academic obsession with the truth claims of scholarship. I do not mean to imply that the obsession with truth and certitude was born only in the modern academy but that the academy has inherited this obsession and is responsible for its perpetuation. As Heschel puts it, "During the medieval epoch in Europe, the theologians were the chief sinners in respect to dogmatic finality. During the last three centuries, their bad pre-eminence in this habit passed to the men of science."[42] Heschel argues that scholarship that obsesses over the truth runs the risk of concealing the part that Torah study plays in attaining religious insight. Torah study (along with prayer) is one of the primary meditative Jewish practices. It is a path to experiencing wonder and to witnessing such visions as that of Eleazar ben Arakh, who saw the trees opening their mouths and singing. The textual canon is the arena in which religious beliefs, ideas, and legal practices can be pondered, tested, rejected, and affirmed. The outcome of this affirmation should not be confused for certitude about the truth or the accuracy of a biographical or academic account of the law. On the contrary, the dissent, dispute, and complexity that comprise rabbinic literature prevent any single conclusion—however complex and multifaceted—from gaining too much ground. No single position, experience, or encounter can ever win the day. The student of rabbinic texts inevitably stumbles upon adversity, incongruity, and paradox that he cannot reduce to his own perceptions, preferences, or predilections. This experience of study and its outcomes is well captured by Dilthey's term *autobiography:*

> Autobiography is the highest and most instructive form in which the understanding of life confronts us. Here is the outward, phenomenal course of a life, which forms the basis for understanding what has produced it within a certain environment. The man who understands it is the same as the one who created it. A particular intimacy of understanding results from this. . . . Between the parts we see a connection which neither is, nor is it intended to be, the simple likeness of the course of a life of so many years, but which, because understanding is involved, expresses what the individual knows about the continuity of his life.[43]

Autobiography is inevitably the reference through which humans understand human experience. This is not to say that it is the reduction of every encounter with external reality to the subjectivity of the reader. Rather, autobiographical experience is something that is accumulated through intersubjective contact with what is learned. Autobiography is an unfolding, developing, cumulative process in which the subject grows through experience. The idea that a text may have an effect upon a reader is thought to confirm the authenticity of the encounter with Otherness in which experience gained through reading becomes a constitutive part of the study process. In other words, the experience of study leaves its mark on both the understanding of the text and the person of the reader. One might say that a pendulum swings between the reader and the text and touches both. Only when both are touched by the encounter can we know that a meeting of the two has actually taken place. An affirmative evaluation of this description moves the orientation of study away from the discovery of truth and toward the goals of self-edification, wonder, and perhaps even holiness.

The presence of an implicit dimension in Torah study allows for the loosening of the bonds between religious study and the epistemic region of discourse.[44] According to Gianni Vattimo, religion can surpass metaphysics and truth claims when it is allowed—as with Eleazar ben Arakh's study of Merkavah—to move inward into the realm of the private soul and its religious experiences. An implicit notion of Torah study finds its ultimate purpose in the generation of personal religious insights. Summarizing Richard Rorty, Santiago Zabala says something similar about philosophy: "The ultimate goal of philosophical investigation after the end of metaphysics is no longer contact with something existing independently from us, but rather *Bildung*, the unending formation of oneself."[45] Following upon the "weak" notion that self-formation comes from the scholar's conviction to "proceed in the opposite direction," away from truths, *Bildung* seems—perhaps ironically— to refer to the acquisition of a humble disposition of the kind that led Rabbi Yochanan ben Zakkai to descend from his donkey, saying, "It is not proper that I shall hear about the glory of my Maker while riding on a donkey." Can the study of Torah be considered authentically in these terms?

There are rabbinic passages that suggest that meekness and humility are qualities that the rabbis admired. If rabbinic study can be experienced as immersion in a world of deliberately baffling and overwhelming varieties, combinations, contradictions, and paradoxes, the encounter with it recognizably breeds humility. In Heschel's figurative words:

> A person cannot correctly grasp the matter of "Torah from Heaven" unless he is on a ladder standing on earth with its head reaching the sky. But who will ascend a ladder standing straight up? The purist tends to believe that his reason corresponds to reality and forgets that reason is to reality as a dwarf is to a giant. The visionary knows that truth is expressed only in fragments and is revealed only through the lens of metaphors and parables.[46]

In *Torah Min Hashamayim,* Heschel seems to be arguing, as I am, that Jewish learning is a conundrum that breeds humility. Jewish thought is nourished from two sources that follow parallel and apparently irreconcilable paths: one of vision and one of reason. These paths are ultimately united in a mystical unity that—as he shows throughout his book—contains the contradictory theologies of Rabbi Akiva and Rabbi Yishmael. Similarly, the rabbis resolve the conflicting legal rulings of Hillel and Shammai with the aphorism "All the contradictory teachings of the Torah were given by the same shepherd—uttered by the same God."[47] For Heschel, a full perception of this unity will not come through the rational resolution of contradictions. Deep study is only possible when an appreciation is gained of the Torah's complexity. The scholar's sense of wonder at the divine is deepened through his experience of the Torah as a marvel. Ultimately, the scholar must experience his own rational powers vis-à-vis the elusive truth like a dwarf standing in the shadows, looking at the soaring height of a mysterious giant.

So far, I have suggested that the scholar and the accomplished rabbi acquire humility through their accumulated experience with study. But the role of humility runs deeper. Humility forged in experience is also intrinsic to the practice of scholarship itself. Without humility, it is impossible to feel overwhelmed by the text. Hubris propels the conviction that any conundrum can be unraveled. However, experience and humility engender the self-doubt that calls attention to what we do not and cannot know. Humility releases the scholar's mind from some of its limitations and—perhaps counterintuitively—emboldens his interpretive powers. Humility is thus a mature state of mind, forged in experience. It is this experience that opens our minds. In Gadamer's words:

> The experienced person proves to be . . . someone who is radically undogmatic; who, because of the many experiences he has had and the knowledge he has drawn from them, is particularly well equipped to have new experiences and to learn from them. The dialectic of experience has its proper fulfillment not in definite knowledge but in openness to experience that is made possible by experience itself.[48]

Perhaps the best-known expression of rabbinic humility is the explanation given for the institutionalized preference for the rulings of the house of Hillel over those of the house of Shammai (see the epigraph to this section). It may seem strange that the law is determined by deference and forbearing. One might think that, when all other things (i.e., claims to truthfulness) were equal, the rabbis broke the stalemate between Hillel and Shammai by turning to an extraneous consideration for the tiebreaker. But the humility of Hillel can also be understood as intrinsic to his knowledge of the law itself:

> It has been taught, R. Jose said: Originally there were not many disputes in Israel, but one *beth din* [law court] of seventy-one members sat in the Hall of Hewn Stones, and two courts of twenty-three sat, one at the entrance of the Temple Mount and one at the door of the [Temple] Court, and other courts of twenty-three sat in all Jewish cities. . . . But since the disciples of Shammai and Hillel who had not adequately served their masters increased in number, quarrels were increased in Israel, and it seemed as if the law came from two different lawgivers. From the court of the great Sanhedrin they used to write and send to all the cities of Israel: Whosoever is wise, modest, and is liked in the eyes of his people may be a judge in his own city. And thereafter, if he deserved it, he was advanced to the court at the gate of the Temple Mount; and further on, until he reached to be a member in the court of the Temple treasury. A message was

sent from Palestine: Who is the man who has surely a share in the world to come? He who is modest, bends his head when he goes in, and the same when he goes out; is always studying the Torah, and does not become proud thereof. And the rabbis gave their attention to R. Ula b. Abba [who possessed all these qualifications]. (Talmud Sanhedrin 88b)

The idea that there was once a single revealed law is expressed by the use of "originally" at the beginning of this passage. This word introduces the past of the text as mythical and hence—like "once upon a time" at the beginning of a children's story—it is outside of the actual time frame of the text. As we move into real time, the task at hand—or so it would seem—is the faithful preservation of that law, its reconstruction where possible, and its application. The text describes the students of Hillel and Shammai who failed in this task. They failed because they did not serve their masters adequately. This is a complaint that—though open to multiple interpretations—suggests a connection between inattention, arrogance, and ignorance. The result was quarreling, conflict, and confusion. Despite an apparent concern for the absolute loss of singular law, the original law appears to be of little interest in the discussion that follows. Instead, a new typology of judges is offered, one in which humility is presented as a path to heavenly reward. The original law now appears only as a shadow, a reminder perhaps that the great paradox of the law has another—explicit—axis. But here, the primary concerns are implicitly religious and not legal. Legal erudition is supplemented (though not replaced) with a new ideal. Scholars who bow their heads, resist self-congratulation, and engage constantly in the study of Torah are favored. Men of humility such as Ula b. Abba come to put an end to legal conflict. It is significant that nothing is said of his knowledge or genius. His rulings are never put to the test in epistemological terms. No heavenly voice appears to vindicate him. Instead, Ula and others like him are evaluated in implicitly religious, even soteriological, language: "Who is the man who has surely a share in the world to come? He who is modest."

The Humor and Humility of the Law

> Legal fiction: An assumption that something occurred or someone or something exists which, in fact, is not the case, but that is made in the law to enable a court to equitably resolve a matter before it.
>
> —American Law Encyclopedia

Urban legend has it that a student at Oxford University once raised his hand during a final exam to demand a keg of beer and a wedge of cheese from the adjudicator. When challenged for this seemingly outrageous request, the cocky student whipped out a copy of the university's statutes and ordinances. The letter of the law (composed in the seventeenth century) clearly stated that he was entitled to order refreshments from the local inn during the course of his final exams. Somewhat baffled, the adjudicator was left with no choice but to comply. The beer and cheese were served at the university's expense while the student believed that the last laugh was his. Several weeks later (after the results of the exam had been posted), the same student was called to the office of the dean, where he was fined for turning up for a final exam without his sword!

I have no idea if this story is true. A perfunctory computer search for "cheese, beer, ale, refreshment" in the examinations section of the statutes and ordinances of both Oxford and Cambridge universities yielded no results. So, it seems unlikely. But whoever invented the story and circulated it has provided a wonderful example of the point I now wish to make: humility can be intrinsic to the law itself and not just to its interpretation.

The student's mistake was that he failed to distinguish between the "application" of the law and its "exploitation." In response, the dean taught him a lesson or two learned through years of experience with legal tradition. The dean's response is effective because it shows how the spirit of the law is inviolate even while the law itself is being bent. It is the assumption that law only stands when its spirit is intact that allows us to forgive the law its imperfections. When the letter of the law is exploited, our compliance is disturbed. This is when all kinds of other incongruities planted and nurtured over years of changing tradition begin to emerge. The good will that offers hospitality to legal fossils dissipates. Thereafter, all sorts of remnants, relics, and vestiges come into sight. The dean simply utilized one of these to restore order (and of course to get back the college's money). But justice was not done because the debt was reimbursed. Justice was done because a specific countermeasure was used to preserve the general illusion of the law's propriety. If the dean had used anything more plausible or realistic than the ploy of the sword, it wouldn't have worked. More to the point, it wouldn't have been funny. The humor makes this a good story to tell. But the dean's humor is also the key to his primary accomplishment: the peaceful dissolution of a potential conflict.

It would seem that the law is effective when those who uphold it know how to smile at its own ironies and play with them. A legal system that makes allowances for play lifts a significant bulk of its weight from the shoulders of its devotees. They comply with its semblance of authority in the same way that theater audiences willingly suspend their disbelief. But, once the credibility of the performance has been established, the spectator no longer needs to think he is playing along when a moving soliloquy elicits a tear.

I am not a legal philosopher and I do not want to make broad claims about the applicability of this description of consensual submission in legal theory. My point is confined to the model of overtly voluntary legal systems (such as modern religions) whose members have willingly pledged their commitment to the protection and preservation of a tradition they could equally choose to abandon. Such a legal system is quite naturally judged on more than its practicability since its capacity to effectively regulate life and to command authority depends upon a prior acceptance of its grand purpose. The purpose of the law transcends the mechanisms with which it demands obedience, and it is this purpose that must command compliance. In the case of the story about the final exam, the traditions of a glorious English institution are at stake. And it is the charm of Oxonian tradition that ultimately wins the day for the college dean. In the case of Jewish law, the purpose of the law is its capacity to call attention to God. Here too (in all matters other than biblical idolatry, which is the archetypal antithesis of the law), the letter of the law is demonstrably humble. I think a consideration of the rather unusual Jewish brand of legal fiction known as *ha'arama* can show this.

The word *ha'arama* connotes more than a fiction. *Ha'arama* suggests a little purposeful deceit. The law, as it were, deceives itself or consciously turns a blind eye.[49] What is quite remarkable is just how widespread and varied the use of this device actually is in Jewish law. Legal fictions are used to permit interest loans between Jews, to allow certain uses of domestic electricity during the Sabbath, to permit carrying objects in public on the Sabbath, to bypass the injunction against the possession of leaven (*chametz*) on Passover, to allow one person to lend his *lulav* (palm branch) to another,[50] to annul marriages, to rescind gifts, and so on. Perhaps the most famous classical example of *ha'arama* is Hillel's *pruzbul*—a legal trick that resuscitated the practicability of financial loans by removing the threat of their being annulled during the *shmita* year.[51] Tricks such as these are numerous. But, more important, their use is extraordinarily public and widespread.

In a wonderfully elegant volume written in 1961, the Israeli Supreme Court judge Moshe Zilberg offers a misleadingly concise yet highly sophisticated account of the Talmudic legal system.[52] It is significant that in his bird's-eye view of Talmudic legal theory, Zilberg dedicates an entire chapter to the presumably minor legal device of *ha'arama*. This choice underlines Zilberg's appreciation of the singular significance of *ha'arama* to the entire Talmudic system. Indeed, Zilberg's analysis cannot be fully appreciated without an understanding of the primary thesis that he sets out in the opening lines of his book. Paraphrasing Maimonides' bombastic introduction to the Mishneh Torah, Zilberg writes, "The foundation of all foundations and the source of all appreciation of the Talmud's merits is the knowledge that the Talmud is a collective enterprise of an expressly legal nature. This applies to the parts that deal with the laws between man and his fellow man and to those that deal with the laws between man and God" (my translation).[53]

This theme runs throughout the book. In Zilberg's view, the essential innovation of the halakha (relative to both secular and religious legal systems) is its legalization of vertical (i.e., God-oriented) religion. The implications of the idea that "the Lord is a litigant" affect both the civil and ritual dimensions of the law. Zilberg notes that the halakha uses the same legal categories to analyze obligations and transgressions in matters of religious ritual as it employs to determine guilt or responsibility in cases of damages. The complex result is that the Talmud can appear dull, oppressive, and insipid in its formalistic treatment of ritual and perhaps inappropriately sentimental, compassionate, and absolute in its handling of the more technical side of civil and criminal law. The point is that the Talmud brings very distinct realms of law into almost seamless interaction, which produces a complex legal/religious system that merges the implicit spirit of the law with the explicit letter of the law. In such a system, even the most technical aspects of civil litigation are oriented toward God while the weight of the divine in matters of religious dogma is significantly lifted. This buoyant feature of the law is brought into public view by the convention of *ha'arama*.

According to Zilberg, *ha'arama* is a distinctive form of legal fiction precisely because its purpose is not simply to enable a court to equitably resolve a matter before it. *Ha'arama* is not a means of bypassing the law nor of utilizing a specific loophole in the law. The direct object of the deceit is the law itself. *Ha'arama* is public, general, frequent, and normative. It often utilizes the interactions of vastly disparate legal and ritual concerns to expose the fallibilities of "law" itself. *Ha'arama* takes an ironic stand toward the law in the most general sense. *Ha'arama* suggests that the halakha is *law* without *Law*.[54] A proud legal system would not tolerate such outrages; the halakha encourages them. An entire tractate (Eruvin) is dedicated to bypassing certain prohibitions pertaining to the Sabbath. The law of the Sabbath and its loopholes stand side by side—on equal footing—on the classical bookshelf. This normative openness is what is special about *ha'arama*.

Ha'arama keeps the law open to extraneous concerns that attest to the imperfections of the law from the outside. The halakha uses *ha'arama* to expose its own susceptibility to self-deceit. Jewish legal fiction is not based upon the ingenuity of the litigator but upon the inadequacy of the law, whose pretense at formalizing and legalizing religion must be understood as a metaphor. By way of extension, the self-conscious metaphorization of the law supplements (potentially tyrannical) explicit legal authority with a modicum of irony and humor. Through the cracks of the law—through the humility of the law about the Law—the law points away from itself and toward the incomprehensible mystery of God that somehow makes sense of it all.[55]

Ha'arama exposes the *différance* that recalls the imperfections of human legislation and judgment. The self-undermining, auto-deconstructing humility of the law is the key to its compassion and holiness. As with the flaws of prophetic language, the cracks in the illusion that the law is Law are openings to implicit religious experience. Through the study of halakha, one may approach theology apophatically. In the implementation and application of the law, the legislator or judge encounters the law's self-deprecating humility and recognizes that it is not in any explicit sense the word of God. Its wings are clipped and its roots are fickle. The law is not held in place by any metaphysical superstructure. It is God's word only insofar as it is not proud of itself nor self-confident about its own truths. The law is holy because it reminds us to turn a forgiving gaze toward its ironies and imperfections. It reminds us that this law is not God. It is a signpost or a clue with which we engage as part of our search for him. This mechanism by which the law exposes itself is what allows the law to sanctify the mundane. It is also crucial to the limitless tolerance of the Other—*le tout autre*—that is the law's interface with both theology and peace.

Sin, Forgiving, and the Pharisaic Voice

> In order to assume his absolute responsibility with respect to absolute duty, to put his faith in God to work, or to the test, he [Abraham] must also in reality remain a hateful murderer, for he consents to put to death. In both general and abstract terms, the absoluteness of duty, of responsibility, and of obligation certainly demands that one transgress ethical duty, although in betraying it one belongs to it and at the same time recognizes it. . . . Abraham must assume absolute responsibility for sacrificing his son by sacrificing ethics, but in order for there to be a sacrifice, the ethical must retain all its value; the love for his son must remain

intact; and the order of human duty must continue to insist on its rights.

—Jacques Derrida, The Gift of Death

The deconstruction of legal pretense extends beyond the mechanisms of authority and into the realm of the ethical. The great purpose of the law that is exposed by the auto-deconstruction of the law is to shed light on the distinction between religious law and ethics. In this sense, the problematic ethics of the law and indeed of biblical theology are inherent to the law. The narratives that provide the foundations of biblical theology shape and even inhibit the law in ways that curb its potential for justifying violence in the name of ethics and the common good. Derrida's remarkable understanding of the Pharisees will serve here as an example of this argument.

Derrida's most explicit (and rare) statements about rabbinic Judaism appear in the context of his reading of the *akeda* (the sacrifice of Isaac). In his reading, Derrida maintains that the great legislator, the divine litigant, the God in whose name the explicit law speaks and in whose place it stands, delivered a blow to religious moralizers when he commanded Abraham to sacrifice his only son. Starting here, the law must come to terms with the idea that it was the God of Genesis 22 who founded the law at the expense of both law and ethics. Recognizing this, there seems no way out for theologically based legal moralism. Mountains of explanation, theodicy, and justification are unequal to the task of getting God off the hook. The question raised by the *akeda* will always seem so much more compelling than its all too many answers. It seems impossible to move on. The law must somehow reclaim and live with this inexcusable act of ugliness.

By getting the Bible started with an unforgivable act of cruelty, God establishes his ethical law on a principle of sin and makes an impossible demand for forgiveness. There is no law without forgiveness for that act. The law must forgive itself into existence. God *gives* a commandment to Abraham and Abraham *gives* his son (and his humanity) in return. Without these two acts of (for)*giving,* there is no covenant.

In *The Gift of Death* (*Donner la mort*), Derrida offers a full-blown deconstruction of philosophical ethics. He operates on the premise that religious responsibility toward God is singular, intersubjective, and immediate—not general. Derrida argues that only an ugly notion of God's commandment to Abraham—one that compromises ethics—can capture the mystery and singularity of God. In order for the word of God to be the word of God, it must contradict and problematize general ideas about humane ethics.

Derrida's reading plunges the morality of law into the depths and the silences of a *mysterium tremendum*.[56] What we can know of Abraham's outrage makes us tremble. We cannot speak of it. We tremble in the face of the silence that conceals a secret because "[a] secret always makes you tremble." Derrida continues, "I tremble at what exceeds my seeing and knowing although it concerns the innermost parts of me, right down to my soul. . . . Inasmuch as it tends to undo both seeing and knowing, trembling is indeed an experience of secrecy or of mystery."[57] What makes us tremble is our fear of God's cruelty in Genesis 22. We tremble at the discovery that "divine" law and justice are not confined by philosophical ethics. We cannot trust or take comfort in our faith that his convictions (about good and evil, kindness and cruelty, life and death) are the same as our own. In Genesis 22, we tremble at what Derrida calls the "dissymmetry that exists between the divine regard that sees me, and myself, who doesn't see what is looking at me; it is the gift and endurance of death that exists in the irreplaceable, the disproportion between the infinite gift and my finitude, responsibility as culpability, sin, salvation, repentance and sacrifice."[58]

God commands Abraham in silence to sacrifice his son. He is silent in that he doesn't give his reasons.[59] God, though he speaks in the story, speaks only to keep a secret. Saying nothing is always the best way to keep a secret. Something must be said for the fact of the secret to be known. But what is said must be nothing in order for the secret to be kept. In Genesis 22, God speaks, but he is "absent, hidden, and silent, separate, secret, at the moment he has to be obeyed." It is from within this shroud of silence—*ex silentio*—that the mystery of the commandment can be heard as divine. God commands Abraham's obedience by the singularity of his address. He talks only to Abraham, revealing no general purpose or principle that Abraham might otherwise know on his own. The commandment is alien to human law. It demands a sacrifice not only of a son, but also of a principle, a value, and a way of life. God commands Abraham to sacrifice his innocence by asking for "the most cruel, impossible, and untenable gesture."[60] Abraham then duplicates this behavior with Isaac. He speaks, but he says nothing. "God will provide the lamb for the burnt offering, my son," Abraham says. He speaks, but he does not tell Isaac the secret of why they are climbing Mt. Moriah. He cannot tell him because he is bound to keep the secret from Isaac, the secret that he himself does not know. Isaac and Abraham share a secret—a secret that neither of them knows.

Derrida's point here is that secrecy is an act of betrayal. Abraham betrays Isaac because keeping the secret "is hardly designed to save or protect Isaac's best interests." The *akeda* shows that religion always "transgresses the ethical order." It is not reducible to ethics; or, in John Caputo's formulation, "the religious is the movement of exceeding and suspending ethics, of transgressing rule-governed universality vis-à-vis the *tout autre,* even as justice exceeds the law."[61] The religious excess deconstructs the illusion of ethics by exposing the everyday cruelties performed endlessly in the name of ethics. Derrida continues:

> Let us here insist upon what is too often forgotten by the moralizing moralists and good consciences who preach to us with assurance every morning and every week, in newspapers and magazines, on the radio and on television, about the sense of ethical or political responsibility. . . . What the knights of good conscience don't realize is that "the sacrifice of Isaac" illustrates—if that is the word in the case of such a nocturnal mystery—the most common and everyday experience of responsibility. The story is no doubt monstrous, outrageous, barely conceivable: a father is ready to put to death his beloved son, his irreplaceable loved one, and that because the Other, the great Other asks him or orders him without giving the slightest explanation. . . . But isn't this also the most common thing?[62]

Cruelty is the most common thing. It is the direct result of every form of loyalty and ethical responsibility, the product of every law. Our every choice or norm is a rejection of another calling. "By preferring my work, simply by giving my time and attention . . . I am perhaps fulfilling my duty. But I am sacrificing and betraying at every moment all my other obligations; my obligations to the others whom I know or don't know." Derrida's list includes everyone, from those dying of sickness or starvation in Africa to inner-city street cats. "How would you ever justify the fact that you sacrifice all the cats in the world to the cat that you feed at home every morning for years, whereas other cats die of hunger at every instant. Not to mention other people?" The *akeda* for Derrida is not the exception to the rule of religious morality. It is the rule of life with which religious law must be in contact. The *akeda* mirrors the normative laws of life, showing how cruelty and injustice cannot be wished or washed away by morals and ethics. He portrays the world as a landscape of Mt. Moriahs in which—most poignantly—Mt. Moriah itself is yet another "Mt. Moriah."

> It is the place where the grand mosque of Jerusalem stood, the place called the Dome of the Rock near the grand Aksa mosque where the sacrifice of Ibrahim is supposed to have taken place and from where Muhammad mounted his horse for paradise after his death. It is just above the destroyed Temple of Jerusalem and the Wailing Wall, not

far from the Way of the Cross. It is therefore a holy place but also a place that is in dispute, radically and rabidly, fought over by all the monotheisms, by all the religions of the unique and transcendent God, of the absolute other. (*Gift of Death*, 69–70)

For Derrida, the point of the *akeda* is that religion deconstructs ethics by building its foundations on the disputed and blood-soaked soil of Mt. Moriah. Religion's demands can be harsh and sinful. Ask Abraham! Abraham has to become a murderer. He responds to God's demand singularly and immediately not in order to establish religious practice on a principle of blind obedience but to show that he is willing to sacrifice the economics of self-interest and expedience. How vile it would have been had Abraham consented to sacrificing Isaac in return for a covenant. Abraham gives a pure gift—a gift not only of his son but also of his soul. His gift is pure because it is an absolute surprise, given without hesitation through a hateful act of murder and betrayal. There is no general principle or general language that familiarizes the word of God for Abraham. There is only God, and he is a secret. Abraham acts in an instant in the face of a secret, "without a moment's hesitation, without expecting any payback, exclaiming in his best French, *me voici.*"[63] This is the act that consecrates the law as worthy of religion. It is a parody of both ethics and justice. The *akeda* stands on its own, a singular act that shows there is no difference between morality and immorality. The one always connotes the other. The real line is always the one that divides generality from singularity, action from inaction, articulation from silence, humanity from God.

After the *akeda*, it seems that religious law must be conceptualized as a system that gives its first loyalty not to justice but to living in peace with an unpredictable and unfathomable God. God's unpredictability includes cruelty and ugliness. It is this unethical ugliness that Derrida brings to the foreground in *Gift of Death*. "Abraham must assume absolute responsibility for sacrificing his son by sacrificing ethics, but in order for there to be a sacrifice, the ethical must retain all its value." The complex interplay between ethics and ugliness places Abraham in an impossible situation. The right thing to do must be the wrong thing to do. If it is not wrong, it cannot be right. Only in this impossible situation can Abraham act selflessly for God and entrench the notion of serving God in the *tout autre* and not in the self. What does this portrayal of Abraham teach about the rabbis?

Derrida's partially Christological portrayal of Abraham comes perilously close to the kind of thinking that sends Jews into gas chambers. Derrida's critique of hypocrisy and calculating self-interest echoes across time. It spreads from the New Testament's distaste for the Pharisees all the way to Auschwitz.

But having presented Abraham in the apparently Christological terms of the pure gift, Derrida deconstructs his own Abraham, uncovering the reversibility of selflessness, exposing the self-indulgence that always accompanies self-denial (as when snubbed mothers-in-law say things like "don't mind me"). If deconstruction is the manipulative exposure of reversibility, then the Pharisaic rabbis are masters of it. Derrida grasps the ironic, comic tone of the rabbinic voice. It is the voice that insists on the virtues of hypocrisy and on the hypocrisy of sincerity. In John Caputo's words:

> The point of *Donner la mort* then is not to undo faith but to insist on the un-economic character of faith, that faith is always a matter of the gift and giving, not a transaction between a creditor and a debtor. . . . The point of a "demystifying" analysis is to force out into the light of day the secret contract that allows one to do one thing under the cover of its opposite, e.g., to reap rewards under the cover of giving, to be pharisaical under the cover of a critique of the Pharisees.[64]

Abraham was uneconomically cruel, corrupt, hateful, and murderous. This was what he had to be in order to give to—and forgive—God. He was one thing under cover of the other. According to Derrida, this is the key to religious law because this hypocrisy is what distinguishes it from mere ethics. Religious law must be manipulative, duplicitous, and Pharisaic to remain humbly clear of self-interest. The rabbis provide Derrida with a model of lawyers who are unashamed by their inevitable hypocrisies. Thus, under the cover of hypocrisy, they remain pure of heart. Their critics—in this case, the Gospel of Matthew—come off as hypocritical under the cover of high-handed moralizing.

The humility of the law about its own hypocrisy is the key to its radical capacity to live in peace with unethical people (which for Derrida inevitably means all people). Humility is the key to the law's capacity to function in the shade of an unethical God. ("Unethical" is what Derrida means here by the "wholly otherness" of God.) The law is equipped with a capacity to accept and tolerate precisely those forms of radical Otherness (or ugliness) because it is rooted in the implicit religious quest to contend with God. This is what making peace with the ugliest sort of others really takes.

The irenic promise of rabbinic law is therefore founded on a principle of sin and forgiving. Sin does not refer to transgressions against the law, and forgiveness is not reparation for breaking the law. Sin is what is inevitably ugly about all acts of religious legislation and judgment, while forgiveness is the institutionalized recognition of this that gives way to the acceptance of ugliness within a system of law. Sin stands for what is unavoidably lost when

God's will is put into language. Forgiveness represents the tireless conviction that something workable can be salvaged. Forgiveness lies at the base of the hope that a human course of action can be holy even though Justice might not be done. The acceptance of sin and forgiving allows the tradition to retain and encompass its rough edges. It makes the legislators no better than the sinners. It dismantles the potential for legal hubris from the core.

The *akeda* seems to be connected to the tension between sin and forgiveness—between impossibility and the possibility of serving the impossible, containing the uncontainable. It is the ultimate example of *ha'arama* since this time it is God himself who tricks and bends the law. It shows why *ha'arama* is so fundamental to religious law. It is what gives religion the capacity to go beyond law and to establish—through the transcendence of ethics, morality, and law itself—a private sphere in which humanity faces God. In Heschel's words, "we must learn to abandon the view that religion is simply morality tinged with emotion. It is above all a world of its own, a private, secret realm of relationships between God and man."[65]

In this private realm, where ethics, morals, and law are ultimately exposed in all their partiality, there is a special space where judgment is suspended and place is made for ugliness and Otherness. In the individual privacy of this realm that we visit in study and prayer, there is something as plural as the number of people in the world. We all stand alone before God. There is no single legal editor or judge who comes to determine whose version of beauty is beautiful and whose is not. God does not pass judgment and he does not speak. Implicit religion brings us to search for God in private. What we discover is a mystery, a secret. Thus, the implicit law is restrained from passing objective judgment because it is "only the law"—no more. It is a path to God's mystery. With this self-effacing constriction of pretension (*tzim-tzum*), the law can sacrifice justice, ethics, and aesthetics to contain everything in peace. In sum, if religious law exists, it is because it has made peace with God. If it can live in peace with God, it can make peace with anyone!

Rabbinic Peace

> *Consider the great value of peace. Peace was the reward Abraham received for his faith and righteousness (Genesis 15). It was all that Jacob prayed for (Genesis 28). The reward of Aaron was a covenant of peace (Malachi 2); the same was the reward of Pinchas (Numbers 25:12). The Torah could receive no higher dignity than that all its paths are peace (Proverbs 3). Jerusalem is comforted with peace (Isaiah 32).*

> On the other hand, when Ammon and Moab incurred retribution they were to be deprived of peace (Deuteronomy 23). When Israel receives the priestly benediction, it is that of peace.
>
> —Bemidbar Rabba 115; trans. Samuel Rapaport

The "sacrifice of Isaac" that took place on November 4, 1995, came as a great shock to me. Like many others, my first thought was, "I hope the shooter isn't Jewish." I knew that if he was, this murder could potentially rip the soul of Israel in two. As it turned out, he was and it did. My second thought—"If he is Jewish, I hope he isn't religious"—was, perhaps, even more disturbing. A religious assassin acting in the name of my religion would tear my soul in two. Again, he was and he did.

The day after Yitzhak Rabin was gunned down at a peace rally in Tel Aviv, I attended morning services at my local synagogue in Jerusalem. I was completely dumbfounded by what I heard in the chatter that preceded the beginning of the service. I knew that most religious people in Israel passionately opposed the Oslo Accords. But on my way to prayers that morning, I had not imagined that people would say things like "He had it coming," "Yigal Amir is God's emissary," "That's what God does to you when you meddle with the Jewish hold on the land of Israel," "Now his soul will pay for his sins." This uninhibited hate astonished me. Maybe I was naïve or out of touch, but after the shock of the night before I had not anticipated this response—at least not so soon.

For the first time since settling in the state of Israel, I became uncomfortable with my *kippah*. As I walked through the streets, I felt strangely visible and watched. My *kippah* burned on my head in ways that were familiar to me from my Birmingham days. I felt implicated and guilty—as if I had to explain myself to everyone who looked at me. "Yes, I am wearing a *kippah*, but . . ."

A little over a week later, my wife gave birth to our second son. We had been toying with names and had not yet found the right one. My father had died only a few months previously and we had been exploring without success creative ways of rendering his name, Bernard, into Hebrew. The dark events of that Saturday night, November 4, gave us our solution. As we explained to our family and friends who gathered to celebrate with us, we chose the name Noam to reassert our faith that the ways of the Torah are pleasantness (*noam*) and that all its paths are peace (Proverbs 3).

Given the widespread opposition of the Jewish religious community in Israel to Rabin, Shimon Peres, and the peace process, the assumption that religion and peace are antithetical seemed well established in political reality. The consistent and repeated opposition of the religious parties to peace initiatives has led me to wonder if it is not the very concept of peace that religious people in Israel object to. Is it possible that peace itself (and not the price in land or the national security risk) threatens the religious camp and moves it to protest every reconciliatory initiative between Israel and the Arab states? Did the opposition to Oslo reflect a general antipathy to peace or only specific objections to the particular flaws of that political process? Is peace perceived in general terms as a religious regression, a temptation that entices Israel away from its triumphant messianic destiny?

I recognize the ideological complexities that motivate religious opposition to the specific peace proposals generated by Israel's political left since the mid-1990s. I even empathize with many of the objections that have been raised by the religious right. But, as my questions suggest, I am also very aware that a price has been paid for the consistent opposition of religious people to peace in Israel. Peace has ceased to function as a core religious value in contemporary Israel. The word *shalom* has been culturally hijacked by one political understanding of its meaning and by one political strategy. Conversely, the other wing of Israel's vibrant political culture has commandeered both Judaism and Zionism. The two camps have been in stalemate for years. After the assassination of Rabin, people like me were left torn, confused, lost, frustrated, and isolated in the middle.

Certain factions in Israel's religious society have occasionally advanced the argument that Judaism has a message of peace. This message, though not necessarily the heart of Jewish faith, is one that allows a compromise over territory in return for national security. According to this halakhic strategy, when politicians and military experts can demonstrate beyond reasonable doubt that a particular peace agreement will save Jewish lives, land can be exchanged and the agreement is halakhically permissible. This position utilizes the powerful halakhic principle of *pikuach nefesh* (protecting Jewish lives).[66] Yet, as long as the future efficacy of political agreements remains impossible to predict, a commitment to the primacy of *pikuach nefesh* is not the same as religious devotion to peace. It is merely a halakhic argument for supporting Oslo or other peace accords.

This halakhic argument is built upon a principle of expediency. It is subject to strategic, political, and military assurances. It is hardly the transcendent stuff that passionate religious ideologies are made of. It sees peace as a consideration that enters the heart of the halakhic system, but only from the margins. Peace is not an organizing principle of religious life. The approach I am advancing proposes a different interface between peace, politics, and religion. In many ways, my dream is to emulate the passion for the land that one finds among the settlers. This passion is organic to their faith (and mine). It endures even when the dream seems impractical or impossible to realize in full. It motivates and animates the study of Torah and the experience of prayer. But there is one big difference between us. As opposed to the ideology of Israel's religious right, my placement of peace at the passionately beating heart of Judaism drives a wedge between religious aspirations and politics. This wedge takes the form of the mechanism that I have termed *theological disarmament.*

In my discussions of both prophecy and rabbinic Judaism, I have suggested a description of religion that combines explicit law (with its concrete aspirations for political, legal, and ethical outcomes) with an implicit language or law that deconstructs, inhibits, and disarms these concretizations. I have suggested that the implicit dimension of religion exposes the imperfections of the law in the hope of transcending the limitations of possibility. In this sense, peace as an implicit religious value transcends the debate about specific strategies for resolving the conflict in today's Middle East. The concept of peace that I propose animates the whole of religious life and in this sense it must be broad enough to contain the biblical claim that "all the paths of the Torah are peace." Or, in the words of the Talmudic scholar Abaye:

> Abaye said to Rav Yosef, "Was this order [that *cohanim* and *levi'im* are called up first to the reading of the Torah] instituted because it is one of the ways that fosters peace? But have we not just proven that it is biblically ordained?" Rav Yosef replied, "It is biblically ordained, but the Torah decreed it because it is one of the ways that fosters peace." Abaye responded, "All the laws of the entire Torah were decreed because they are the ways which foster peace! As it is written, 'Her ways are of pleasantness, and all her paths are peaceful.'" (Talmud Gittin 59b)

The various arguments presented in this chapter thus far culminate in the claim that rabbinic Judaism—like biblical prophecy—can be taken in its entirety as a system that fosters peace. This chapter has been an attempt to lay the foundations for a full understanding of Abaye's broad claim. According to my reasoning, all of the laws of the entire Torah culminate in one great incomprehensible combination that amounts to a religious philosophy—or theology—of peace. I have attempted to give substance to this claim by calling into question the assumption that divine law is exclusively associated with truth by the rabbis. I have made the case that the confusion and obstruction of explicitly truthful legal outcomes is central to rabbinic hermeneutics.

The hermeneutic methodology that I have associated with Derrida's notion of auto-deconstruction allows for the duplication of prophetic esotericism by establishing a second axis of implicit readings that live in paradoxical unity with the explicit legal processes of the halakha. In this sense, the rabbinic claim that one should follow the rabbis even when they say that right is left and left is right can be taken as having a dual meaning. On the explicit plane, the principle of obedience to rabbinic authority is established. (It is striking that, even here, this obedience undermines the value of absolute truth by institutionalizing a kind of fictional legal truth and subjecting it to the authority of the courts.) But a second reading is also implied. Rabbinic interpretations generate impossible contradictions that dismantle the singular truth of left- or right-wing interpretations and indeed of any statement. Ultimately, when the rabbinic treatment is complete, there is no difference between left and right since the two options auto-deconstruct into each other. Each one always connotes the other while a principle of reversibility moves between them. The philosophical complexity of the implicit reading is further compounded by the superstructure of the rabbinic genre—the paradox of explicit and implicit language—that combines explicit statements about rabbinic power with implicit interpretive practices that undermine and overwhelm the singularity or power of any rabbinic statement. Thus, in the final outcome, authority is simultaneously established and undermined by rabbinic hermeneutics. This is the characteristic that distinguishes the halakha as a religious law.

Religious law has religious purposes that can be isolated from political translation and implementation—even in the relatively limited context of ritual practice. Despite the importance of practical law and unequivocal dogma to the rabbinic project, the rabbinic voice is not one that only edits, limits, reduces, or confines the legitimate boundaries of the legal tradition according to a preordained standard. Thus, the practical halakha—however one conceives it—is not simply the product of (even a highly elaborate) selective decision-making process. Rather, rabbinic thought proliferates opinions, venturing quite deliberately beyond the reasonable boundaries of an interpretive project.

Implicit rabbinic inquiry does not seek its own conclusion in finite clarity. It culminates in an overwhelming experience of the law as uncontained—defiantly resistant to any organized structure or absolute coherence. Within this implicit discourse, a paradoxical unity may be established between radically opposing positions. The paradoxical unity of rabbinic positions does not contradict divine revelation; it duplicates its mystery. The purpose of rabbinic debate is therefore to ground the explicit law with humility in the impossible and incomprehensible foundations of the implicit quest for the divine.

This combination of explicit and implicit religion simultaneously allows the law to be the law of a community—to command and obligate from within an integral or organic sense of tradition—while at the same time reminding the members of that community that the law is only the law. Both the law and prophecy are structured to remind us that neither of them is God. God, who is concealed by the law in the same way as he is concealed by his names in the Bible, is suspended behind an impenetrable barrier. In more traditional terms, we might say that he is waiting to burst into the light in a messianic age when language will be cleared of its ambiguities (Zephaniah 3) and all opposites will culminate in peace. This, for example, is the vision of Rav Kook, who wrote, "The Lord will bless his people with peace. And the blessing of peace, which comes with the [blessing of] strength, is the peace that unites all opposites. But we must have opposites so that . . . something might be united, and the blessing is evident in the power of these and these are words of the living God."[67]

Peace is a culmination of an impossible set of combinations that somehow join together in a unity of opposites that lies beyond human perception. Without what I have called "ugliness" and "wholly otherness" (in God and human beings), there can be no peace. Conflict is the result of inadequate variety. Peace comes when judgment is suspended, where variety is unlimited, and when no single voice is allowed to stand for the truth. At the heart of the rabbinic project, peace is the product of a limitless process of auto-deconstruction applied on an infinite scale to every aspect of the law. Like the refraction of light into the colors of the rainbow (through which God expresses his covenant of peace with humanity), bringing peace into the light of day requires the integration of all shades of opinion. Peace is the culmination of *all* options blended, and it is thus an endless quest. An inadequate blend of colors produces a murky quality of light or, in Rav Kook's words:

> Some err to think world peace will be built only through one color, one quality of opinions and characteristics. Therefore when they see that as scholars research the wisdom and knowledge of the Torah through their research different opinions and points of view flourish, they think that causes strife, the opposite of peace. This is really not the case. Real peace can come about only through the value of the flourishing of peace.[68]

As with prophecy, this notion of the multivocal rabbinic tradition implies a principle of peace that operates on two levels. On one level, peace is the impossible culmination of infinite legal possibilities. It is the timeless outcome of an endless process of interpretation that seeks to undermine and reverse the law so that it may overwhelm itself and culminate in divine unity. This is a form of messianism that, like prophecy, is messianic without being concretized. It demands a tireless and passionate belief in the possibility of the impossible, which is the implicit prophetic aspiration of rabbinic hermeneutics. It animates the law, calling our attention away from its pose as metaphysical truth and toward its susceptibilities to reversal, paradox, and self-contradiction. The tireless and endless quest for the unity of an ultimately impossible infinite variety of legal options is the impossible quest for God, who is Shalom. *Shalom* is the organizing principle of the rabbinic notion of *makhloket* that extends all the way from the most explicit clashes over points of legal detail to the esoteric dimensions of rabbinic mysticism, as in the following passage from the Zohar:

> Conflict is a distancing of peace, and whoever is in conflict about peace is in disagreement with His holy name, because His holy name is called "Peace." . . . Come and behold: the world does not exist except through peace. When the Holy One, blessed be He, created the world, it could not endure until He came and made peace dwell upon them. What is it? It is the Sabbath, which is the peace of the upper and the lower grades. And then the world endured. Therefore, whoever creates dissension about peace will be lost from the world. Rabbi Yosi says that it is written "great peace have they who love your Torah" (Psalms 119:165). The Torah is peace, as it is written "and all her paths are peace" (Proverbs 3:17). And Korach came to blemish that peace above. (Numbers 16)[69]

Peace, as I have already argued in the discussion of prophecy and in the instance of the Oslo Accords, can be the subject of conflict. People fight over peace all the time. The Zohar here is distinguishing between a debate conducted for the sake of heaven and one that is not. The former is a debate— or even a conflict—that is motivated (perhaps paradoxically) by the desire for cosmological peace. The notion that peace is the opposite of conflict, though simple, is counterintuitive to the liberal worldview in which peace is the by-product of conflict resolution. Peace is what remains to be built when conflict is removed. It is a political rather than a religious concept. In the Zohar's formulation, peace is a religious term. It is the active antidote to conflict. The conditions required for achieving this kind of peace are in many ways quite the opposite of those needed for the liberal resolution of conflict. While conflict resolution requires a compromise—the relinquishing of certain demands in the quest for common ground or a shared system of law—peace is the culmination of infinite differences that must be generated and developed, as it were, from below. Peace must therefore transcend the limits of tolerance and pluralism. It cannot be reached without reclaiming what is ugly, unpleasant, and counterintuitive.[70] It demands the sacrifice of ethics and a radical openness to the impossibility of prophetic surprise. It is the quest that motivates endless generations of study, tireless dedication to minute details, limitless explication, deliberation, and dissent—all of which proliferate and ferment, filling pages and pages of uninviting rabbinic texts that often have no applicability to the practice of explicit law. This is the first level of the rabbinic message of peace.

On a second level, the rabbinic voice speaks to the question of how we wait for ultimate peace. The implicit and impossible aspiration for ultimate peace that animates the religious energy of the rabbinic project imposes a damper of irenic humility on the law as it is explicitly practiced and legislated in the meantime. The law as we know it and understand it commands without metaphysical pretensions. It is humbled by the impossibility of its ultimate implicit task. In its self-awareness, the law is cognizant of the foundational hypocrisy that undermines the claim of human beings to wield the word of God. This is the same cognizance that protects the law from the abuse of ethics. Rabbinic literature is thus humbly eager to expose and disarm itself and is filled with constant references to the flaws of its heroes, their failings, transgressions, and violations.[71] This is the crucial contribution of humility to the law, and it is in this context that ha'arama—which undermines the law so as to expose its deeper meaning—enhances the law's irenic quality.

Though the law is in constant search of resolution and legislation, even its most explicit legal impulses remain open-ended. Even the most final and authoritative of finite legal codes soon emerge as the setting for a new wave of explication, dispute, and exegesis.[72] The codifying instinct has only contributed to the construction of a complex web of legal rulings that interchange and interrelate without ever actually resolving themselves into emphatic legal statements. As a result, the halakha is able to pass for explicit law while in effect it is a religious practice that rules variously and gently. It is religious law that lies beyond the control of those who seem to master it. It endures beyond their capacity to legislate, because it is a religious law that defies human constructions of systems, consistency, and even logic.[73]

In order for religion to play a role in peacemaking, the cantankerous side of religious belief must be confronted head-on—as it were, from within religion. What does this mean for our understanding of rabbinic Judaism? Can rabbinic Judaism stand for—and perhaps even engender—peace? Is there a notion of peace that emerges from the rabbinic tradition that can contain all dissent? Can the rabbinic tradition be spoken for nonselectively and bring even those (the vast majority of the religious camp in Israel) who oppose specific (leftist) visions of peace into an irenic dynamic of peaceful interaction with others?

In seeking affirmative answers to these questions, I have attempted to present the rabbinic conversation as one that culminates in a messianic vision of peace. In the paradoxical, multivocal rabbinic voice, all colors, legitimate and illegitimate, sinful and forgiven, ultimately unite in peace to transcend the limits of "civilized" or rational discourse. Transcending the limits of fully comprehensible discourse is the hermeneutic strategy for generating the final rabbinic outcome of prophetic peace. In the meantime, in the world as we know it, the rabbinic voice is indeed a voice of law. But this law is one that is aware of its own partiality. It is explicitly aware of its unfulfilled ultimate purpose and its flawed ethics. Hence, it carries a message of humility, irony, and humor along with enduring patience and boundless acceptance of the Other. Ultimately, it provides a model of radical openness with the assumption that it takes a kind of peace between all of humanity to allow for the ultimate peace to be made—between humanity and God. I pray that my efforts to present the rabbinic voice in these peaceful terms will vindicate Rabbi Hanina's famous (and perhaps ironically humorous) words, *talmidei chachamim marbim shalom ba'olam* (the teachings of the sages spread peace throughout the world) (Talmud Berachot 64a).

Chapter 7

A Prayer for Peace

And when you go to war in your land against the adversary
that oppresses you, then you shall sound an alarm with the
trumpets and you shall be remembered before the Lord your
God, and you shall be saved from your enemies.

—Numbers 10:8

Praying in a Combat Vest

The obligation to pray as it is mandated by the halakha catches you, three times each day, in the midst of life. It requires you to find some space in the middle of whatever you are doing to stand before God. The formal obligation of prayer is perhaps little more than a ceremonial commitment that can be fulfilled even when the prescribed texts in the prayer book (*siddur*) are uttered in a rush and without thought.

Given the potential for degeneration to which this formalization is prone, times of special need are apt to stand out as times of special prayer. When the obligation to pray presents itself in the middle of a day spent at the side of a hospital bed caring for a loved one, the heart and the soul are the beneficiaries of a welcome interruption. In times of need, the regulated prayer is easily transformed into a seemingly spontaneous self-expression that originates in the soul and overflows in the uttering of the prescribed words: "Heal us!" Special moments of prayer such as these perhaps set the highest standard to which we must aspire routinely when nothing more than a formal commitment calls us into God's presence. Sometimes, we are successful and throw our hearts and our souls into the words of the *siddur*. Sometimes, we fail. Whether we are successful or not, the ideal seems clear—to refresh rote repetition with waters drawn from the fountains of spontaneity.

But what if the special moments of prayer—moments when the distance between the prescribed words and their utterance seems to disappear entirely—are hateful to us? What if our greatest moments of accomplishment in prayer are memories that distress us? What if our souls are most eloquent when we call out to God—with the words of the prayer book on our lips—to beg for things we later regret? What if our souls are most profoundly intertwined with the words of the *siddur* when we are at war and begging for the destruction of others? What then?

Perhaps, there are those who can draw refreshment from the blood-stained wellsprings of war. Perhaps, there are those whose prayers can suckle upon the bloody memories of their wartime pleas. Prayers said in perfect supplication to God—beseeching him to annihilate, slaughter, and humiliate enemies—are, perhaps, a source of inspiration for some. But not for me. After praying so avidly at war, I find myself with a serious predicament. I cannot strive in my daily practice to emulate my greatest prayers. My most urgent supplications to God and my most complete experiences of communion with the words of the *siddur* are of no use to me. They are no use because I am ashamed of them.

It is this problem above all others that has been hardest to face in my attempts to reevaluate the place of peace in my religious thinking. It has been especially awkward to reconsider and reconstruct my understanding of prayer because my obligation to pray three times each day has not relented while I rethink. An ideal of prayer that I struggled for so many years to live up to was fulfilled with spectacular ease in Lebanon. And now, rather than savoring its memory, I seek to repress and replace it. This is no easy task.

I prayed hard at war. I prayed because I was afraid. I was desperate to take comfort in an all-powerful God who would protect me. But beyond the difficulties I have today either duplicating or repressing the intensity of those prayers, I face an additional challenge. In Lebanon, the words of the prayer book came enticingly, irrepressibly alive for me. As I read my *siddur* at war, it erupted with new meanings. I prayed to the ethnic "God of Israel" with a sense of special entitlement that I "knew" with certainty was reserved only for his most beloved children: "For the Lord takes pleasure in His people." I prayed to the God of my fathers Abraham, Isaac, and Jacob, who takes more pleasure in my people, my country, my army, my division, my platoon, and my unit than he does in anyone or anything else. The words of the *siddur* lit up to show me that God *is* "a man of war," and as I turned its pages each morning, afternoon, and evening, there he was again and again. "Who then is the king of glory? The Lord strong and mighty, the Lord who is mighty in battle." It felt as if he were coming out of hiding from some secret page or space between the lines of my *siddur.* "It is He who smote great nations and slew mighty kings." I begged him "to deliver me this day, and every day, from a bad companion and from a bad neighbor . . . or the adversary that destroys . . . and from a hard opponent, whether he be a son of the covenant or be not a son of the covenant." The words seemed to strike their mark as they never had before. My right to God's protection was crystal clear. "We are thy people. ... So, let our horn be exalted and raised on high." How could the simple logic of this have ever passed me by? Holding the *siddur* in my hand like a child with a new toy, I turned to "God who gave Israel the land of Canaan as the lot of your inheritance when you were but a few in number" and reminded him of his promise to be a God "who suffered no man to oppress Israel; and rebuked kings for their sakes [saying], 'Touch not my anointed ones and do my prophets no harm.'" My *siddur* throbbed in my hands as if my combat vest had somehow activated it and armed it for action. I wielded "the God of Israel, who gives strength and power unto His people. Blessed be God" like a sword. I prayed to God "with a two-edged sword in my hand; to execute vengeance upon the nations, and punishments upon the peoples; to bind their kings in chains and their nobles with fetters of iron." With neither self-doubt nor reproach I thundered my demands, "O God of retribution, Lord, O God of retribution, shine forth. Lift up thyself, Judge of the world and render to the proud what they deserve. Save thy people and bless your inheritance. ... Rise up for our help and set us free for your loving kindness."

I found this cache of hidden word weapons in my *siddur* as if it had been concealed in a secret compartment of a gift that I had been carrying around since I was a child. The formal obligation to say the words of the *siddur* daily—with or without thought or focus or meaning—suddenly made sense. Regularity and halakhic obligation created the habit that made sure the words would be there—in my heart and in my combat vest—when their time came. As they burst alive before me, the meanings of the words that I uttered with no comprehension as a child now seemed so obvious. I dusted off the words of the prayers and fired them up as if God had been waiting patiently for me to discover them and finally use them. I felt that God had been expecting me to grow up, move to Israel, learn Hebrew, and go to war so that I could finally crack open his code. The words burned on my lips as if they had been specially written for me. My most violent fantasies seemed to ooze out of them and into my prayers with such ease that I can now barely open the *siddur* without feeling powerless to suppress them. I begged God to protect me so that I could kill his enemies.

Repressions and Sublimations

> Our rabbis taught, he who prays must focus his thoughts
> on heaven.
>
> —Talmud Berachot 31a

After my return home and after the urgent sense of imminent danger passed, the intensity of my prayers dampened. For a while, I drew inspiration from the thought that my wartime petitions and demands had been answered (after all, I returned unscathed along with my entire division, which suffered no fatalities and only a few casualties). I channeled my postwar energies into spontaneous expressions of gratitude to God. I tried to ignore the bellicose prayers I no longer needed, giving almost exclusive attention to the words *modim anachnu lach*: "We give thanks unto thee, for thou art the Lord our God and the God of our fathers forever and ever. . . . We will give thanks unto thee and declare thy praise for our lives which are committed unto thy hand, and for our souls which are in thy charge, and for thy miracles, which are daily with us."

But as time passed, even my gratitude became hard to sustain. How many times can you thank God for the same thing? Refreshing regularity with waters drawn from the fountains of spontaneity requires that the prayers be kept alive with fresh thoughts. My concentration weakened. I found myself backtracking in the text of the daily prayers to say the words of *modim* again and again because I had failed to give them adequate attention on previous attempts. This was especially awkward—not only because I felt guilty about the inadequacy of my concentration (and hence of my gratitude)—but also because I knew that the repetition of *modim* is disapproved in the Mishnah and Talmud.[1]

As I gradually laid my lame obsession with gratitude aside and turned my attention back to the rest of the *siddur,* I found it difficult to duplicate the intensity of my wartime prayers in the safety and security of my home life. More to the point, while my thoughts and concerns turned to peace and the articulation of a peaceful philosophy for Judaism, the words of the *siddur* that had served me so well as weapons felt horribly out of place, like radioactive plutonium in a kindergarten. I tried to teach myself to pray peacefully. But how is one to pray peacefully with the same passionate urgency that one has when begging for the destruction of enemies at war? How was I supposed to use the words of the *siddur* to pray for peace after the stunning transformation they had undergone?

I began focusing upon the frequent (though not ubiquitous) mentions of peace that appear in the *siddur.* There are blessings, benedictions, and petitions that ask God: "Grant peace, welfare, blessing, grace, loving kindness, and mercy unto us and unto all Israel, thy people . . . and may it be good in thy sight to bless thy people Israel at all times and in every hour with thy peace. Blessed art thou, O Lord, who blesses thy people Israel with peace."

My concentration surged as I asked, "may He make peace for all of us and for all Israel," and again as I said, "Depart from evil and do good—Seek peace and pursue it." But, in the long run, grabbing onto tidbits such as these proved no more satisfying or religiously compelling than my failed attempts at sustaining gratitude. And besides, turning my attention to the prayer book's references to peace did little to subdue the grimacing words of war that still flashed their shining teeth at me from almost every page. I needed to get away from the words.

For some time, I sought to draw inspiration from the silent, inarticulate sensation I had experienced of hands resting on my shoulders during the last week of the war. I focused my energy away from the words and into song, soaring on melodies that emanated in my stomach and passed effortlessly through my throat into the air around me. I prayed through song, free from the guttural obstructions of wordiness. On occasion, I sought to avoid sound altogether by simply praying above the words, allowing my thoughts to soar toward God in silence as I mumbled inattentively and imperceptibly under my breath. I pressed the soles of my feet firmly to the ground as I imagined my praying self lifting off like a space rocket from the confines of my body. And I looked down at the text as one looks at miniaturized houses and cars from the window of an airplane after takeoff. Prayer was, for a while, an inner expression of my yearnings, an attempt to feel near to God without actually trying to speak to him.[2]

These silent or musical expressions of my inner longing for intimacy with God felt peaceful. I could fulfill my formal obligations to pray without pestering him. I didn't need to make any assumptions about him. I made no demands of him. I could accept him as a transcendent mystery and seek only to know the sensation of his presence as one knows the caress of a loved one. I could leave my throbbing *siddur* behind. I was finally making progress. This, at last, felt like peaceful prayer. But it was not enough. It was not enough because it missed the point of praying.

A Dialogue with Franny and Zooey Glass

> *I am convinced God will kindly wear a human head, quite capable of nodding, for the benefit of some admirer who enjoys picturing him that way, but I personally am not partial to His wearing a human head. . . . Is it not highly tempting to take off one's hat to someone who is both free to move in mysterious ways as well as in perfectly unmysterious ways?*
>
> —Seymour Glass in Salinger, "Hapworth 16, 1924"

As a teenager, I read and reread J. D. Salinger's *Franny and Zooey* several times a month. After the war, for the first time in a long time, I took my tattered copy off the shelf as I experimented with peaceful prayer. I went back to the book because my attempts at meditative prayer made me feel the need for a scolding from Franny's older brother Zooey.[3]

Franny and Zooey are the youngest children in Salinger's Glass family. All of the Glass children, following on the coattails of the eldest brother, Seymour,[4] were regular panelists on a radio show called *It's a Wise Child*. Like their siblings, Franny and Zooey were precocious, melodramatic, and startlingly bright children. In *Franny and Zooey,* we encounter them, at the respective ages of twenty and twenty-five, embroiled in a family crisis that Franny has instigated. Franny is an overly critical college student whose demands of her teachers and classmates verge on an almost frantic obsession with what Seymour calls being "first-hand."[5] Seymour's taste for freshness and non-imitative originality has manifested in the hypersensitivity and intolerance of his younger siblings, whom he brought up on an overdose of religious philosophy. As a result, Zooey has a disturbingly misanthropic side while Franny has an ugly tendency to regard normally intelligent people (the type who use their intelligence to try and get ahead in life) as egotistical, ill-motivated phonies. Franny is horribly exasperated at college and self-destructively critical of everyone there, as she tells Zooey:

> "What happened was, I got the idea in my head—and I could *not* get it out—that college was just one more, *dopey, inane* place in the world dedicated to piling up treasure on earth and everything. I mean treasure is *treasure,* for heaven's sake. What's the difference whether the treasure is money, or property, or even *culture,* or even just plain knowledge? It all seemed like *exactly* the same thing to me, if you take off the wrapping—and it still does! Sometimes I think that *knowledge*—when it's knowledge for knowledge's sake, anyway—is the worst of all. The least excusable, certainly." Nervously and without any real need whatever, Franny pushed back her hair with one hand. "I don't think it would have all got me quite so down if just once in a while—just *once* in a while—there was at least some polite little *perfunctory* implication that knowledge *should* lead to *wisdom,* and that if it *doesn't,* it's just a disgusting waste of time!" (146)

After a rough semester putting up with all this inane cleverness, Franny decides to indulge herself in a mini-breakdown. She travels to the Glass family home in Manhattan and plants herself on the sofa, clutching a little pea-green book. The book is the Russian Orthodox religious classic *The Way of a Pilgrim*[6] and its subject is the constant, unyielding, mantric recitation of the Jesus prayer, "O Lord Jesus Christ have mercy on me, a sinner." Seeing their daughter in this state of collapse—and perhaps a little impervious to its religious overtones—the Glass parents (Les and Bessie) summon Zooey to come and talk Franny out of her mess. Zooey's somewhat preachy attempts at shaking his sister out of her depression—peppered with her remonstrations—amount to a subtle treatise on prayer that fills nearly half of the book. Since Salinger weaves all this religious philosophy into highly alluring descriptive prose, the theoretical content of Zooey's speech is difficult to separate from its narrative context.

Zooey begins (quite exasperatingly for Franny) by telling her off for worrying her parents. At first, this feels like a regular brotherly pep talk about how to behave in the family. But, as Zooey's argument unfolds, he soon gets straight to the point, i.e., that the Jesus prayer is no use—as a prayer—if you upset your parents by saying it. He continues:

> [I]n going ahead with the Jesus Prayer, aren't you trying to lay up some kind of treasure? Something that's every goddam bit as nego-tiable as all those other, more material things? Or does the fact that it's a prayer make all the difference? I mean by that, is there all the difference in the world, for you, in which side somebody lays up his treasure—this side, or the other? . . . As a matter of simple logic, there's no difference at all, that *I* can see, between the man who's greedy for material treasure—or even intellectual treasure—and the man who's greedy for spiritual treasure. (148)

> [Franny to Zooey] Don't you think I have sense enough to *worry* about my motives for saying the prayer? That's exactly what's *bother-*ing me so. Just because I'm choosy about what I want—in this case, en*light*enment, or *peace,* instead of money or pres*tige* or *fame* or any of those things—doesn't mean I'm not as egotistical and self-seeking as everybody else. If anything, I'm more so! (149)

Don't you think I've agonized over my entitlement to long for intimacy with God? Don't you think I know it's vulgar to assume that access to God is up for grabs as long as you have enough imagination to press the soles of your feet to the ground and pretend your inner self is taking off? Is it so powerful a spiritual virtue to be able to both recite and ignore the words of the *siddur* simultaneously? Doesn't God get to decide whom he is going to caress, where, and when? Perhaps the only reason I can think of myself as being in his presence in the first place is because I am commanded to pray. Anything else would be greedy. You can't expect to satisfy your greed for God. Is the choice to invade God's presence with my yearnings a choice that

I am entitled to make? Who am I to make such choices when my track record with choices is so pitiful? How can I dare use my power of free choice to give myself license to turn up on God's doorstep uninvited when so many of my other choices have been simply shameful?

> The trees stand like guards of the Everlasting; the flowers like sign-posts of His goodness—only we have failed to be testimonies to His presence, tokens of His trust. . . . Amidst the meditation of mountains, the humility of flowers—wiser than all alphabet—clouds that die constantly for the sake of His glory, we are hating, hunting, hurting. Suddenly, we feel ashamed of our clashes and complaints in the face of the tacit glory in nature. It is so embarrassing to live![7]

Back in Salinger's novel, Zooey responds: "if you don't know it yet, you're beginning to give off a little stink of piousness. God damn it, there isn't any prayer in any religion in the world that justifies piousness" (159).

Piousness is so sanctimonious. It is actually violent. How can we be holy without feeling it? How can we speak to God without demanding his attention? Can prayer be about God without being about us? Who or what else could it be about? "A word is a focus point at which meanings meet and from which meanings seem to proceed. In prayer, as in poetry, we turn to the words, not to use them as signs for things, but to see the things in the light of the words. In daily speech it is usually we who speak words, but the words are silent. In poetry, in prayer, the words speak."[8]

Zooey goes on:

> I don't know if you remember, but I remember a time around here, buddy when you were going through a little apostasy from the New Testament that could be heard for miles around. . . . I'm not bringing this up with the idea of throwing anything back in your teeth—my *God*. I'm bringing this up for a good reason. I'm bringing this up because I don't think you understood Jesus when you were a child and I don't think you understand him now . . . and I *don't* see how you can go ahead with the Jesus Prayer till you know who's who and what's what. Do you remember at all what started off that little apostasy? . . . Well, I do, it happens. Matthew, Chapter Six. I remember it very clearly, buddy. I even remember where I *was*. I was back in my room putting some friction tape on my goddam hockey stick and you banged in—all in an uproar, with the Bible wide open. You didn't like Jesus any more, and you wanted to know if you could call Seymour at his Army camp and tell him all about it. And you know why you didn't like Jesus any more? I'll tell you. Because, *one*,

you didn't approve of his going into the synagogue and throwing all the tables and idols all over the place. That was very rude, very Unnecessary. You were sure that Solomon or somebody wouldn't have done anything like that. And the *other* thing you disapproved of—the thing you had the Bible open to—was the lines "Behold the fowls of the air: for they sow not, neither do they reap, nor gather into barns: yet your heavenly Father feedeth them." *That* was all right. That was lovely. That you approved of. *But,* when Jesus says in the same breath, "Are you not much better than they?"—*ah,* that's where little Franny quits the Bible cold and goes straight to Buddha who doesn't discriminate against all those nice fowls of the air. All those sweet lovely chickens and geese that we used to keep up at the Lake. . . . You *still* can't love a Jesus as much as you'd like to who did and said a couple of things he was at least reported to have said or done—and you know it. You're constitutionally unable to under*stand* any son of God who throws tables around. And you're constitutionally unable to understand any son of God who says a human being, *any* human being . . . is more valuable to God than any soft, helpless Easter chick. (163–165)

I cannot pretend I never prayed to God to help me kill others. I cannot pretend I never felt that those prayers could reach his ears and stir his compassion to choose me over them. I thanked him with all my soul for defending me in war. I prayed for the war to go away, but I uttered far more pugnacious and destructive prayers than that. How can I pray peacefully to God without being grateful to him for allowing others to die in my place? For allowing my side to kill instead of being killed? How can I pray when I know that the people killed were praying to him too? Praying for my death. Men have been calling out his names on all sides of holy wars for centuries. In the war, bombs exploded, rockets maimed, bullets and shrapnel pierced skin—but not mine. How can I thank God for that? What else can I do but thank God for that?

Zooey is still scolding Franny:

You take a look around your college *campus* and the *world,* and *pol*itics, and one season of summer *stock,* and you listen to the conversation of a bunch of nitwit college students, and you decide that everything's ego, ego, ego, and the only intelligent thing for a girl to do is to lie around and shave her head and say the Jesus Prayer and beg God for a little mystical experience that'll make her nice and happy. (167)

"My heart finds its peace in the highest, in spiritual things and not in earthly and material ones" (John of Cronstadt).[9] When the world is contrary, the natural impulse is to flee from it. Run for the hills. Fly for the heavens. Kid yourself into believing that you can meet with God there on peaceful terms—on *your* terms—without all the murkiness and confusion of the world he created. The world he created is the world as it is, not the world as I would have it. Can prayer be a journey away from that? An escape? Do I have the right to run away from him—deluding myself about his plan for creation—just to be near to him? Can prayer be real when it is an attempt to escape the world from which it must emanate? Is it not our humanity that makes us pray? Why should he pay attention to my self-indulgence? Is it wrong to long for peace and spirituality—and not "earthly material" things—in prayer? Is it not a blasphemy to pray peacefully in a violent world?

Zooey:

> No matter what I say, I sound as though I'm undermining your Jesus Prayer. And I'm *not,* God damn it. All I *am* is against why and how and *where* you're using it. I'd like to be convinced—I'd *love* to be convinced—that you're not using it as a substitute for doing whatever the hell your duty is in life, or just your daily duty. Worse than that, though, I can't *see*—I swear to God I can't—how you can pray to a Jesus you don't even understand.... If you're going to say the Jesus Prayer, at least say it to *Jesus*, and not to St. Francis and Seymour and Heidi's grandfather all wrapped up in one. Keep *him* in mind if you say it, and him only, and him as he was and not as you'd like him to have been.... The Jesus Prayer has one aim, and one aim *only.* To endow the person who says it with Christ-Consciousness. *Not* to set up some little *cozy,* holier-than-thou trysting place with some sticky, adorable divine *per*sonage who'll take you in his arms and relieve you of all of your duties. (169–172)

In the final scene of the book, Zooey talks to Franny on the phone. She is still on the sofa, quietly moving her lips, saying the Jesus prayer under her breath. At first, as the conversation starts, she thinks Zooey is someone else (their oldest surviving brother, Buddy Glass). When she realizes who is really on the phone, she agrees to continue the conversation. What Franny does not know is that Zooey is speaking to her from the phone in Seymour and Buddy's old bedroom:

> [Zooey] I started bitching one night before the broadcast. Seymour told me to shine my shoes just as I was going out the door.... I was

furious. The studio audience were all morons, the announcer was a moron, the sponsors were morons, and I just damn well wasn't going to shine my shoes for them, I told Seymour. I said they couldn't see them *any*way, where we sat. He said to shine them anyway. He said to shine them for the Fat Lady. . . . He never did tell me who the Fat Lady was, but I shined my shoes for the Fat Lady every time I ever went on the air again. . . . This terribly clear, clear picture of the Fat Lady formed in my mind. I had her sitting on this porch all day, swatting flies, with her radio going full-blast from morning till night. I figured the heat was terrible, and she probably had cancer, and—I don't know . . . I don't care where an actor acts. It can be in summer stock, it can be over a radio, it can be over *tele*vision, it can be in a goddam Broadway theatre, complete with the most fashionable, most well-fed, most sunburned-looking audience you can imagine. But I'll tell you a terrible secret—Are you listening to me? *There isn't anyone out there who isn't Seymour's Fat Lady. . . . Don't you know that? . . . And don't you know—listen to me now—don't you know who that Fat Lady really is? . . .* Ah, buddy. It's Christ Himself. Christ Himself, buddy. (200–202)

Explicit and Implicit Prayer

> *The* siddur *is a book, which everyone talks about, but few people have really read; a book, which has the distinction of being one of the least known books in our literature. Do we ever ponder the meaning of its words? Do we seek to iden-tify our inner life with what is proclaimed in the* nishmat: *"The soul of every living being blesses Thy name, Lord our God . . ."? And yet, there are those who claim that the* siddur *does not express the needs, wants, aspirations of contempo-rary man. We must learn how to study the inner life of the words that fill the world of our prayer book. Without intense study of their meaning, we indeed feel bewildered.*
>
> —ABRAHAM JOSHUA HESCHEL,
> "The Vocation of the Cantor"

In explicit prayer, we face the task of saying the prayers as if we were great stage actors. Spontaneity is achieved through skill and through prac-tice. Like method actors, we may cultivate our ability to say the words of the *siddur* as if they were our own. To pray implicitly is to listen to the words of the prayer book, resigning ourselves to them as they throw us around from pillar to post or like a pinball in a machine or like a baby in a basket floating perilously on the stormy waves of a great river. In explicit prayer, we trust ourselves. We take control over the intentions, meanings, and purposes of the words we utter. In implicit prayer, we give ourselves over to the words of the *siddur,* allowing them to comfort, upset, affirm, and affront us. Occasionally, the thoughts and the feelings that were there before the prayer began coincide with the meanings the words assume as we utter them. If this happens, the *siddur* will give us fleeting moments of explicit expression—but not by our design. Implicit prayer is birthed in surprise.

Explicit prayer is individual prayer. In it, the intentions and desires of the individual follow the words of the *siddur.* The words yield to the prayers of the soul, which flow in them—like a direct current of electricity passing through a metal conductor—straight to God. The purposes and meanings of the supplicant are premeditated and clear while the distinct nature and identity of the "blessed art thou" is vividly envisaged. Explicit prayer is exoteric individual communication with God. It has content and moral consistency. It can be truthful or false, good or evil, kind or cruel, bellicose or peace loving. It is subject to moral judgment. Implicit prayer is communal and collective. It is the prayer of *everything* sprayed out in alternating directions. It rises and falls, concentrates and dissipates, flashing on and off with the seething, tumbling rhythms of created life. It squirts from the soul and splashes itself around like the blood of a slaughtered animal splattering a sacred altar. The words of the *siddur* address themselves to God but only by piercing the soul of humanity; their semantic meanings make no metaphysical journey to the heavens. They travel between the page and the praying mind, disturbing, disrupting, and arousing it. At one moment, we beg unknowingly and expectantly for God's forgiveness, and at the next we tell ourselves with certitude that he is a forgiving God. We beseech him to hear us, and then tell ourselves that he can hear. We ask him to heal us, and tell ourselves that he can and will heal our sicknesses and wounds. The words of the *siddur* electrify and charge the soul like an alternating current, flowing through it in every direction till the soul erupts indiscriminately in praise. Implicit prayer is a response to the *siddur* and to its associations with the world. It is life at peace with its violent tenor.

The alternation between implicit and explicit moments of prayer and the acceptance of the paradox that they comprise are together the most distinct method or means by which creation can collectively, variously, and perhaps even completely acknowledge the Creator. We ask for triumphs that we know we can only accumulate at the expense of others. We ask for them knowing all the while that those very others beg for the same triumphs themselves, and do so at our expense. In order for prayer to be peaceful, the full conflicted variety of the created world—along with the multiple imaginings of God's traits, preferences, and politics that are part of it—must be drawn in. The created world comprises an inconceivably numerous diversity of beings, moods, thoughts, positions, activities, concerns, hopes, dreams, convictions, feelings, and emotions. Prayer spans continents and centuries, engulfing all creeds, races, tribes, faiths, particularisms, desires, and identities, encompassing everything that can clash. Creation is a prayer for peace. A prayer for peace is all prayers combined. It is a cacophony in which only God can find harmony, a skein so tangled that only God can see its individual threads. Only an expression this mottled might be imagined as equal to the task of making peace with God. That is what makes Seymour's secret so terrible.

> *Nishmat Kol Chai.* . . . The soul of every living thing shall bless thy name, O Lord our God, and the spirit of all flesh shall continually glorify and exalt thy memory, our King; from ever and forever you are God and besides you we have no King who redeems and saves, sets free and delivers, who supports and has mercy in all times of trouble and distress. . . . If our mouths were full of song as the sea, and our tongues of exultation as the multitude of its waves, and our lips of praise as the spacious skies; if our eyes shone with light like the sun and the moon, and our hands were spread forth like the eagles of heaven, and our feet were swift as hinds, we should still be unable to thank you and bless your name, O Lord our God and God of our fathers, for one thousandth or one ten-thousandth part of the bounties which you have bestowed upon our fathers and upon us. . . . For every mouth shall give thanks unto thee, and every tongue shall swear unto thee; every knee shall bow to you, and whatsoever is lofty shall prostrate itself before you; all hearts shall fear you and all the inner parts and feelings shall sing unto your name, as it is written, All my bones shall say, Lord, who is like you?

Ultimately, the words of the *siddur* brought me back to the words of the *siddur*. It was as if a plane that had taken off from one airport had landed in an identical airport. I found solace in the hyperbole, in the defiantly self-contradicting psalms, songs, petitions, and benedictions that abound in the *siddur*. I delighted in the peacefulness with which I could resign myself to the simple task of praising God with all the variety of the text—the variety that echoed the conflicted complexity of my soul, the variety that mirrored all the uncontainable and contradictory diversity of the world. The regulated regimen of daily prayer became an opportunity for acknowledging my total dependence upon the plurality of the *siddur*'s language (heal *us,* forgive *us,* hear *us*) for prayers that did not project only *my* desires, needs, predilections, convictions, and preferences upon him, but gave voice to all of creation. I found peacefulness in imagining the unbridled diversity of human prayers breaking free of the insufficient collective political and sociological identities that human minds impose on the world. I stood before God to praise him from within the noise of creation, not to lobby him on my own behalf in solitude. The pages of the *siddur* finally began to light up again:

> Happy are they that dwell in thy house; they will ever be praising thee. I will extol thee, my God, O King; and I will bless thy name forever and ever. Great is the Lord, and exceedingly to be praised and his greatness is unsearchable. One generation shall laud thy works to another.... On the majestic glory of thy splendor, and on thy marvelous deeds, I will meditate.... My mouth shall speak of the praise of the Lord; and let all flesh bless his holy name forever and ever. ... I will praise the Lord while I live: I will sing praises unto my God while I have my being. Put not your trust in princes, in a son of man who is no help.... Happy is he that has the God of Jacob for his help, whose hope is in the Lord his God ... who keeps truth forever; who executes judgment for the oppressed; who gives food to the hungry. The Lord releases prisoners; the Lord opens the eyes of the blind; the Lord raises up those who are bowed down; ... the Lord guards the strangers; he upholds the orphans and the widows.

When we pray at war, we give vent to fear, anger, hatred, love, desire, attachment, and shame—all of which we must acknowledge in order to make peace with God. As we read the *siddur,* we pray by reminding ourselves that its words are not God's. Their references do not and cannot transcend the boundaries of their fleshy, linguistic limitations. They are symbols for the soul, stimuli for the mind, evocations that stir us into praying by challenging us to endure the discomfort of the mind's confines. Up against the walls of our anguish and our yearning, we withdraw from God. Taking three steps backward, we say:

> He who makes peace in His heavens, He will bring peace upon us and let us [all] say,
>   Amen.

CHAPTER 8

Peace Education

*I want to suggest that making our universities just is no lon-
ger enough. . . . There has been, since September 11th, a
series of appeals in print for something new under the sun:
"intellectual philanthropy" could be a tentative name for
it. Lorraine Daston has argued in the* London Review of
Books *that our public problems are now hermeneutic more
than technical and has expressed the hope that "students of
the symbolic" will now deal with [the] "enormously complex
problems" of commensuration that we have been ignoring
and can no longer ignore. Keith Thomas has lectured the
British Academy on "the need for scholars to dispel mutual
incomprehension," a need that he traces historically but that
he goes on to assert is at the present time more pressing than
ever. Similar assessments have come from journalists like
Flora Lewis in the* Herald Tribune *and Peter Beinart in the*
New Republic. *Universities cannot in themselves be expected
to take on tasks such as those defined by these writers, but
intellectuals without frontiers—working together through
journals, centers, and ad hoc associations—can certainly
do so, and must. Scholars in the humanities and human
sciences have particular skills, much as the physicians who
volunteer for Médecins sans Frontières do, to offer in times
of crisis. Scholars are less uniquely talented at solving public
problems than at clarifying what a problem (as opposed to
a pseudo-problem) is and what counts as a solution. Our
task, then, is to find and fund limited and well-defined
projects that will apply our theoretical training and experience to urgent problems whose full complexities have as yet*

gone untended. . . . For if we do not undertake these vital
hermeneutic tasks today, who will do so and when?

—Stanley N. Katz, "Excellence Is by No Means Enough"

Educational Philosophy

Perhaps the most fundamental methodological assumption that runs through all the chapters of this book is that scholarship can be grounded in educational philosophy. While the philosophy of education seeks to articulate and conceptualize the practices of educators, educational philosophy is itself a form of education in which scholars and intellectuals engage. Resting upon the opinion that positivistic notions of academic and scholarly truth have been satisfactorily discredited by the modern projects of hermeneutics and deconstruction, I present educational philosophy as an alternative methodological foundation upon which scholarly interpretation can be built.[1] Not discounting the depth, detail, complexity, and rigor necessary for extracting plausible readings out of primary sources, from the perspective of an education-conscious philosopher it is still hard not to notice that a social, political, cultural, ideological, indeed *educational* agenda is always served when a scholar writes. My claim is that this agenda can and, indeed, should be chosen openly, owned publicly, and articulated deliberately—even autobiographically.

The approach that I am calling *educational philosophy*—or *intellectual philanthropy,* to use the term Katz does in the epigraph above—calls into question the whole purpose of higher education and scholarship as it is understood and practiced in the majority of Jewish studies departments in universities today. While schools of Jewish education are typically marginalized, some departments of Jewish studies are remarkably oblivious to the educational role they play in shaping the ways in which classical Jewish texts are understood, interpreted, and taught by their students. Indeed, in many cases, scholars are uncomfortable with (if not vehemently resistant to) the notion that their research can be evaluated not only for its "scientific" validity but also for the educational effect it has on those who read it. While it is clear that for many (if not most) Jewish studies scholars, academic work is a vital arena in which intellectual interests reflect existential concerns, construct personal identities, and provide opportunities for expressing personal beliefs—this is often kept secret, denied, or treated as cause for embarrassment. You don't get tenure for educating your reader or even for articulating in your scholarship an informed and learned expression of personal belief. Such things are "self-indulgent" and inappropriate to the practices of higher learning. Universities reward invisible loudspeakers for demonstrating their acumen transparently, for allowing texts to speak objectively and—as it were—for themselves.

Not only is this ideal philosophically implausible, but its effect on academic Jewish studies, especially in Israel, has contributed to a growing cultural vacuum in wider Israeli society—adding to a widespread estrangement from academic Jewish learning. This is beginning to show inside the universities where student registration for Jewish studies is in decline and where a cultural identity crisis threatens the future of many Jewish studies departments.[2] I therefore begin this chapter on education and practice by suggesting that—methodologically speaking—this book might be seen as an example of what I mean by *educational philosophy*. To return to the positions I voiced in chapter 3, I will use educational language as a means of justifying what I referred to there as *irenic scholarship*. I will then go beyond the realm of theory and describe some of my attempts at implementing the theory of this book in educational practice.

If you have read your way through to this point from the start, it should be clear that what I mean by "education" is in no danger of being confused for populism or for the kind of writing that is patronizingly dummied down to make it "useful" for schoolteachers. While I hope that my arguments and interpretations are intelligible, I recognize that they are often not easy and that both the autobiographical and interpretive passages in this book hardly make for light reading. What makes this "educational philosophy" is connected both to the autobiographical dimension of my thinking and to my sense of my work's purpose. That purpose has been to begin a conversation about possible Jewish understandings of peace today. I have sought to do this in two ways, the first of which is personal while the second is general.

Personally, I have sought to reconcile my religious (and religious Zionist) convictions with my belief in the sanctity of peace. I believe that the central ideas that I have presented resonate with the classical and canonical texts of the Jewish tradition. I trust that this tradition confirms my conviction that peace as I have described it is an ultimate value and furthermore that Jewish texts yield to a reading of Judaism's deepest principle as the pursuit of peace. This perhaps counterintuitive idea works because it is associated with Judaism's most obvious belief—the unity of God. As I have presented it, monotheism—which describes a single God, whose incomprehensible unity encompasses all the forces that span created time and space—is a peaceful idea captured in (among many other expressions of it) the divine name Adonay-Shalom.

The most explicit rabbinic articulation of this principle is Rav Kook's.[3] For Kook, peace is organically connected to the theological principle of *achdut hahafachim* (the unity of opposites).[4] Rather than focusing attention on Kook's version of this thesis, however, I built mine by exploring the structures of paradoxical unity that are implicit in both biblical prophecy and rabbinic disputation. I drew upon linguistic-turn philosophers for the method of my analysis with an open sense of their educational relevance to the attitudes of present-day secular Western philosophy. The upshot of this is my claim that a contemporary reading of the various genres of the Jewish religious tradition that mediate the will and word of God suggest that they do so peacefully because of the self-effacing consciousness with which Jewish texts acknowledge the role of language in the imperfect and paradoxical refraction of divine revelation.[5] Both biblical prophecy and rabbinic law are paradoxical, contradictory, and humble testimonials to their own legal, moral, and indeed epistemological inadequacies, which come to the fore when one thinks of them as representatives of a mysterious divine will.

Within such a tradition, religious faith is thus connected to a state of radical openness to diversity (and even stark contradiction) and the conviction that the unity of God cannot be imagined as consisting in anything less complex or more harmonious than a cosmic network of resolute paradoxes. Similarly, Jewish law is built upon a paradoxically peaceful construction of explicit religion and implicit religiosity, two components of faith whose coexistence defies the logic of their diametrically opposite purposes. The explicit or exoteric Torah enables the practice of law by leaving the mysteries of its theological foundations necessarily unexamined, while the implicit path of religiosity that I have described seeks—by theological necessity—to intensify religious experience through the sublimation of conflict, the absorption of paradox, and the containment of enmity. Buber's distinction between religion and religiosity has been central to my presentation of this. Within the context of *religion,* we know God and the law. However, in *religiosity,* he is mysterious and the object of a quest. Law is an indication of its own inadequacy when compared to God. This is why the halakha instrumentalizes the law, changes it, and, most important, uses it as a form of practice in the quest for divine intimacy. The peaceful outcome of this combination is an unrequited quest for intimacy with or love for God that is conducted through practices (such as prayer and study) that are inexplicably (and hence gently—or even ironically) perceived as normative commandments. This paradoxical theological description of Judaism is what I call *prophetic peace* and—since my return from war—it is my religion.

My second and more general purpose has been to engender a conversation about peace that strays from the (liberal) norm by acknowledging the irenic potential of the illiberal religious cultures embroiled in the Middle East conflict. It has not been my purpose to have the last word in this conversation. Indeed, I have developed only one of several possible Jewish paths to peace. In terms of its more general purpose, this book seeks only to demonstrate how a philosophy of peace *can* organize a Jewish understanding of prophetic revelation, rabbinic learning, and communal prayer. I am aware of how individual and particular my own approach is. I have cited the work of Christian theologians and postmodern philosophers whose writings have made an impression upon me even though their ideas and identities are likely to alienate many of the Jews whom I would ultimately like this book to address. Moreover, I have said virtually nothing about Islam. Perhaps there are readers out there who identify with my interdisciplinary and interdenominational choice of bibliography. But I am sure that many might not share my tastes. To them, this book is an invitation to articulate other and perhaps very different paths to peace that fit with their beliefs, loyalties, and bibliographical preferences. Put differently, my conviction that "all her paths are peace" is stronger than my loyalty to the particular path that I have walked.

The general purpose of this book, therefore, should be understood as part of an *educational* project. Starting with the premise that peace—however it is understood—is a binding normative concern for anyone committed to the Jewish tradition, my suggestion is that the question Jews should be asking each other is not "Why do you support or oppose this or that particular peace proposal?" but "What do you mean by peace?" We are less accustomed to asking this question and are often unable to offer anything concrete as an answer to it. Moreover, we tend to confuse it with the—related but different—question "How do you want things to look when the conflict is over?"

In addition to providing my own Jewish answer to this question, I would like to take part in a wider conversation in which Jews and Muslims—separately and together—offer each other their versions of peace's meaning for careful and thoughtful consideration. The outcomes of these conversations might supplement the debate about the Middle East conflict and its proposed political solutions with new alternatives. Better still, this conversation might generate organically Jewish and Muslim motivations for putting an end to the hostilities. While it is commonly argued that a silent majority supports peace in the Middle East, I urge people to notice that the workings of a silent majority are inadequate to the challenge at hand. By engendering an ideological discussion about peace and its potential meanings, my ultimate hope is to create a varied and extremely vocal majority of Jews and Muslims who see peace—as they understand it—as the ultimate fulfillment of their aspirations and who are prepared to pursue peace with the same passions and convictions that currently fuel the perpetuation of hatred and violence.

Educational Practice: The Talking Peace Project

As I have been writing and editing this book, I have also been working on a small-scale—but significant—project that grew out of the aspiration to create a fresh discourse about peace in the Middle East. The practical/educational question I have been asking myself is, "Can the ideas outlined in this book actually help with the creation of peace in modern Israel?" The answer to this question has yet to be determined, but conversations that I initiated with two people, Avinoam Rosenak and Sharon Leshem-Zinger, have made some progress possible. Avinoam is a scholar of Jewish thought and an expert in the teachings of Rabbi Abraham Kook. Sharon is an expert in facilitating cross-conflict dynamic group processes. Together, we set out to engage people in conversations about peace and to bring together populations who had never met constructively or meaningfully over this issue in the past.

The formulation of peacefulness that I have presented here resonated significantly with Avinoam's research on the paradoxical complexities of Kook's theology. Avinoam's articulation of this thesis in the writings of Kook could give us the ability to demonstrate to rabbis on the ideological and religious Zionist right that peace can be understood in ways that belong authentically and comfortably inside the scope of their existing ideological convictions.[6] Sharon brought the remarkable human sensitivity of an expert in group dynamics to our thinking. In particular, she brought a unique approach to the facilitation of group dynamics. Her method seeks to overcome a group's tendency to reach compromise and consensus and works to cultivate the feeling that a group situation can include radical differences.

Our premise was that an ideological debate about peace that takes place in a group that includes prominent public figures of radically different perspectives could contribute significantly to the challenge of creating a vocal majority in favor of peace in Israel. We rejected the popular notion that a silent majority is enough to empower negotiators to broker agreements. This notion has repeatedly been seen as inadequate to the task of overcoming the motivations and convictions of radical factions on both sides. In Israel, radicals and opponents of peace successfully present themselves as authentic loyalists to the national cause while compromising proponents of peace are easily discredited as guilty of betraying core national and religious values. This is, in my mind, the most serious problem impeding progress toward peace in Israel today.

The objective, as I saw it, was to begin the work of building a vocal majority in favor of peace. We believed that this could be accomplished by extending the notion of what peace means beyond the confines of any specific compromise or negotiated solution. We sought to bring together significant agents of change who represent the full scale of Israel's political spectrum. We invited chief rabbis from the settlements along with thinkers, intellectuals, and institutional leaders of influence to engage in a year-long process of intranational discourse. It seemed obvious that respectful interest in the unwavering tenacity of conflicting ideological positions in Israeli society would yield more support for peace than aggressive lobbying for the existing paradigm. The group sessions would be built around the varying peace visions of each participant, who would be given an opportunity to present their perspective while the others witnessed both the personal angst and the theoretical thinking that comprise a complex worldview.

As we started looking for members to join our group, the idea that an illiberal or radical (rather than compromise-based) philosophy of peace would encourage political rivals to explore each other's convictions peacefully seemed to work. Some of the most telling and striking examples of this took place at the interviewing stage as we noticed how our willingness to accept varying understandings of peace helped to earn the confidence of the group's members. On one occasion, we traveled to the beaches of Nitzan in the south of Israel to meet with one of the most influential rabbinic leaders of the Gush Katif settlements. Nitzan was now the home of settlers who had lost their homes in the summer of 2005. As we sat in the rabbi's temporary home, we listened carefully to his account of the disengagement and its devastating impact on the social fabric of his community. He spoke with passion about the efforts he had orchestrated to win support in Israel for his cause. Steering the conversation around to the subject of peace and its meaning in the teachings of Rav Kook, we were able to demonstrate to that rabbi that peace was a sorely neglected value among the settlers. After listening to his deeply moving account of the efforts to rebuild his community, I simply asked him to imagine what an impact he could have if he made the same efforts to win support for peace—as he understands it. He heard me and looked at his wife, who was sitting with us, and said, "What should I say to that?" She said, "I think you should listen." He did and joined our group.

Getting leaders and thinkers from the left wing to attend was also not an easy task. It often seemed that they were far less willing to engage with the settlers than the settlers were to engage with them. But through personal contacts, we were able to assemble a remarkable group that we believed could have a tremendous impact on Israeli society if we were successful.

The meetings of the group produced many moments of dramatic epiphany. The atmosphere was open and honest. People spoke freely and shared the most honest versions of their moral and ethical judgments. Sometimes, group members were shocked by what others had to say. But certain moments were truly transformative. At the beginning of one meeting, for example, a settler rabbi asked if he could address the group before we let the discussion planned for that evening get under way. He wanted to describe a dream he had had. He told the group that he dreamed that, on the way to one of our meetings, he had stopped at the gate of his settlement to pick up hitchhikers. The car filled with Jewish young men and headed to Jerusalem. It was only at a later stage in the ride that he realized that one of the men was a Hamas bomber, also heading for Jerusalem. The rabbi described how he stopped the car, ordered everyone out, and went to engage the Hamasnik in discussion. In the dream, he protested that it was not fair of him to behave in such a way. "I gave you hospitality. I picked you up in my car! Why are you doing this? It is against your faith as much as it is mine!" Ultimately, the bomber was convinced and agreed to remove the explosives belt. The rabbi took him to the police and handed him over. He emphasized at this point how he instructed the police officers to behave decently. "He is our enemy," he said, "but you must not violate his honor." This was the end of the dream. Members of the group sat flabbergasted by this medley of associations. I gently asked the rabbi what he felt the meaning of the dream was. His answer amazed me. He asked to be introduced to Palestinians to whom he could talk.

The most important conclusion to be drawn from this story is not that the rabbi turned into a liberal and started to see the Palestinian point of view. The most important aspect is his associations with the journey to our meeting. Clearly, this was a setting that forced him to confront the complexity of the conflict in which his ideology plays a role. But it was also a setting in which he could do this without having to compromise or alter his convictions. It is not his belief system that changed but his openness to engage with the Other, who remains his enemy but within a context in which a radical form of coexistence seems possible without the resolution of their significant differences. This is perhaps what is meant by the wolf lying with the lamb. As paradoxical and intractable as this conflict is, it seems possible to imagine a form of coexistence that requires of the wolf to continue being a wolf so that his coexistence with the lamb might be theologically meaningful.

A Blessing of Peace

The point of this book has not been to model an overall political solution to the Arab-Israeli conflict. It has been to articulate a prayer that this specific conflict might not distract the Jewish people from our wider and deeper purpose—the humble pursuit of world peace. It seems unlikely that the Arab-Israeli conflict will be solved locally. It is always expanding and will only be dealt with on a global level. But I believe that, whether it helps to solve the conflict or not, the state of Israel will fulfill its highest purpose if it helps the Jewish people to fulfill our ultimate purpose of bearing witness to the name of God. In modern—and perhaps secular—terms, this means that the state of Israel must become an emblem of peacefulness and build a collective culture whose declared purpose is the pursuit of world peace. By serving as the national religion of a state, a peaceful articulation of Judaism can represent peace to the world. This is my closing thought and with it goes my closing prayer. The daily prayers, the priestly blessings, the sacrifices of the Temple, and even the six books of the Mishnah all end with peace, as it says:

> And one concludes with the blessing of Peace, because it is true of all the blessings that their endings are about peace. (Palestinian Talmud, Berachot 2:4)

> R. Shimon ben Chalafta said, "you have no better vessel with which to hold blessing than the vessel of peace. And what is the source? God wishes to give might to His nation; God will bless His nation in peace. (Mishnah Uktzin 3:12)

AFTERWORD

Beating Softly

The summer of 2006 was my first experience of full-scale war, but it was not my first taste of military conflict. During the years between my conscription in 1987 and the Lebanese war, I found myself in numerous situations of low-grade combat inside Lebanon, at the Lebanese border, and in the territories of Judea, Samaria, and Gaza.

The intifada that erupted in 1987 literally blew up in my face. I was patrolling the silent streets of the Jabalya refugee camp when it started. The camp had been under curfew for days, and we had become accustomed to walking the empty streets as if Jabalya were a ghost town and not the most densely populated spot on the planet. Other than the smells of burnt refuse and cooking and the sounds of barking dogs and children playing behind walls and gates, it was hard for us to believe that there was anyone there. I was completely blind to the lives the Palestinian refugees were living. As a young soldier, I felt too oppressed by the discipline of the army to imagine the oppression of others.

Against the backdrop of this silence, the shock I experienced (along with the other members of my unit) was alarming when we turned a corner to find hundreds, if not thousands, of angry youths pouring onto the streets—as if from nowhere—to pelt us with stones and broken bottles. It is amazing that we never even heard them before we saw them. We were absolutely at a loss. We had no idea what to do. There were only thirty of us against thousands of them. We were carrying semi-automatic rifles and had enough live ammunition in our combat vests to gun them down in droves. But shooting into a stone-throwing crowd did not seem right. None of us even thought to use our weapons. We just watched the crowd in disbelief.

My officer soon took control. He was quick to grasp just how perilous our situation was. It was clear that his first priority was to get us out of there alive and not to disperse the crowd. It is strange, but I do not remember feeling afraid. The civilian population in the refugee camps had not yet established itself as a threat. We were astonished, but did not panic. My officer was especially resourceful in coming up with a creative solution to our predicament.

We were each instructed to empty one of the magazines in our set of all its bullets. With empty magazines in our guns, we ran forward, screaming *Esh, esh* (Fire, fire). We leveled our guns and charged the crowd without shooting a single round. As if by magic, the mob stopped in its tracks. With a strange mixture of incredulity and fear they let us pass, dispersed, and then completely disappeared. In minutes, we stood alone once again in the silent street. Whatever it was that had happened, it felt for a moment as if it had never happened at all. We continued our patrol in shocked silence.

When we returned to our base, we discovered that similar incidents had taken place that day all over Jabalya and throughout the Gaza Strip. We had been well led and lucky. But we knew that trick was only going to work once. Now what?

The army had no idea how to respond to the low-grade uprising of the first intifada. It was the first time the Israel Defense Forces (IDF) had faced widespread civilian unrest. This was no war for soldiers to fight. We weren't up against either soldiers or hardened terrorists. The enemy was made up of teenagers and even small children, throwing the "stones of freedom" from behind the walls of their impoverished homes—from behind washing lines, trees, playgrounds, and hospitals. Sticks and stones *can* break bones; they can smash the windshields of cars, knock out eyes, shatter teeth. They can kill. But they are also only stones, thrown by incited children who have nothing to lose.

A few weeks later, my unit was positioned in Khan Unis. We slept near the greenhouses of Gadid, one of the settlements of the Katif bloc that would be disbanded by Ariel Sharon in the summer of 2005. In 1987, Gadid was our refuge. We came there to sleep, pray, and eat, spending the bulk of our time in the huge refugee camp nearby. The people of Khan Unis had been involved in the unrest, and the IDF had arrived in numbers. The Israeli government and the IDF were resisting the calls from the political right to gun down a few hundred of them in one go, to nip the intifada in the bud before it got out of control. "This could go on for years," they claimed, "thousands—not hundreds—could be killed on both sides." They argued, "Do you think the Egyptians or the Jordanians would look for humanitarian ways of handling this situation? . . . The international community will scream for a while, but then they will forget. If we gun a few hundred of *them* down now, *they* will never forget it, and then there will be peace and quiet for years." The government and the army had to find a way of dealing humanely with the uprising without succumbing to this pressure. They never did.

This was a confusing time for me. As a young soldier, barely past basic training, I was not in a position to appreciate just how unusually imprecise our orders were. Our officers told us that the instructions were coming from "very high up." We were to patrol Khan Unis and "show the anger of the state of Israel." How does one do that? The army seemed to have decided that the Palestinian uprising was "misbehavior" and that the youthful culprits needed to be "taught a lesson." The intifada was to be subdued with corporal punishment. We were issued truncheons and, eventually, tear-gas canisters. Armed with these, and carrying the full weight of our combat gear, we launched an assault on the streets of Khan Unis. We stood on street corners for hours on end, waving our truncheons in the air and breathing the stench of the overflowing sewers. We jeered at the muezzin whom we heard on the loud-speaker, clearing the phlegm of sleep from his throat and swallowing a glass of water noisily before calling the believers to morning prayers. We eyed him as he climbed the stairs of the tower time after time—five times—throughout the course of each day. We watched poverty and desolation with contempt. Sometimes, we chatted too much and annoyed our officer. When he got angry, he would punish us by leading us on patrols of Khan Unis at break-neck speed, carrying all our equipment. We would trail after him, gasping for breath, trying to keep up like naughty children. We dragged through the streets for hours on end till our legs and shoulders ached. More experienced soldiers watched us and jeered at our youth and our misfortune.

Many seemed to understand "the anger of the state of Israel" in terms of the disciplinary measures typically dished out by NCOs to green military trainees like us. Palestinian civilians were forced to march in time or to run around distant landmarks—trees or pylons—carrying heavy rocks and sand-bags. They were forced to do pushups or kneel on all fours or hold their hands in the air, to paint rocks with white plaster and lay them on the ground in the shape of a Star of David. Objectionable graffiti was painted over by the nearest passerby, who was given a sharp deadline to complete the task in the best tradition of IDF basic training. Some were forced to take all the furniture out of their houses and then put it all back. Others had to unpack their bags or empty their pockets in the streets on demand. The uprising brought every Palestinian civilian face to face with the kind of correctional hostility a rebellious conscript meets at the hands of his higher-ranking superiors.

During those days in Khan Unis, I learned to bark in Arabic: *Jib elaweeya!* (Give me your ID card!), *Iftach el baab!* (Open the door!), *Saaker el motor!* (Turn off the car engine!). It is amazing how the selective use of another person's language can breed mutual contempt in place of communication. We barked our orders at the Palestinian population just as we had been barked at weeks earlier in basic training. What could be more humane than that? "Do unto others as you have had done unto yourself." The contempt experienced and then stored up by young conscripts was unleashed on the suspected perpetrators of the intifada in the stupid belief that peace among enemies and the good behavior of a well-trained platoon were much the same thing—and achieved in the same way.

I spent several weeks in Khan Unis, but one day stands out. It began with a morning patrol in which we were ordered, once again, to show the anger and dissatisfaction of the Israeli government with the behavior of the Palestinians. However, this time, the method of our madness was a little more prescribed. That day, we made our way through Khan Unis with clear orders. A curfew was called after which we patrolled the refugee camp slowly and deliberately, like a plague of locusts with a craving for glass. The platoon formed two long lines on either side of the road with two armored personnel carriers (APCs) driving between them. We moved forward, and with rocks, boots, and truncheons we shattered every piece of glass we could find. There was not a streetlight, a headlight, or a window intact when we had finished. We used our truncheons to shatter the windows of cars and buses and threw heavy rocks from the ground up to the "receivers" perched on the APCs; from that angle, second-floor windows were easy prey. Now and again, the officers took potshots with their guns at rooftop water tanks, but we were not allowed to join in the target practice. So, we contented ourselves knocking out lightbulb after lightbulb and filled the streets with glass. As we approached the market—the notoriously dangerous casbah—we were pelted with iron pokers. I was standing inside one of the APCs with my head sticking out of the top, passing slabs of concrete to my friend, who was dropping them onto nearby solar panels. One poker slid past my face and chest and smashed loudly on the iron floor of the vehicle, just missing the toe of my black army boot.

Our outraged response was swift. We sprang from our patrol into a fierce chase. No one knew who had thrown the poker, but we saw roughly where it had come from: one of the third-floor balconies of a building overlooking the casbah. We burst into each of the homes on that floor. In minutes, the windows were shattered and the TV sets were thrown overboard along with plates, dishes, and anything else breakable we could put our hands on. My Arabic-speaking officer barked loud warnings at the families inside as we pointed our guns at them menacingly, for his protection. After all the excitement was over, we returned with boiling blood and sweaty foreheads to the deliberate routine of our slow-moving path of destruction.

When the patrol was completed, we returned to Gadid, our boyish faces deceptively coarse with the sand kicked up by the tracks of the APC. We returned from our long day of destruction to the news that a huge operation was planned for that night and that we were to play a dramatic part in it. We were given a few hours to sleep in our humid tents and prepare for the grand action ahead. Again, the orders had come from "very high up." Forces were gathering in Gadid from all over Gaza. The entire Givati brigade moved into our silent little field along with hundreds of men from other units of military police, border guards, tanks, and infantry. Around 10 PM, we piled into buses for the short drive to Khan Unis where the forces made their final preparations for the operation that lay ahead. The first wave began with the Arabic-speaking border guards, who sped through the streets of Khan Unis in jeeps, announcing on loudspeakers that all men between the ages of fifteen and thirty-five were to report to the dilapidated football stadium at midnight for detainment. The grand idea of someone "very high up" was to keep all the feisty youths in Khan Unis awake all night. A night without sleep would make them too tired to throw stones the next day. With a drowsy day of inaction working against them, so the theory ran, the insurrections would lose their momentum and fizzle out. Somebody seems to have thought that all the Palestinians needed was to sleep it off for a day and the intifada would go away.

After the border guards had finished screeching their instructions, the foot soldiers were sent in. Flanked with tanks and APCs, we began making our way through Khan Unis, banging on door after door, waking up family after family. Again, my Arabic-speaking officer shouted orders at the civilians, who were then supposed to know precisely where to go and what to do. Having been on the wrong end of his sharp tongue and gruff voice, I remember thinking, "better them than me." We waited for the streets to fill with young men and when they did not, we burst into houses, pointing our guns, gesturing with our arms, and began pulling people indiscriminately from their beds. Again, we waited for the streets to fill with neat files of clearheaded young men heading purposefully for the stadium in an orderly fashion. But that is not what happened. The streets filled—but not only with young men. Within a few moments, hundreds and probably thousands of people of all ages, men, women, and children, poured into the streets, into the drippy sewage that flowed in the dank pathways and alleys of Khan Unis. This was no planned insurrection. It was an unholy mess.

It now became my job to sort the men from the women, the young from the old. Waving my gun in the air, I motioned to the hordes that stood before me to sit down. The alleys were wet with flowing sewage. The stink was horrible. But the hundreds of women with flimsy white scarves over their heads and flowery patterns on their long black dresses all complied. Kicking off their sandals, they crouched down on their haunches and wailed. One woman came over to me and stroked my beard, speaking loudly in Arabic that I could not understand. She seemed to believe that facial hair was a sign of softness and compassion. Gently, I pushed her away and moved on. Finally, when the men had been separated from the women and were now sitting in a group at the other end of the road, my task was to send the women back to their homes and to their beds. I signaled that they were to get up and go home. *Roch el beit,* I called out feebly and unconvincingly in my newly acquired military Arabic. As they rose from the crouching positions they had held unflinchingly for nearly an hour, it became clear that most of them had neglected to keep track of their sandals. The streets and alleyways were filled with hundreds of lost sandals and plastic shoes. Some of the women scrambled for their lost footwear; most moved away barefoot and disappeared. For weeks after that night, as we patrolled the streets of Khan Unis, we kicked our way through piles and piles of lost shoes.

With the women on their way home, we now turned our attention to the men. Older men were to be sent home after inspection. We flipped through ID cards, looking for anyone born before 1952. Everyone younger was sent off along the soldier-lined streets in the direction of the stadium. After a long and messy night, and after the last house in our zone had been either emptied or put back to bed, we began making our own way to the stadium. There, we discovered just how huge the scale of this operation had been. The army had been in action all over Khan Unis that night, and the stadium was now filled with thousands of young men who stood in rows with their hands tied behind their backs. High-ranking officers were marching to and fro with megaphones in their hands, shouting warnings at the prisoners who stood accused of pissing off the Israeli government whose displeasure should, by now, have been made very clear.

While I was impressed with the restraint I had seen and displayed that night—horrible as this ordeal no doubt was, no one in my zone had been hurt, no bones had been broken—I was appalled to discover that some Israeli soldiers had behaved disgracefully, violating some of the basic standards of human decency. One Arab youth had been thrown into a pit that soldiers from another unit had been using as a crapper. I was young and powerless to rebuke them. I watched in horror as they sat around hurling insults at him in Arabic from the nearby bleachers. My Hebrew was still inadequate to the task of assuming an authoritarian tone and my accent was still so obvious that every unfamiliar soldier I addressed still responded by mimicking whatever I said in an overdone American accent. I slinked away and rejoined the boys in my unit who had at last been given permission to curl up inside the APC for a couple of minutes' sleep.

When the dawn broke, it was time to release all the detainees and send them on their way. "Surely," we reasoned, "they learned their lesson from a night like this. They don't want to go through this again." Neither did we. "Surely," we reasoned, "the stone throwing will now come to an end." I was told to stand at one of the stadium's exits with a scowl on my face and a truncheon in my hand. My job was to make sure that the Palestinian men went straight home with no further trouble. Minutes after I assumed my position, they started flowing by. They came past me at a sprint and headed for home. I waved my truncheon in the air, shoving them on like a cowboy moving his herd.

As I stood there, I was joined by Ronen. Ronen was a nonreligious NCO who had been "imported" from the Golani brigade to guide my unit through basic training. I despised him. Standing at the exit of the stadium, I soon became the object of Ronen's snide humor. I was too weak for his tastes, too white-skinned, too dovish, too Ashkenazi. "Isaacs," he called out, "when are you going to understand that the only thing Arabs understand is force? What are you standing there for? When they run by, give it to them where it hurts." My body filled with fear. It ran through my veins and into my fingers, fear of Ronen. I was a young conscript and he was my sergeant. He could do what he liked with me. I could resist his order and take the risk of complaining, or I could comply. But I could not ignore him. I froze on the spot, scared to speak for fear of being mocked. I looked at him, imploring him with my gaze to leave me alone to get on with it as I saw fit. But he was not going anywhere. "Give me that truncheon and sit over there while I show you how it's done."

I sat and watched as Ronen took my position. With his cigarette between his teeth, he began smashing away at the continuous stream of youths who ran by. They stopped in their tracks with eyes like wild, hunted animals as they spotted him, the shrewd ones timing their steps to slip by while Ronen unleashed his wrath on another. He smashed with the wooden truncheon at their skulls, their ankles, and their wrists, stopping people to put their hands on the ground so he could stamp on their fingers. "That will put an end to their stone throwing," he jeered in my direction. "When will you understand that this is the Middle East, not America?" (It didn't seem to matter how many times I claimed my Scottish birth and English childhood. The rest of the world was America for Ronen, and all its children were pampered do-gooders who had no business serving in the Israeli army.) Less than twenty-four hours before, I had smashed windows and thrown TV sets off third-story balconies, and even more recently I had pulled women and children from their beds in the middle of the night. Watching Ronen, I began to feel the terrible sense of confusion that, over the years, would become resentment, bitter loneliness, and deep shame. I watched him batter and smash; he grabbed clumps of hair, burning the foreheads of Palestinian youths with the smoldering end of his cigarette. I watched him take hold of teenagers and children by the hair. I watched him yell at them as he burned them with his cigarette. I watched him burn their heads and their necks. I heard them screaming with the pain. I could stand it no more. I had to act.

What was I to do? Stop him? Complain about him? Reason with him? What was I to do? Hit them? Burn them? Frighten them? Show them the anger of my new country? Show them the anger of Ronen's grandparents at their Arab neighbors in Morocco? What was I to do? A voice inside me said, "Do nothing." Leave Ronen alone. It is his business. He is the sergeant. I am a private, a soldier with no experience in the country, no experience in the army. Another voice said, "You have to act." What did I know of such things? How was I to take on Ronen? Since my arrival in Israel thirteen months earlier, I had spent almost all of my time studying the legal precepts of the Talmud in a yeshiva. I had exerted all the intellectual energies I could muster trying to make up for my vastly inferior British Jewish education. I had learned almost from scratch how to read the slanted letters of Rashi script, how to decipher the sometimes cryptic and more often telegraphic apologetics of Talmudic reasoning. I had sweated over abstract legal concepts and binary distinctions whose comprehension required a mastery of biblical, Mishnaic, and Talmudic texts which I was only now encountering for the first time. The experience had been invigorating and stimulating, but overwhelming. I had struggled to find religious meaning in it, and had failed. Instead, I focused my religious and ethical energies on a self-deprecating regime of penitence for the cardinal sins of wasting time and sexual desire. My study and my prayer had been disjointed, though the energies I had invested in them both stretched my soul to the limits of its capacity. I had studied and prayed, but had gained no wisdom. I stood now before Ronen with sharpened powers of reason, but without the character or experience to know how to act.

"Now I see how it's done," I said. "Give me the truncheon back. I want to have a turn." Ronen smiled approvingly as I returned to my position. Taking the truncheon from his hands, I began smashing away with all my strength at every man who ran past. I bashed and I smashed at backs, shoulders, and hips, trying to avoid contact with fragile bones, fingers, and heads. Some squealed with pain as I hit them. I made sure that the force of my blows was hard enough to keep Ronen at bay. One young lad ran toward me with his hand held high as if he were trying to hit me. I landed my truncheon on his face and I think I broke his nose. I watched as he ran off, struggling to keep my composure as I turned to hit the next guy in line. Ronen, who was killed in a car accident only a few months later, stayed in his seat, smoking. Nobody else was burned that day. May God forgive me!

My participation in the IDF's struggle against the intifada (now known as the *first* intifada) in 1987 had a very strong impact on me. The night in Khan Unis and the terrible decision I had to make the next morning plunged me into deep confusion. Only a year had passed since I had left England and now I was discovering all too fast that my decision to settle in Israel was one that raised as many (if not more) questions about my Jewishness than it answered. My encounters with Israeli youth had been equally disturbing. On the one hand, I discovered in yeshiva that by the time they completed their high school education, religious boys in Israel had acquired a depth and breadth of Jewish knowledge that I could hardly imagine or ever hope to equal. I revered them for it and naïvely believed them to have hailed from a higher caste of humanity. They were the new Jews, the children of good fortune whose childhoods had been forged in the realization of the (religious version of the) Zionist myth. I idealized their culture and made every effort to join their society. On the other hand, I was deeply disappointed with their conduct in the army. I expected more of them than I did of myself. I thought their superior knowledge of Judaism and halakha should dictate a quality of behavior that I never even aspired to. I lacked the perspective to understand how disorienting the special circumstances of our service were, and I lacked the years to appreciate how young and inexperienced we all (including the veteran officers who seemed so tested) were. All the same, when faced with the challenge of behaving humanely in the face of adversity, my idealized Israelis had failed appallingly. My disappointment and anger were only made worse by the nagging awareness that I had failed too.

Notes

Preface

1. Isaacs, "Lebanon II."

1. Politics, Anti-Politics, and Religion

1. Hegel, "Addition G," 310.

2. Arguably, the change of attitude that I observed among Israeli reservists during the war reflects a broader change taking place, particularly in European society today, that has been summed up effectively by James Sheehan in his *Where Have All the Soldiers Gone?* 223. Writing about the future of the civilian state in contemporary Europe, Sheehan comments, "The blend of commitment and coercion that once motivated people to fight and die for their nations is gone forever.... Europe has become a 'non-war community' which means that its citizens live in a 'post-heroic age,' sustained by private ambitions and individual desires. In the early twenty-first century, national defense is no longer the duty of each citizen; it is a matter for professionals who are paid to assume the risks and bear the burdens that come with their jobs."

3. James Sheehan argues that the "peace" that has evolved in the past sixty years among European states should not be mistaken for a global phenomenon because it is, in Sheehan's words, "a product of Europe's distinctive history in the twentieth century." See ibid., xvii, 172–197.

4. Williams, *Silence and Honey Cakes,* 62.

5. Ibid.

6. Mishnah Avot 2.

7. Soloveitchik, *Halakhic Man,* 5.

8. Ibid., 5–6.

9. Ibid., 7.

10. Though the halakhic man whom Soloveitchik goes on to portray in much greater detail is the religious hero of his essay, I believe that the religious integrity of *homo religiosus,* as Soloveitchik presents him, is to be taken seriously indeed. Similarly, Soloveitchik's emphasis on the halakhic system does not preclude the utmost seriousness with which he addresses the scientific method of cognitive man's system of thought.

11. To avoid confusion, I should mention that the use of this phrase is not intended to suggest rejection or disdain for the political process. On the contrary, politics is inevitable and essential. As I hope will become clear, the notion of anti-politics will be used here to suggest that religion best participates in the political process by flowing against the stream of political activity. In other words, it has a role, but this role is deconstructive and not ideological. My primary concern is not the delegitimization of politics but the dislocation of religion's ultimate concerns from political ideologies and ambitions. See Konrad, *Anti-Politics.*

12. Goodman, "*Anti-Politics* by George Konrad."

13. Taylor, "A Catholic Modernity?"

14. Ibid., 34.

15. Ibid.

16. Ibid., 28.

17. Shea, "A Vote of Thanks to Voltaire," 42–47.

18. I will discuss the biblical evidence for this claim in chapter 5.

19. Hegel, "Addition G," 307.

20. This biblical reading will be dealt with in detail in chapter 5.

21. These lines were written in the context of Heschel's protest against the Vietnam War and express his conviction that religious thinkers had a crucial religious responsibility to protest the war. By quoting Heschel here, I admittedly pull him out of context. My purpose is to use his words to echo my convictions that peace is a religious cause and that religious leaders have a significant role to play in drawing the attention of religious people to its importance.

22. The title of this section is wordplay lifted directly from the title of Dennis Ross's book about his experiences as an American diplomat working on the Middle East peace process during the tenure of Presidents G. H. W. Bush and Bill Clinton. See Ross, *The Missing Peace*.

23. Ibid., 765.

24. Ibid., 761, 766.

25. While it is clear that not only religious motivations were behind the opposition to the Oslo Accords, my point is that the tremendously powerful role played by religion should not be overlooked. Precisely because Barak sought to bring the conflict to its "ultimate" end, through settling the issue of Jerusalem, his secularized version of what "ultimate" might mean stirred up the passionate (sometimes messianic) objections of Israel's religious citizens. This was especially true of the religiously motivated settlers, who did everything in their power to prevent the notion that peace could be achieved through compromising sovereignty over parts of greater Jerusalem from winning the majority support of the Israeli public. Likewise, within the narrower context of the Knesset, Barak was unable to win the support of Israel's religious parties for his idea.

2. Irenic Scholarship

1. This passage is from Hartman's short but eloquent foreword to the first volume of an annotated anthology of classical Jewish texts designed to serve as a resource for the double-sided project he proposes here: the reinterpretation of the Jewish legal tradition in light of a Jewish polity and the reevaluation of Jewish political behavior as inspired by classical Jewish law. See Hartman, Foreword, xiv.

2. *Common Knowledge* is an interdisciplinary quarterly published by Duke University Press that is dedicated to the advancing of peace through scholarship. Its founding editor, Jeffrey Perl, and its offices are based at Bar-Ilan University, Tel Aviv.

3. Bynum is a professor of historical studies, Institute for Advanced Study (Princeton, N.J.), formerly a MacArthur Fellow, and a professor at Columbia University. Geertz was the Harold F. Linder Professor of Social Science, Institute for Advanced Study. Nusseibeh is the president of Al-Quds University and a former

minister for Jerusalem affairs in the Palestinian Authority cabinet. Yuval is the academic head of Scholion: Interdisciplinary Research Center in Jewish Studies and a professor of Jewish history, Hebrew University of Jerusalem. Perl is the founder and editor of *Common Knowledge* and a professor of English literature at Bar-Ilan University.

4. Bynum et al., "Conference Working Group Recommendations." See also Perl, "Irenic Scholarship and Public Affairs."

5. See, for example, Geertz's two classic collections of essays on interpretive anthropology, *The Interpretation of Cultures* and *Local Knowledge: Further Essays in Interpretive Anthropology*.

6. The scholars mentioned have dedicated multiple studies to the comparison of Jews and Christians in medieval Europe and late antiquity. See, for example, Bonfil, *As by a Mirror;* Yuval, *Two Nations in Your Womb;* Marcus, *Rituals of Childhood;* Boyarin, *Border Lines.*

7. Durkheim, *Suicide,* chapter 6; Beteille, *Some Observations on the Comparative Method;* Burke, *History and Social Theory,* chapter 2, 22–28. See also Perl and Isaacs, "A Postscript on Method."

8. The juxtaposition of Synagoga and Ecclesia is a case in point. In decorated manuscripts and on church walls all over Europe, the younger sister with her bold gaze and her crown is placed quite deliberately next to Synagoga, who stands with her broken staff, bound eyes, and overturned Torah scroll. For Synagoga, this comparison speaks only to her disadvantage. It proclaims God's rejection and gloats at her loss of former glory. See, for example, "Ecclesia and Synagoga in the Initial T," a fourteenth-century French manuscript.

9. See Babylonian Talmud, Yoma 69b: "For were it not for God's awe, how could one nation survive among the nations?" See also Midrash Tanchuma Toledoth 5: Adrinus asked Rabbi Joshua, "How great is the sheep that stands between seventy wolves [meaning the Jewish people, who survive among the seventy Gentile nations of the world]?" Rabbi Joshua replied, "How great is the shepherd who protects it."

10. Gentiles, too, have celebrated the incomparable marvel of Jewish survival. Jean-Jacques Rousseau notably said, "it is an astonishing and unique spectacle to see an expatriated people . . . scorned by all nations, nonetheless preserving its characteristics." See Rousseau's unpublished manuscript in Poliakiv, *The History of Anti-Semitism,* vol. 3, 105.

11. See his treatments of the Barcelona and Paris debates in Baer, *A History of the Jews in Christian Spain,* and Baer, *Studies in the History of the Jewish People,* vol. 2, 128–143.

12. These are two of the many criticisms unleashed by Fleischer, who effectively led the assault on Yuval with his response article, "Christian-Jewish Relations in the Middle Ages Distorted."

13. An example of this is Daniel Boyarin's startling preface to *Border Lines*—a book in which he proposes a rather controversial account of the process whereby Judaism and Christianity emerged with distinctive religious identities in late antiquity. He begins, "As long as I can remember I have been in love with some manifestations of Christianity. . . . Tennessee Ernie Ford singing on television the hymn 'The Garden' moved me to tears when I was a child. . . . later on it was medieval Christian art and architecture, the cathedrals of Europe, the spirituality of Meister Eckhart and

Jacob Böhme." Later, he considers the implications of this affection and its connection to his scholarship: "Implicitly through this scholarship and explicitly right here, I suggest that the affiliation between what we call Judaism and what we call Christianity is much more complex than most scholars, let alone most layfolk, imagine and that that complexity has work to do in the world." Boyarin, *Border Lines,* ix–xi.

14. The group known as the New Historians is a striking example of this. This group argued for a historical reevaluation of the events that led up to the establishment of the state of Israel and the Israeli victory in the 1948 War of Independence. They argued for a reversal of the Zionist understanding of this period, claiming that the British had been instrumental supporters of the Jewish state, that the Palestinian refugees had not fled their homes but had been evicted from them and chased away, that the arms and resources of the fledgling Jewish state outnumbered those of the Arab states, and finally that it was primarily the decisions of the Israeli government that prevented the early establishment of an Israeli-Arab peace settlement. Some examples of the work of the New Historians include Morris, *Righteous Victims* and *The Birth of the Palestinian Refugee Problem Revisited.* See also Pappé, *The Making of the Arab-Israeli Conflict.* For reactions to the New Historians, see Karsh, "Rewriting Israel's History" and "Benny Morris and the Reign of Error." For a more general reflection on the New Historians, see Myers and Ruderman, *The Jewish Past Revisited.*

15. Horowitz, *Reckless Rites.*

16. It is worth noting that, despite the author's anticipation that his book would spark considerable opposition—unlike the books of the New Historians—it has not, and it has generally been well received and favorably reviewed. Horowitz has succeeded in conveying his audacity without being unnecessarily provocative.

17. Horowitz's fear that his use of an extremely wide variety of subjects and areas of expertise might undermine the validity of his claims and elicit the displeasure of his colleagues motivated him to invoke the great (though controversial) French historian Renan, who offered his readers the option of adding the word "perhaps" wherever they saw fit. Horowitz, *Reckless Rites,* 19–20.

18. Ibid., 23.

19. Ibid., 144–145.

20. Ibid.

21. Ibid., 315.

22. Ibid., 10.

3. Theological Disarmament

1. My distinction here echoes Michael Rosenak's distinction between explicit and implicit religion. According to Rosenak, "Explicit religion concerns itself with what we believe and practice as loyal adherents of a specific faith, as members of a believing community; it sets down norms that prevail in our fellowship, norms that are incumbent on those we call religious. Implicit religion deals with existential encounters, occasioned by looking within and up in an attitude of faith; it connotes reverence, openness and a search for meaning." *Commandments and Concerns,* 112–113. As Rosenak points out, these terms echo Martin Buber's distinction between "religion" and "religiosity," Paul Tillich's "cosmological" and "ontological" faith, and William James's "institutional" and "personal" religion.

2. Maimonides, *The Guide for the Perplexed,* chapter 65. In this edition, Friedlander translates the Arabic *alkol* as "word." The more recent Hebrew translation

by Michael Schwartz translates *alkol* as *kol,* meaning "voice." See Schwartz, *Moreh Nevuchim LeRabbi Moshe Ben Maimon,* 167n4.

3. Wittgenstein, *Tractatus Logico-Philosophicus.*

4. John D. Caputo discusses the play on "Babel" as "babble" in his *The Prayers and Tears of Jacques Derrida,* 91.

5. Derrida, "Des tours de Babel": "First in what tongue was the tower of Babel constructed and deconstructed? In a tongue within which the proper name of Babel could also, by confusion, be translated by 'confusion'" (166).

6. My liberal inclusion here of names that, with some justification, one might consider excluding from the cadre of those applicable to the biblical (monotheistic) God echoes the position that Rabbi Adin Steinsaltz articulated in a paper entitled "Peace without Conciliation." See also my "Benamozegh's Tone: A Response to Rabbi Adin Steinsaltz."

7. Derrida identifies the sin of Babel, the sin that provoked God to descend in confusion, as the desire "to make a name for themselves, to give themselves the name, to construct for and by themselves their own name" ("Des tours de Babel," 169).

8. Zabala, "A Religion without Theists or Atheists," 9.

9. This argument has been developed by Ranjit Chatterjee in his *Wittgenstein and Judaism.* See also Caputo, *Prayers and Tears,* 263–280.

10. I am using the term *advanced introduction* in conversation with the subtitle of Buber's *On Judaism,* where the notion of an "introduction to an essence" connotes a new beginning that is clearly not designed for truly uninitiated beginners to appreciate.

11. The formulation is Gide's, but it rests on the Schopenhauerian notion that one faces mortality at a point of departure since "every parting gives a foretaste of death." In our context, my quote hints at the correlation that Gianni Vattimo establishes between religion (Christianity) without metaphysics and Nietzsche's death of God. In Rorty's formulation: "The incarnation was an act of *kenosis,* the act in which God turned everything over to human beings. This enables Vattimo to make his most startling and important claim: that secularization . . . is the constitutive trait of authentic religious experience." Rorty, "Anticlericalism and Atheism," 35.

4. Deconstruction and the Prophetic Voice

1. This is the classical formulation of the relationship between revelation and rabbinic law as portrayed in Mishnah Avot 1:1: "Moses received the Torah from Sinai and passed it on to Joshua who passed it on to the elders, the elders to the prophets and the prophets handed it down to the men of the Great Assembly."

2. Following the flood, the rainbow was a symbol of the peaceful covenant between God and humanity (Genesis 9:12–17). The rainbow in the cloud also represents the image of God himself, as in Ezekiel 1:28: "as the appearance of the bow that is in the cloud in the day of rain . . . this was the appearance of the likeness of the glory of the Lord."

3. The possibility that postmodernism might inform an ethic of peace was raised by Jeffrey Perl in his essay "Postmodern Disarmament," 326–347.

4. Kearney, *The God Who May Be,* 2.

5. Ibid.

6. This description of the prophet's fearlessness is an interesting echo of Maimonides: "The prophets must have these two forces, courage and intuition, highly

developed, and these were still more strengthened . . . under the influence of the Active Intellect. . . . In the same manner you discover that all prophets possessed great courage." Maimonides, *The Guide for the Perplexed,* chapter 38, 229.

7. See Monk, *Ludwig Wittgenstein.*

8. See Chatterjee, *Wittgenstein and Judaism,* 104–107.

9. Wittgenstein, *Culture and Value,* 9e. See also Chatterjee, *Wittgenstein and Judaism,* 104.

10. Quoted in Chatterjee, *Wittgenstein and Judaism,* 104.

11. Wittgenstein, *Tractatus Logico-Philosophicus.*

12. Wittgenstein, *Philosophical Investigations,* 255.

13. See Chatterjee, *Wittgenstein and Judaism,* 43–52. Wittgenstein's disturbing habit of recommending Weininger's anti-Semitic and misogynistic book *Sex and Character* to his friends is generally understood as an expression of his distaste for his Jewish ancestry.

14. Quoted in Chatterjee, *Wittgenstein and Judaism,* 69.

15. Ibid., 6.

16. Ibid.

17. In a chapter called "Confessions," Monk describes how Wittgenstein almost tortured his friends and family by insisting they hear his confessions. He traces the records of these confessions in the notes and letters left behind by Engelmann, Rowland Hutt, Fania Pascal, Maurice Drury, G. E. Moore, and Francis Skinner. The list of sins included an act of cowardice at war, an act of deceit, an act of violence against a child. Among his sins, Monk describes Pascal's report of Wittgenstein "allowing most people who knew him to believe that he was three-quarters Aryan and one-quarter Jewish, whereas, in fact, the reverse was the case." Monk makes light of this confession, since Wittgenstein did not tell Pascal that not one of his three "Jewish" grandparents was actually a practicing Jew. Monk, *Ludwig Wittgenstein,* 369. Chatterjee (*Wittgenstein and Judaism,* 90–92) reads the significance of this element in Wittgenstein's confessions differently, arguing that his concealed Jewishness is crucial to Wittgenstein's sense of guilt. He is in a trap. Unable to reveal what his work conceals, he only hints at it. Wittgenstein is thus tormented by the price in deceit that he pays for concealment.

18. Monk, *Ludwig Wittgenstein,* 366.

19. Heschel, *The Prophets,* xxi.

20. Ibid., 3.

21. Heschel, "No Religion Is an Island," 8.

22. Buber, *I and Thou.*

23. Rorty, *The Linguistic Turn.*

24. Rorty, *Philosophy and the Mirror of Nature,* 3.

25. Ibid., 4–5.

26. Similarly, in "Anticlericalism and Atheism," Rorty uses military imagery to make his point: "The battle between religion and science conducted in the eighteenth and nineteenth centuries was a contest between institutions, both of which claimed cultural supremacy." In Zabala, *The Future of Religion,* 39.

27. Rorty, *Philosophy and the Mirror of Nature,* 4.

28. Zabala, *The Future of Religion.*

29. See Caputo, *Prayers and Tears,* 117–160.

30. Zabala, "A Religion without Theists or Atheists," 14.

31. Ibid., 13.

32. Wittgenstein, *Tractatus Logico-Philosophicus,* 6.53.

33. Rorty, "Anticlericalism and Atheism," 33.

34. Caputo, *Prayers and Tears,* 288.

35. Derrida, "Circumfession," 154.

36. I thank Benjamin Sommer, who assisted me in the translation of this complex phrase. The use of YHWH underlines the idea that this is a personal name and not a title. The use of this name emphasizes the personality of the Jewish God as the true God, in contrast to Baal, Marduk, or any other. This translation is taken from T. Muraoka. See Joüon-Marouka, *A Grammar of Biblical Hebrew* (Rome: Pontificum Institutum Biblicum, 1991), section 154j.

37. Caputo, *Prayers and Tears,* 42–44.

5. Messianic Peace

1. The tank developed and used by the IDF is called the Merkava. The Hebrew word literally means "chariot," while the term also connotes the mystical vision of Ezekiel 1. The same term is used to denote the mystical experience of beholding God's truth that Maimonides called "metaphysics" in his introduction to *The Guide for the Perplexed.*

2. This is the Egyptian name given to Joseph by Pharaoh in Genesis 41:45. The literal meaning of the name is "the breaker of codes" or "the interpreter of hidden messages."

3. The way in which repeated cycles of liturgical time bring about ritual reenactments of the biblical narrative was identified by Yosef Haim Yerushalmi as one of the features of Jewish "memory." His example is Joseph's release from prison, but the point is still the same. Yerushalmi writes, "We must realize that the very incorporation of those ritualized public readings had also endowed the . . . past with the inevitably cyclical quality of liturgical time. True, Joseph had lived many years ago, but in the fixed rhythm of the synagogal recital, he is in prison this week, next week he will be released, next year in the very same season both events will be narrated once more, and so again in every year to come." Yerushalmi, *Zakhor,* 41–42.

4. See Ashkenazi (Manitou), *Hesped LaMashiach,* 48.

5. Ezekiel says, "My servant David shall be prince over them." In this, he might be implying a victory of Judah. But it is not the rule of Judah that the messianic David of the future promises, but the rejection of idolatry and the rule of God. Hence, the verse continues, "and there shall be one shepherd for them all; they shall live by my statutes and carefully observe my decrees."

6. Ashkenazi (Manitou) speaks of there being a messiah and a king for each tribe, that are somehow united and brought together when the miracle of redemption unfolds in God's ultimate plan for Israel. I propose that it might be helpful if this notion could be expanded beyond the internal varieties of the Jewish world to include the monotheistic prophecies and messianisms of Jesus and Muhammad, since they, too, must find their place in the ultimate reconciliation that constitutes the miraculous peace of Jerusalem.

7. Vattimo, "Dialectics, Difference, and Weak Thought."

8. See Geller, *Sacred Enigmas.*

9. See Richard Kearney's analysis of God's enigmatic answer to Moses, "I am Who may be," in *The God Who May Be*, 20–38.

10. See Sommer, "Revelation at Sinai."

11. Ibid., 423.

12. Ibid., 427.

13. Ibid.

14. Ibid., 432.

15. As Sommer shows (ibid., 436), this position is significantly echoed in the Mekhilta of Rabbi Yishmael and in the commentary of the Rashbam.

16. The idea that only the first two commandments were delivered directly by God is common. It is reinforced by the frequently cited switch from the first-person "*I am* the Lord" and "Thou shalt have no other gods before *me*" to the third-person "Thou shalt not take the name of *the Lord* thy God in vain." This theme is echoed in Shir Hashirim Rabba and in the commentary of the Bekhor Shor.

17. The reference is to Maimonides, who denies the possibility of hearing articulate divine speech.

18. Sommer, "Revelation at Sinai," 439.

19. Yehuda Gellman has criticized Sommer's reading of the Ropshitzer, claiming that Sommer's rendition of the *aleph* as a "guttural stop" is different from the Ropshitzer's intention in Zera Kodesh in which he implied that the *aleph* was supplemented by the vowel *kamatz*, giving the divine utterance an intelligible sound. All the same, this does not affect the claim that the epiphany, according to the Ropshitzer, was wordless, as in 1 Kings 19. See Gellman, "Welhausen and the Hasidim" and "Conservative Judaism and Biblical Criticism."

20. Sommer, "Revelation at Sinai." See also Gellman, "Conservative Judaism and Biblical Criticism," 442; Sommer, "Unity and Plurality in Jewish Canons."

21. Sommer, "Revelation at Sinai," n. 50. See, for example, Job 4:16 and Knohl, *The Sanctuary of Silence*. In his book, Knohl distinguishes between the holiness school and the priestly Torah, arguing that the ritual of the sanctuary as described by the priestly Torah is one devoid of articulation and revelation of God's name and involves a sublimation of the silent God. For a similar reading of the mystery of God's will as ensconced in the ineffability of his name, see the commentary of Ibn Ezra on Exodus 3:15. See also Sommer, "Unity and Plurality in Jewish Canons."

22. As Sommer shows, this is a position echoed by Heschel, Buber, Hasidic writers such as the Besht, and multiple rabbinic texts that develop the theme of there being a primordial heavenly Torah that preceded creation and was never revealed to humanity. Sommer, "Revelation at Sinai," 446–447.

23. Ibid.

24. See Heschel, *Torah Min Hashamayim*, in particular chapters 2, 14, 17–20, 30–32, and 34.

25. Dillard, *The Writing Life*, 46.

26. Hegel, "Addition G," 307.

27. Agamben, *Homo Sacer*, 133.

28. Ibid., 114.

29. The centrality of this paradoxical mystical structure to the writings of Rav Kook is the thesis of Avinoam Rosenak's *Prophetic Halakha*.

30. Williams, *Silence and Honey Cakes*, 70.

6. The Rabbinic Voice

1. The Mishnah and Talmud in Sanhedrin marginalized and ultimately did away with the biblical injunction that a rebellious child must be brought to judgment by his parents and stoned at the city gates. That this radical rabbinic interpretation is evidence of the importance of ethics to rabbinic readings of "troublesome" biblical texts has been explicated in detail by Moshe Halbertal in *Interpretive Revolutions in the Making*, 42–67.

2. The Talmud here is referring to the passage in Deuteronomy 22:6: "If a bird's nest shall chance to be before thee in the way on any tree, or on the ground, whether with young ones, or eggs, and the mother sitting upon the young, or upon the eggs, thou shalt not take the mother with the young."

3. Pelikan, *The Vindication of Tradition*, 60.

4. There can be little doubt that the dovish left seems as pugnacious to the chief rabbi of Safed as he does to them. Peace must be built upon a philosophy that allows them both to "contain" both ends of this spectrum. Finally, peace between Jews and Muslims will require an even greater breadth of acceptance.

5. This economic phrase sums up quite concisely the essentialist or positivist project of interpreting revelation to determine the law. The phraseology is Julia Kristeva's who uses it in "Rethinking Normative Conscience," 221.

6. Pelikan, *The Vindication of Tradition*, 46 (my emphases).

7. Ratzinger, "Homily Pro Eligando Romano Pontifice," 451–455.

8. Sagi, *The Open Canon*, 1.

9. It seems that the struggle against idolatry is something of an exception to the rules of biblical and rabbinic justice. The pursuit of idolaters is atypically uncompromising and, as the following passage suggests, judges are given extraordinary punitive power.

10. Indeed, this theme is established in Deuteronomy 18:20, in which Moses warns against the prophet who dares to speak presumptuously in God's name: "that same prophet shall die." This theme is taken up quite famously by Maimonides, who insists on the exclusion of prophets from the halakhic process and on scholarly learning as a prerequisite to the attainment of prophetic revelation.

11. Sagi, *The Open Canon*, 1.

12. I will add at this point that the scholarship I am analyzing in this section was written with the express purpose of gaining academic insight into the literature of the rabbis. This is achieved through the use of contemporary interpretive prisms that have ideological implications. Despite this, it is important to note that neither of the authors whose work I discuss wrote with ideological intentions.

13. Fisch, *Rational Rabbis*, 61.

14. Ibid., 38.

15. Ibid., 51.

16. Ibid., 84.

17. The reference here is to the much-cited passage usually referred to as "Akhnai's oven," which appears in Talmud Baba Metzia 59b.

18. Fisch, *Rational Rabbis*, 188.

19. See Sagi's account of "The Halakha Follows Bet Hillel: The Harmonic Version," in Sagi, *The Open Canon*, 116.

20. Ibid., 210.

21. Since "fundamentalism" is a loaded term that is not appropriately applied to every nonliberal understanding of religion, I should add a brief qualification of my use of it here. I am employing this term as Mordechai Rotenberg uses it, for example, in *Re-biographing and Deviance*. For Rotenberg, "fundamentalism" refers to a theological or religious orientation in which the content and meaning of divine revelation is believed to have originated at a specific point in linear time and whose meaning is thereafter presumed to be self-evident. The fundamentalist is therefore in a position to claim his single view of a text's meaning as the only truthful one.

22. My reading of *The Open Canon*'s broader implications aligns its purpose with the programmatic approach to contemporary Jewish thought expressed by Sagi's colleague David Hartman, who wrote in his foreword to *The Jewish Political Tradition*: "The rebirth of Israel provides the Jewish people with a public arena where they themselves must take charge, *drawing on the strength of their tradition to give a direction to political life* and a content to popular aspiration" (vol. 1, xiv; my emphasis). My purpose is to test the limits of this worthy project. I recognize, however, as I mentioned above, that Sagi's interests in this study were primarily historical.

23. Sagi, *The Open Canon*, 88.

24. See Talmud Baba Metzia 59b. In order to support his point of view, Rabbi Eliezer resorts to the performance of miracles. In the first of these miracles, a carob tree is uprooted. This represents a threat to life since elsewhere in Talmudic lore (Talmud Shabbat 33b) the carob is a symbol of food and sustenance. In the second miracle, water flows upstream, diverting the most crucial resource for agriculture and civilization. In the third (though Rabbi Yehoshua prevents lethal damage from occurring), the walls of the study house are brought down on the scholars within.

25. The phrase *lo kiblu heymano* (they did not accept from him) clearly suggests that it was the man who was being rejected and not the substance of his arguments.

26. Mill, *On Liberty and Other Essays,* chapter 1.

27. God's acceptance of this defeat is conventionally taken as an expression of his approval of Rabbi Yehoshua's position. I propose an alternative reading on the grounds that the need for God's approval undermines the whole point of the story. Ultimately, Rabbi Yehoshua's claim that the law can be wielded without divine intervention is enough to allow the story to end with his emphatic statement that the law is not in heaven.

28. "Merkavah" refers to the esoteric teachings concerning images of God's celestial presence, emblematically described in Ezekiel 1.

29. This translation is from Abraham Joshua Heschel's *Torah Min Hashamayim Beaspaklaria Shel Hadorot,* which appears almost in its entirety in translation as *Heavenly Torah as Refracted through the Generations,* 281.

30. Theories of revelation are, I think, crucial to any understanding of rabbinic interpretation. In his critique of the monist view of halakha, Sagi says: "Monism is presumably forced to assume a maximalist theory of revelation whereby the Torah given at Sinai includes, at least implicitly, the entire range of rulings appropriate to every situation. This theory of revelation appears to be the basic assumption of views supporting unconditioned objectivity ... since all assume that, in every state of affairs only one halakhic decision is unconditionally right—the decision resting on revelation." Sagi, *The Open Canon*, 60. I am continuing the thrust of this critique by applying

it to the explicit theory of metaphysical truth that even the most pluralistic halakhic attitudes share with fundamentalism.

31. Heschel, *God in Search of Man,* 336.

32. Talmud Eruvin 13b.

33. Caputo, *Prayers and Tears,* 220.

34. Talmud Eruvin 13b.

35. This translation is taken from Walzer et al., *The Jewish Political Tradition,* vol. 1, 258.

36. This prayer, attributed to Rabbi Elazar Hakalir (sixth–seventh centuries), was recited in medieval Ashkenazi Jewish communities on the Sabbath of Parah, which falls immediately after the festival of Purim. On this Sabbath, the passage from Numbers 19 dealing with the laws of the red heifer is read in the synagogue service.

37. Judah Loew b. Bezalel, *Derekh Hayyim* (Jerusalem: Ryzman, 1971), 258–259 [Hebrew], as translated by Sagi in *The Open Canon,* 115.

38. Sagi, *The Open Canon,* 124.

39. For examples of rabbinic proclamations about the prophetic status of scholarship, see the rabbinic sources collected in the section "Beyond Prophecy" in Walzer et al., *The Jewish Political Tradition,* vol. 1, 257–263.

40. The most striking example of this appears in Talmud Gittin 56a–b. In this passage, the founder of the Yavne School—Rabbi Yochanan ben Zakkai—is caught in the Roman siege of Jerusalem. He makes a remarkable decision to give up on Jerusalem and make peace with the Romans. Symbolically, he exits the city in a coffin, suggesting that there is no living future for the Judaism of the Temple, and he offers the life of legal study and prayer as its replacement. The Judaism of the Temple metaphorically dies in this act and a new Judaism is born outside the city walls. When Rabbi Yochanan reaches the Roman camp, he greets General Vespasian as if he were Caesar. For this impertinence, Vespasian tells him he must forfeit his life. Rabbi Yochanan responds by insisting that Vespasian *must* be Caesar since only an emperor could conquer Jerusalem. As Vespasian pronounces Rabbi Yochanan's death sentence, a messenger arrives proclaiming the death of Caesar in Rome and announcing Vespasian's ascent to the throne. The significance of this passage to our discussion lies in the hermeneutic or midrashic technique with which Rabbi Yochanan "divined" the future from an allegorical cross-referencing of biblical passages. His rabbinic reading is portrayed as prophetic. By confounding the semantic independence and coherence of three distinct and separate biblical passages, Rabbi Yochanan gains prophetic insight into political circumstances. At this juncture, the new Caesar grants Ben Zakkai a request. Instead of asking to save Jerusalem, Rabbi Yochanan asks the Roman's permission to found the academy of Yavne. This symbolic moment is arguably one of the rabbinic project's most significant foundational myths.

41. Though a full answer to these questions will be the subject of the remainder of this discussion, the story of Rabbi Yochanan and Vespasian already implies my position. Rabbi Yochanan makes peace by considering the inconceivable. This is true both in terms of his abandonment of Jerusalem and the Temple and also in his willingness to do business with Rome.

42. Heschel, *God in Search of Man,* 44.

43. Dilthey, *Pattern and Meaning in History,* 85–86. See also Dilthey, *Hermeneutics and the Study of History* and *Introduction to the Human Sciences.*

44. This is a paraphrase of Santiago Zabala's phraseology in *The Future of Religion,* 43.

45. Ibid., 4.

46. Heschel, *Heavenly Torah,* 710.

47. Talmud Hagiga 3b.

48. Gadamer, *Truth and Method,* 355.

49. I do not intend to discuss this concept in full but rather will focus on one single analysis that illustrates the connections between *ha'arama,* humility, and the spirit of the law. For fuller discussions of *ha'arama,* see Desberg, "*Ha'arama* b'dinei torah uvetakanot chazal"; Shiloh, "*Ha'arama* B'Talmud"; Hayes, "Authority and Anxiety."

50. Here, *ha'arama* is necessary to bypass the requirement to purchase a *lulav* on the festival of Succot.

51. *Shmita* is the seventh fallow year in which all financial loans are automatically annulled by biblical injunction (Numbers 25).

52. Zilberg, *Kach Darko,* esp. 26–44.

53. Ibid., 1.

54. This formulation echoes Derrida's notion of religion without Religion or messianism without Messianism, suggesting the idea that specific concepts can exist without belonging to any general or universal categories. For a fuller discussion of this, see Caputo, *Prayers and Tears,* 117–160.

55. Zilberg, *Kach Darko,* 40. See n. 60 where Zilberg suggests that the notion of *ha'arama* might account for the rabbinic statement "every ordinance of the rabbis is like a law from the Torah."

56. Derrida's reading closely follows Kierkegaard's. See Kierkegaard, *Fear and Trembling, and Repetition.* Despite the many overlaps between them, in the discussion that follows, I will focus my attention on Derrida without further acknowledgment of Kierkegaard.

57. Derrida, *Gift of Death,* 56.

58. Ibid.

59. Ibid., 57.

60. Ibid., 58.

61. Caputo, *Prayers and Tears,* 189.

62. Derrida, *Gift of Death,* 67.

63. Caputo, *Prayers and Tears,* 188.

64. Ibid., 218–219.

65. Heschel, *A Passion for Truth,* 322.

66. See, for example, Yosef, "Mesirat Shetachim Me'eretz Yisrael Bimkom Pikuach Nefesh."

67. Kook, *Olat ha-Rayah,* 331, cited and translated in Sagi, *The Open Canon,* 121.

68. Ibid.

69. "Now Korach," in *The Zohar,* vol. 18, 225–226.

70. It is pertinent to mention here the halakhic category of *avera lishma.* The Talmud suggests in a number of places (e.g., Nazir 23a–b and Berachot 61a) that certain transgressions are necessary for preserving the law. These are categorized as transgressions that are performed in "its name"—in the name of God or in the name of the law. The examples discussed in the Talmud include sexual intercourse between

King Ahasuerus and Queen Esther and also the incestuous rape of Lot by his daughters. In both cases, the law is not so much the issue as survival. The Talmudic discussion in Nazir 23b reaches the somewhat conservative conclusion that such transgressions are accepted in the hope that they will lead to more pious behavior. However, later rabbinic texts toy with the idea that certain transgressions are of spiritual and religious importance in their own right since religious expressions sometimes require transcending the legal boundaries of the halakha. See, for example, the stories of the three confessors in the twelfth-century text *Sefer Hasidim*. In these stories, confessors come to a wise man to describe sins that they have performed, claiming that they only transgressed in order to bring themselves close to temptation so as ultimately to overcome it and repent. But, in order to get there, they needed first to sin. Judah ben Samuel, *Sefer Hasidim*, sections 52–53. Though the confessors are censured for their conduct in this story, later Hasidic writers, such as Rabbi Tsadok Hakohen of Lublin, maintain paradoxically that the annulment of the Torah is also its foundation since God's will is served when the law is transgressed in his name.

71. For a fascinating collection of rabbinic stories that fall into this self-deprecating category, see Kosman, *Men's Tractate*. Kosman's primary concern in this book is the reappraisal of Daniel Boyarin's claim that rabbinic heroes are essentially effeminate and passive. Kosman's close readings of a broad selection of rabbinic texts are designed to support the claim that the rabbis are active, "masculine" manipulators of power. The overwhelming impression that I received when reading this collection is that the stories that Kosman rallies to support his case expose the ugly, manipulative, and violent side of rabbinic conduct as much (if not more than) the supposed masculinity of the rabbis. Arguably, stories that describe the ugly conduct of many great rabbinic legislators and sages have the primary effect of calling into question the moral fabric of the rabbinic elite. The effect of this is decidedly unheroic—and hence disarmingly modest. See also Boyarin, *Unheroic Conduct*.

72. Two striking examples of this stand out: the Maimonidean code (Mishneh Torah) and the Shulchan Arukh. Though Maimonides' express intention was to replace the multivocalism of the Talmud with the clarity of his code, printed editions of the Mishneh Torah are now swaddled in layers of commentary. Joseph Karo's Shulchan Arukh suffered a similar fate. This monumental halakhic codex, designed by its author for an international audience and made accessible by the invention of the printing press, never even went to print before the Ashkenazic adaptations of Rabbi Moses Isserles were added. Like the Maimonidean code, today's printed editions of the Shulchan Arukh (and indeed all subsequent attempts at codification) are layered with questioning commentary. Despite this, it should be noted that these books are understood by many as definitive and authoritative statements on the obligations of Jewish law.

73. See Scholem, *Major Trends in Jewish Mysticism*, 158.

7. A Prayer for Peace

1. "One who says *modim, modim* [we give thanks, we give thanks], we silence him . . . because it appears as if he was thanking two deities one after the other" (Talmud Berachot 33b). While the most likely understanding of this Talmudic passage does not actually forbid repeating the prayer in the way that had become my habit, the similarity made me feel very uncomfortable.

2. This form of prayer, called "meditative ascension," is an ancient Jewish practice described, for example, by Gershom Scholem in his *Origins of the Kabbalah,* 209, 243–248, and esp. 299–308 and 412–420.

3. *Franny and Zooey* originally appeared in the form of two short stories in the *New Yorker.* "Franny" appeared in January 1955 and "Zooey" in May 1957.

4. Seymour was born in 1917. He features in several of Salinger's short stories, most famously in "A Perfect Day for Bananafish," originally published in the *New Yorker,* January 31, 1948.

5. This taste of Seymour's is one of the themes in Salinger's last published Glass family story, "Hapworth 16, 1924." Here, Salinger finally reveals that the source of Seymour Glass's genius was at least in part his ability to "glimpse" the knowledge and wisdom accumulated in his previous "appearances" on this earth. This Buddhist theme, along with the many other references to Zen, Christianity, Hinduism, "the Greeks," and even a little Judaism that recur in Salinger's stories about the Glass family, contributes to the religiously hypersensitive aroma that—at least for me— makes Salinger's writing so appealing.

6. See Fedotov, *The Way of a Pilgrim.*

7. Heschel, *Man's Quest for God,* 5.

8. Ibid., 26.

9. John Sergieff of Cronstadt, "Prayer: The Spirit of Prayer," 351–352.

8. Peace Education

1. This is an argument that I have made elsewhere with reference to historical scholarship. See Isaacs, "The Role of the Historian in Jewish Education," 247–255.

2. A striking example of this is the Department of Jewish Thought at the Hebrew University, which in December 2008 conducted a heated internal debate about its symbolic purpose and about the ideological implications of the university's decision to relocate the department in a school of general religion. An unpublished report of this discussion was edited by Avinoam Rosenak: "Jewish Philosophy and the Future of Jewish Studies."

3. Kook, *Olat ha-Rayah,* 331.

4. The unity of opposites is found in the writings of many religious thinkers, including the Zohar, the Maharal of Prague, Nachman of Breslov, and the Catholic philosopher Charles Taylor—who all appear in the section "The Rabbinic Voice." It is also the subject of several papers by Avinoam Rosenak, who has studied the centrality of this principle in the work of Rav Kook and considered its implications for peace. See Rosenak, *Prophetic Halakha,* 44–56; David and Rosenak, "Judaism and Peace." See also Rosenak, "Prophecy and *Halakhah*" and "Hidden Diaries and New Discoveries."

5. While explicit Jewish mysticism has not been my subject, this linguistic feature is clearly one of the central characteristics of the Jewish esoteric canon. See, for example, Idel, *Language, Torah, and Hermeneutics,* 1–28.

6. See the sources in n. 4 above.

BIBLIOGRAPHY

Agamben, Giorgio. *Homo Sacer: Sovereign Power and Bare Life.* Translated by Daniel Heller Roazen. Palo Alto, Calif.: Stanford University Press, 1998.

Ashkenazi (Manitou), Rabbi Yehuda Leon. *Hesped LaMashiach* [Eulogy for the Messiah]. Efrat: Manitou Institute, 2006 [Hebrew].

Baer, I. *A History of the Jews in Christian Spain.* Philadelphia: Jewish Publication Society, 1961–1966.

———. *Studies in the History of the Jewish People,* vol. 2: *The Jewish People in the Middle Ages.* Jerusalem: Historical Society of Israel, 1985.

Ben Samuel, Judah. *Sefer Hasidim.* Translated by Jehuda Wistinetzki. Frankfurt am Main: M'kize Nirdamim, 1924 [Hebrew].

Beteille, A. *Some Observations on the Comparative Method.* Amsterdam: Centre for Asian Studies, 1990.

Bonfil, Robert. *As by a Mirror: Jewish Life in Renaissance Italy.* Jerusalem: Zalman Shazar Center for Jewish History, 1994 [Hebrew].

Bouwsma, Oets. *Wittgenstein: Conversations 1949–1951.* Edited by J. L. Craft and Ronald Hustwit. Indianapolis, Ind.: Hackett, 1986.

Boyarin, Daniel. *Border Lines: The Partition of Judaeo-Christianity.* Philadelphia: University of Pennsylvania Press, 2004.

———. *Unheroic Conduct.* Berkeley: University of California Press, 1997.

Buber, Martin. *I and Thou.* Translated by Walter Kaufman. New York: Touchstone, 1970.

———. "Jewish Religiosity." In his *On Judaism: An Introduction to the Essence of Judaism by One of the Most Important Religious Thinkers of the Twentieth Century.* Edited by Nahum N Glazer. Tel Aviv: Schocken, 1996 [1967].

Burke, Peter. *History and Social Theory.* Ithaca, N.Y.: Cornell University Press, 1992.

Bynum, Caroline Walker, et al. "Conference Working Group Recommendations." *Common Knowledge* 12:1 (Winter 2006): 13–15.

Caputo, John D. *The Prayers and Tears of Jacques Derrida: Religion without Religion.* Bloomington: Indiana University Press, 1997.

Chatterjee, Ranjit. *Wittgenstein and Judaism: A Triumph of Concealment.* New York: Peter Lang, 2005.

Cohen, Jeremy. *The Friars and the Jews: The Evolution of Medieval Anti-Judaism.* Ithaca, N.Y.: Cornell University Press, 1982.

———. *Living Letters of the Law: Ideas of the Jew in Medieval Christianity.* Berkeley: University of California Press, 1999.

David, Joseph E., and Avinoam Rosenak. "Judaism and Peace: Between Responsibility and Identity." In *The Role of Religious and Philosophical Traditions in Promoting World Peace: An Asian Perspective,* edited by Imtiyaz Yusuf. Singapore: Select Books, 2007.

Derrida, Jacques. "Circumfession: Fifty-Nine Periods and Periphrases." In *Jacques Derrida,* edited by Geoffry Benington and Jacques Derrida. Chicago: University of Chicago Press, 1993.

———. "Des tours de Babel." In *Difference in Translation,* edited and translated by Joseph P. Graham, 165–248. Ithaca, N.Y.: Cornell University Press, 1987.

———. *The Gift of Death.* Translated by David Willis. Chicago: University of Chicago Press, 1992.

———. "*Sauf Le Nom* (Post-Scriptum)." In *On the Name,* edited by Thomas Dutoit. Translated by John Leavey Jr. Palo Alto, Calif.: Stanford University Press, 1995.

Desberg, Uri. "*Ha'arama* b'dinei torah uvetakanot chazal" [Legal Fiction in Torah and Rabbinic Law]. *Shana beShana* (1992): 215–218 [Hebrew].

Dillard, Annie. *The Writing Life.* New York: Harper Perennial, 1989.

Dilthey, W. *Hermeneutics and the Study of History.* Princeton, N.J.: Princeton University Press, 1996 [1949].

———. *Introduction to the Human Sciences: An Attempt to Lay a Foundation for the Study of Society and History.* Detroit, Mich.: Wayne State University Press, 1988 [1942].

———. *Pattern and Meaning in History: W. Dilthey's Thoughts on History and Society.* London: HarperTorch, 1961.

Durkheim, Emile. *Suicide.* New York: Free Press, 1951 [1895].

"Ecclesia and Synagoga in the Initial T." Bibliothèque Nationale, Paris, Cod. Th.26.

Fedotov, G. P., ed. *The Way of a Pilgrim and Other Classics of Russian Spirituality.* Mineola, N.Y.: Dover, 2003.

Fisch, Menachem. *Rational Rabbis: Science and Talmudic Culture.* Bloomington: Indiana University Press, 1997.

Fleischer, Ezra. "Christian-Jewish Relations in the Middle Ages Distorted." *Zion* 59:2–3 (1994): 267–316 [Hebrew].

Foucault, Michel. *The Archaeology of Knowledge and the Discourse on Language.* Translated by A. M. Sheridan-Smith. New York: Pantheon, 1972.

Gadamer, H. G. *Truth and Method.* Translated by Joel Weinsheimer and Donald G. Marshall. London: Continuum, 1975.

Geertz, Clifford. *The Interpretation of Cultures.* New York: Basic, 1973.

———. *Local Knowledge: Further Essays in Interpretive Anthropology.* New York: Basic, 1983.

Geller, Stephen A. *Sacred Enigmas: Literary Religion in the Hebrew Bible.* London: Routledge, 1996.

Gellman, Yehuda. "Conservative Judaism and Biblical Criticism." *Conservative Judaism* 59:2 (2007).

————. "Welhausen and the Hasidim." *Modern Judaism* 26 (2006): 193–207.

Goodman, Walther. "*Anti-Politics* by George Konrad." *New York Times,* May 17, 1984.

Halbertal, Moshe. *Interpretive Revolutions in the Making: Values as Interpretive Considerations in Midrashe Halakha.* Jerusalem: Magnes, 1997 [Hebrew].

Hartman, David. Foreword to *The Jewish Political Tradition,* vol. 1, *Authority,* edited by Michael Walzer, Menachem Lorberbaum, and Noam Zohar. New Haven, Conn.: Yale University Press, 2000.

Hayes, C. "Authority and Anxiety in the Talmuds: From Legal Fiction to Legal Fact." In *Jewish Religious Leadership: Image and Reality,* edited by J. Wertheimer. New York: Jewish Theological Seminary, 2004.

Hegel, Georg Wilhelm. "Addition G." In *Outlines of the Philosophy of Right,* translated by T. M. Knox. Oxford: Oxford University Press, 2008 [1952].

Heschel, Abraham Joshua. *God in Search of Man: A Philosophy of Judaism.* New York: Farrar, Straus and Giroux, 1955.

————. *Man's Quest for God: Studies in Prayer and Symbolism.* Santa Fe, N.M.: Aurora, 1998.

————. "No Religion Is an Island." *Union Theological Seminary Quarterly Review* 21 (January 1966): 3–22.

————. "No Time for Neutrality." In his *Moral Grandeur and Spiritual Audacity.* New York: Farrar, Straus and Giroux, 1996 [1970].

————. *A Passion for Truth.* Philadelphia: Jewish Publication Society, 1973.

————. *The Prophets.* New York: HarperCollins Perennial, 2001 [1962].

————. *Torah Min Hashamayim Beaspaklaria Shel Hadorot* [Heavenly Torah as Refracted through the Generations]. Edited and translated by Gordon Tucker. London: Continuum, 2007.

————. "The Vocation of the Cantor." In his *The Insecurity of Freedom: Essays on Human Existence.* New York: Schocken, 1975.

Horowitz, Elliott. *Reckless Rites: Purim and the Legacy of Jewish Violence.* Princeton, N.J.: Princeton University Press, 2006.

Idel, Moshe. *Language, Torah, and Hermeneutics in Abraham Abulafia.* Translated by Menahem Kallus. New York: State University of New York Press, 1989.

Isaacs, Alick. "Benamozegh's Tone: A Response to Rabbi Adin Steinsaltz." *Common Knowledge* 11:1 (Winter 2005).

————. "Lebanon II." *Common Knowledge* 15:1 (Winter 2009): 96–152.

————. "The Role of the Historian in Jewish Education." In *Languages and Literatures in Jewish Education: Studies in Honor of Michael Rosenak,* edited by Jonathan Cohen, Elie Holzer, and Alick Isaacs. Jerusalem: Magnes, 2007.

James, William. *The Varieties of Religious Experience.* New York: Random House, 1902.

Karsh, Efraim. "Benny Morris and the Reign of Error." *Middle East Quarterly* 6:1 (1999).

———. "Rewriting Israel's History." *Middle East Quarterly* 3:2 (1996).

Katz, Stanley N. "Excellence Is by No Means Enough: Intellectual Philanthropy and the Just University." *Common Knowledge* 8:3 (Fall 2002): 427–438.

Kearney, Richard. *The God Who May Be: A Hermeneutics of Religion.* Bloomington: Indiana University Press, 2001.

Kierkegaard, Søren. *Fear and Trembling, and Repetition,* vol. 6 of *Kierkegaard's Writings.* Edited and translated by Howard V. Hong and Edna H. Hong. Princeton, N.J.: Princeton University Press, 1983.

Knohl, Israel. *The Sanctuary of Silence: The Priestly Torah and the Holiness School.* Minneapolis, Minn.: Fortress, 1995.

Konrad, George. *Anti-Politics: An Essay.* Translated by Richard E. Allen. New York: Quartet, 1984.

Kook, Abraham Isaac. "Eulogy in Jerusalem." In *Igrot Haraa'ya.* Jerusalem: Mossad Ha-Rav Kook, 1984 [Hebrew].

———. *Olat ha-Rayah.* Jerusalem: Mossad Ha-Rav Kook, 1963 [Hebrew].

Kosman, Admiel. *Men's Tractate: Rav and the Butcher and Other Stories on Manhood, Love and Authentic Life in Aggadic and Hasidic Stories.* Jerusalem: Keter, 2002 [Hebrew].

Kristeva, Julia. "Rethinking Normative Conscience: The Task of the Intellectual Today." *Common Knowledge* 13:2–3 (Spring–Fall 2007).

"Legal Fiction." *American Law Encyclopedia,* vol. 6. http://law.jrank.org/pages/8149/Legal-Fiction.html.

Maimonides, Moses. *The Guide for the Perplexed,* 2nd ed. Translated by M. Friedlander. Mineola, N.Y.: Dover, 2000 [1904].

Marcus, Ivan. *Rituals of Childhood: Jewish Acculturation in Medieval Europe.* New Haven, Conn.: Yale University Press, 1996.

Medding, Peter Y. Preface to *Jews and Violence: Images, Ideologies, Realities,* edited by Peter Y. Medding. Oxford: Oxford University Press, 2002.

Mill, John Stuart. *On Liberty and Other Essays.* New York: Oxford University Press, 1991 [1859].

Monk, Ray. *Ludwig Wittgenstein: The Duty of Genius.* New York: Penguin, 1990.

Morris, Benny. *The Birth of the Palestinian Refugee Problem Revisited.* Cambridge: University of Cambridge Press, 2004.

———. *Righteous Victims: A History of the Zionist-Arab Conflict 1881–2001.* New York: Vintage, 1999.

Myers, David N., and David B. Ruderman, eds. *The Jewish Past Revisited: Reflections on Modern Jewish Historians.* New Haven, Conn.: Yale University Press, 1998.

Pappé, Ilan. *The Making of the Arab-Israeli Conflict, 1947–1951.* London: Tauris, 1992.

Pelikan, Jaroslav. *The Vindication of Tradition: The 1983 Jefferson Lecture in the Humanities.* New Haven, Conn.: Yale University Press, 1984.

Perl, Jeffrey M. "Irenic Scholarship and Public Affairs: A Report on the Skidmore Conference." *Common Knowledge* 12:1 (Winter 2006): 1–12.

———. "Postmodern Disarmament." In *Weakening Philosophy*, edited by Santiago Zabala. Montreal: McGill-Queen's University Press, 2006.

Perl, Jeffrey M., and Alick Isaacs. "A Postscript on Method: Editorial Note." *Common Knowledge* 8:3 (Winter 2002): 147–151.

Poliakiv, Leon. *The History of Anti-Semitism*, vol. 3. Philadelphia: University of Pennsylvania Press, 2003.

Ratzinger, Joseph. "Homily Pro Eligando Romano Pontifice: Address to the College of Cardinals in the Vatican Basilica." Translated by the Holy See Press Office, reproduced in *Common Knowledge* 13:2–3 (Spring–Fall 2007): 451–455.

Rorty, Richard. "Anticlericalism and Atheism." In *The Future of Religion*, edited by Santiago Zabala. New York: Columbia University Press, 2005.

———. *The Linguistic Turn: Essays in Philosophical Method*. Chicago: University of Chicago Press, 1967.

———. *Philosophy and the Mirror of Nature*. Princeton, N.J.: Princeton University Press, 1979.

Rosenak, Avinoam. "Hidden Diaries and New Discoveries: The Life and Thought of Rabbi A. I. Kook." *Shofar: An Interdisciplinary Journal of Jewish Studies* 25:3 (Spring 2007): 111–147.

———. "Jewish Philosophy and the Future of Jewish Studies: A Debate about the Department of Jewish Thought in the Hebrew University." Unpublished report [Hebrew].

———. "Prophecy and *Halakhah*: Dialectics in Rabbi Kook's Meta-Halakhic Thought." *Jewish Law Annual* (forthcoming).

———. *Prophetic Halakha: The Philosophy of Halakha in the Teaching of Rav Kook*. Jerusalem: Magnes, 2007 [Hebrew].

Rosenak, Michael. *Commandments and Concerns: Jewish Religious Education in Secular Society*. Philadelphia: Jewish Publication Society, 1987.

Ross, Dennis. *The Missing Peace: The Inside Story of the Fight for Middle East Peace*. New York: Farrar, Straus and Giroux, 2004.

Rotenberg, Mordechai. *Re-biographing and Deviance: Psychotherapeutic Narrativism and the Midrash*. New York: Praeger, 1987.

Sagi, Avi. *The Open Canon: On the Meaning of Halakhic Discourse*. Translated by Batya Stein. London: Continuum, 2007.

Salinger, J. D. *Franny and Zooey*. New York: Bantam, 1961.

———. "Hapworth 16, 1924." *New Yorker*, June 19, 1965.

Scham, Paul, Walid Salem, and Benjamin Pogrund, eds. *Shared Histories: A Palestinian-Israeli Dialogue*. Jerusalem: Palestinian Center for the Dissemination of Democracy and Community Development, and Yakar Center for Social Concern, 2005.

Scholem, Gershom. *Major Trends in Jewish Mysticism*. New York: Schocken, 1974.

————. *Origins of the Kabbalah*. Edited by Zvi Werblowsky. Translated by A. Arkush. Philadelphia: Jewish Publication Society, 1986.

Schwartz, Michael. *Moreh Nevuchim LeRabbi Moshe Ben Maimon* [Maimonides' Guide for the Perplexed]. Tel Aviv: Tel Aviv University Press, 2002.

Sergieff of Cronstadt, John. "Prayer: The Spirit of Prayer." In *The Way of a Pilgrim and Other Classics of Russian Spirituality,* edited by G. P. Fedotov. Mineola, N.Y.: Dover, 2003.

Shea, William. "A Vote of Thanks to Voltaire." In *A Catholic Modernity? Charles Taylor's Marianist Award Lecture, with Responses by William Shea, Rosemary Luling Haughton, George Marsden, and Jean Bethke Elshtain,* edited by James L. Heft. New York: Oxford University Press, 1999.

Sheehan, James. *Where Have All the Soldiers Gone? The Transformation of Modern Europe.* Boston: Houghton Mifflin, 2008.

Shiloh, Shmuel. "*Ha'arama* B'Talmud" [Legal Fiction in the Talmud]. *Shnaton Hamishpat Haivri* [Jewish Law Annual] 8 (1991): 309–355 [Hebrew].

Soloveitchik, Joseph B. *Halakhic Man.* Translated by Lawrence Kaplan. Jerusalem: Sefer ve Sefel, 2005.

Sommer, Benjamin. "Revelation at Sinai in the Hebrew Bible and in Jewish Theology." *Journal of Religion* 79:3 (July 1999): 422–451.

————. "Unity and Plurality in Jewish Canons: The Case of the Oral and Written Torahs." In *One Scripture or Many? Canon from Biblical, Theological, and Philosophical Perspectives,* edited by Christine Helmer and Christof Landmesser, 108–150. New York: Oxford University Press, 2004.

Steinsaltz, Adin, "Peace without Conciliation: The Irrelevance of 'Toleration' Judaism." *Common Knowledge* 11:1 (Winter 2005).

Taylor, Charles. "A Catholic Modernity?" In *A Catholic Modernity? Charles Taylor's Marianist Award Lecture, with Responses by William Shea, Rosemary Luling Haughton, George Marsden, and Jean Bethke Elshtain,* edited by James L. Heft. New York: Oxford University Press, 1999.

Tillich, Paul. "The Two Types of Philosophy of Religion." In his *Theology of Culture.* Oxford: Oxford University Press, 1959.

Vattimo, Gianni. "Dialectics, Difference, and Weak Thought." Translated by T. Harrison. *Graduate Faculty Philosophy Journal* 10 (1984): 151–163.

Walzer, Michael, Menachem Lorberbaum, and Noam Zohar, eds. *The Jewish Political Tradition,* vol. 1: *Authority.* New Haven, Conn.: Yale University Press, 2000.

Weil, Simone. "The Love of God and Affliction." In her *Waiting for God,* translated by Emma Craufurd. New York: Harper Perennial, 1951.

Williams, Rowan. *Silence and Honey Cakes: The Wisdom of the Desert.* Oxford: Lion, 2003.

Wittgenstein, Ludwig. *Culture and Value.* Edited by G. H. von Wright, with Heikki Nyman. Translated by C. G. Luckhardt and Maximillian Aue. Chicago: University of Chicago Press, 1982.

———. *Philosophical Investigations.* Translated by G. E. M. Anscombe. New York: Macmillan, 1953.

———. *Tractatus Logico-Philosophicus.* Translated by D. F. Pears and B. F. McGuiness. London: Routledge, 1972.

Yerushalmi, Yosef Haim. *Zakhor: Jewish History and Jewish Memory.* Seattle: University of Washington Press, 1982.

Yosef, Rav Ovadiah. "Mesirat Shetachim Me'eretz Yisrael Bimkom Pikuach Nefesh" [Handing Over Territory from the Land of Israel in Circumstances That Save Life]. *T'chumin* 10 (1989): 34–47 [Hebrew].

Yuval, Israel. *Two Nations in Your Womb: Perceptions of Jews and Christians in Antiquity and the Middle Ages.* Translated by Barbara Harshav and Jonathan Chipman. Berkeley: University of California Press, 2006.

———. "Vengeance and Damnation, Blood and Defamation: From Jewish Martyrdom to Blood Libel Accusations." *Zion* 57:1 (1993) [Hebrew].

Zabala, Santiago. "A Religion without Theists or Atheists." In *The Future of Religion,* edited by Santiago Zabala. New York: Columbia University Press, 2005.

Zabala, Santiago, ed. *The Future of Religion.* New York: Columbia University Press, 2005.

Zilberg, M. *Kach Darko Shel Talmud (Principia Talmudica).* Jerusalem: Acadamon, 1984 [Hebrew].

The Zohar. Edited and compiled by Rabbi Michael Berg. New York: Kabbalah Center International, 2003.

Index

messianic zeal, 45; and politics, 12; as prophetic peace, 13, 63–93, 141; and violence, 17
Mishna Avot, 100, 102, 179n1
monism, 107, 184n30
Moses, 76–77, 79–81, 101, 102, 110, 179n1, 182n9, 183n10
mindfulness, 12, 34

Nachmanides, 76, 77

Orthodoxy (Jewish), 99, 107, 108, 111
Oslo peace process, 14, 19, 111, 134, 135, 139, 176n25

Palestinians, author's interactions with, 165–172; and Camp David talks, conflict with, 29; 14; hatred directed against, 97; Jewish empathy with, 163–64; peace agreement with, 19, 24; refugees, 165, 178n14; terrorism, 96
Pascal, Fania, 52, 180n17
Pelikan, Jaroslav, 97, 98
Peretz, Amir, 2
Perl, Jeffrey, ix, 22, 179n3
Plato, 38–39, 40
pluralism, 43, 107–110, 117, 140, 185n30
Popper, Karl, 104, 105
prayer, 33–34, 88, 142–46, 148–55, 164, 185n40, 187n1, 188n2
prophecy, biblical, 12, 45–47, 138, 159; disarming of, 64–68, 79; of Ezekiel, 64, 68, 72, 80, 81; of Isaiah, 48, 49, 84, 86, 89; messianic, 72, 89; nature of, 43, 86, 91–93; and peace, 86, 97; and politics, 80, 84; and rabbinic Judaism, 136, 138–39, 159; and "the unification of the opposites," 90; and violence, 112; and Wittgenstein, 48–49, 81
protest, political, 2, 84, 111, 135, 176n21
Proverbs, 81, 133, 134, 139
Psalms, 33, 69, 80, 90, 111, 139
Purim, 27, 28–29, 96, 185n36

Rabbi Aha bar Hanina, 113–14, 141
Rabbi Akiva, 110, 121
Rabbi Aleazar ben Arakh, 111, 119, 120
Rabbi Eliezer, 108–110, 113, 184n24
Rabbi Jehoshua, 31, 34, 103, 105, 108–110, 184n24, 184n27
Rabbi Jose, 31, 122, 139
Rabbi Meir, 113–114
Rabbi Nehemiah, 113
Rabbi Yochanan ben Zakkai, 111, 121, 185n40
Rabbi Yosef, 136
Rabin, Yitzhak, 19, 134, 135
Rabbinic Literature, 16, 77, 94, 97, 103–104, 106–107, 112–113, 117–118, 120, 140, 183n12
Ras-Bayada, xi–xxi, 48
Rashi, 86, 172
Ratzinger, Joseph, 98, 99
religiosity, 42–46, 56, 57, 159, 178n1
Renan, Ernest, 27, 178n17
revenge, 32, 96–97
revelation, and concealment, 52, 73, 85, 89, 112, 114, 118; as foundation for Jewish texts, 16–17, 42–43, 104, 108, 112, 137, 159–60, 179n1; God's need for, 54; and peace, 34; and politics, 12; purpose of, 35; religious claims about, 56; and silence, 74–79; voice of, 33
Riskin, Shlomo, 28
Rosenak Avinoam, ix, x, 161, 182n29, 188n2, 188n4
Rosenak Michael, ix, 178n1
Rorty, Richard, 41, 54–56, 58, 121, 179n11, 180n26
Rotenberg, Mordechai, 184n21
Rousseau, Jean-Jacques, 177n10

Sagi, Avi, 101, 102, 106–109, 117–18, 184n22
Salinger, J.D., 146–49, 188n4, 188n5
secularism, 55–56, 58, 108
Shabbat, xv, xvi, xvii, xviii, 51, 101, 125, 184n24
Sheehan, James, 175nn2–3
Shiloh, 70, 71

ALICK ISAACS was born in Glasgow, Scotland; grew up in Birmingham, England; and settled in Israel in 1986. He is a research fellow at the Hartman Institute's Kogod Centre for Contemporary Jewish Thought and teaches at the Melton Centre for Jewish Education and the Rothberg School for Overseas Students, both at the Hebrew University of Jerusalem. Isaacs serves as editor of religious affairs for the journal *Common Knowledge* and is co-director of the Talking Peace project sponsored by Mishkenot Sha'ananim in Jerusalem.